WITH FIDDLE AND
WELL-ROSINED BOW

D1522900

D. A. Cole and family, ca. 1898. Cole was born in 1873 in Giles County, Tennessee, and became a champion Limestone County fiddler when he moved to Alabama in the 1920s. Cole's great-grandson, Daniel Carwile, is a nationally recognized fiddler today. Photo courtesy of Mrs. Estelle Cole Carwile.

JOYCE H. CAUTHEN

WITH FIDDLE AND WELL-ROSINED BOW

Old-Time Fiddling in Alabama

THE UNIVERSITY OF ALABAMA PRESS

TUSCALOOSA AND LONDON

Copyright © 1989 by
The University of Alabama Press
Tuscaloosa, Alabama 35487–0380

Manufactured in the United States of America

Designed by Laury A. Egan

Library of Congress Cataloging-in-Publication Data

Cauthen, Joyce H., 1944–
With fiddle and well-rosined bow.

Bibliography: p.   Includes index.
1. Fiddlers—Alabama. 2. Fiddle tunes—
Alabama—History and criticism. 3. Folk
music—Alabama—History and criticism.
4. Folk dance music—History and criticism.
I. Title
ML3551.C38 1989   787.1'09761   87–38080
ISBN 0-8173-0403-7

British Library Cataloguing-in-
Publication Data is available.

To Jim and Carey

CONTENTS

In 1924, Dr. W. H. Johnson described the opening of the Old Fiddlers' Convention at Athens Agricultural School: "At eight o'clock the curtain went up and seated on the stage were many citizens of the county and adjoining counties with fiddle and well-rosined bow, ready for the contest, each eager for the start."[1] The phrase "with fiddle and well-rosined bow" captures the enthusiasm with which fiddlers across the state and across the years have thrown themselves into entertaining their communities at barn raisings, Saturday night square dances, Fourth of July barbecues, and other gatherings; thus I chose it for the title of my book.

In selecting a subtitle, it is customary to leave aside literary flourishes and plainly announce the subject at hand. My subject is fiddling in the state of Alabama, but what sort of fiddling? I would have been happy to use the words *traditional* or *folk* in the subtitle, but they both suggest music of ancient and anonymous origin and are more restrictive than a study of Alabama fiddling allows. Uninterested in the authenticity of their sources, fiddlers have always played music that pleased themselves and their audiences, be it traditional reels and jigs learned from their fathers, parlor tunes and hymns sung around the piano with their families, or popular dance tunes from the radio that their listeners requested.

When commercial record companies began recording fiddle music in the 1920s, they, too, had trouble finding a term for the music. The Victor Company settled on "Olde-Time Fiddlin' Tunes and Hill Country Music" (Victor), and Columbia tried "Familiar Tunes—Old and New." Decca Records, for a time, labeled it "hillbilly" music. Only one of the fiddlers interviewed for this book used that term to define his music, however. In 1900, the *New York Journal* had defined "Hill-Billie" as "a free and untrammelled white citizen of Alabama, who lives in the hills, has no means to speak of, dresses as he can, talks as he pleases, drinks whiskey when he gets it, and fires off his revolver as the fancy takes him."[2] With such connotations, the word *hillbilly* was not popular.

The term of choice in Alabama's rural weekly newspapers seems to have been *old-time,* and I have chosen to use it throughout the book. In the 1920s and 1930s, in hundreds of articles about fiddlers' conventions and community celebrations, the term was used to describe the contests, the music, and the fiddlers themselves. The quality that unites the eclectic mix of tunes in the fiddler's repertoire is oldness. The tunes may be ancient, but if they are not, they are played in a style which makes them sound that way. If you drove to Oneonta and listened to E. H. Allgood fiddle "Yakety Sax," you would know what I mean.

In earlier days, when newspapers reported on old-time fiddling events, they were prone to envelope the subject in nostalgia. More than one article mentioned the old-time fiddler's ability to transport the listener to the joys and pleasures of yesteryear or, as one wrote, to "rekindle the smoldering fires of youth, retouch the golden heart-strings of a broken chord, rejuvenate and transplant the soul to the green fields of memory's ecstatic joys and pleasures of the LONG AGO."[3] While I have tried to avoid overt nostalgia in the book, it is really not possible to remove all traces. Old-time fiddling, having been part of the fun, courtship, and celebrations of earlier days, is actually one of the good things about the "good old days."

With that halfhearted apology for nostalgia, I shall proceed to two more areas which may require apologies. First, there are sure to be omissions. I may have overlooked the best fiddler who ever pulled a bow in the state of Alabama or the biggest fiddlers' convention ever held. Because Alabama has such a rich, full history of fiddling, I knew it would be impossible to cover the subject fully in one book. I tackled the overwhelming task by mentally dividing the state into quadrants, then attempted to interview a number of fiddlers in each, thus learning of fiddling traditions and repertoires in various parts of the state. I also spent countless hours in archives, libraries, and the basements of county courthouses across the state, turning the pages of old newspapers to find articles about fiddling conventions and other local entertainments. I drafted my husband, daughter, and anyone else I could into the dusty business. In the newspapers of Fayette, Lamar, Limestone, Clarke, Marshall, De Kalb, Cullman, and Chilton counties, in particular, we found an abundance of information, while in the newspapers of counties such as Madison and Pike, which I know had good fiddlers and numerous contests, we found almost nothing written about fiddling. Thus some counties and their fiddlers are not represented in the book simply because their newspapers did not report on such activities. And most well-known contemporary fiddlers are not mentioned because I limited my research to the years between the settlement of Alabama and the end of World War II, with only a few general and very brief excursions into the present to show that fiddling is indeed alive in the state.

After five years of research, sixty interviews, and more notes than I could keep up with, I decided to start writing, even though I had not interviewed all the fiddlers and examined all the newspapers I would have liked. It is my hope that this will not be my last writing on the subject and I will have opportunities in the future to address that which was left out of this one.

Second, there may be errors in dates, locations, spelling of names, and the outcomes of contests. Such errors are a result of my heavy reliance on other people's memories and on reports in newspapers. When people are asked to look back forty or fifty years to describe fiddle events, they are bound to make errors. And it seems newspapers are bound to make errors even when looking back at last Tuesday's fiddlers' convention. Yet these are the best sources we have on the subject of old-time fiddling. If you do find errors, I hope you will regard them as small flaws in a fabric woven of memories and written accounts of earlier days. The pattern that emerges in the weaving, I believe, is vivid and true.

Acknowledgments

In the process of my research, many people have given me information, inspiration, and encouragement. I am sure I would not have thought of writing about fiddling had not my husband "turned fiddle" twelve years ago and had I not discovered *The Devil's Box*, a journal about old-time fiddling which has been published in Alabama since 1968. Beside showing me how interesting the subject could be, editors Stephen Davis and Bill Harrison have provided much information for the book. Old-time music scholars Charles K. Wolfe, Guthrie T. Meade, Wayne W. Daniel, Tony Russell, and Norm Cohen were unselfish with their large stores of information, as were Alabama folklorists Joey Brackner and Hank Willett, newsman Bob Kyle, and Marty Everse, director of Brierfield Ironworks Park. Bob Pinson at the Country Music Foundation in Nashville unfailingly answered the stream of questions I directed his way. Of course, librarians across the state provided essential services, particularly those at the Linn-Hinley Research Library and the Archives of the Birmingham Public Library, the Special Collection at Samford University, and the State of Alabama Department of Archives and History. Tinker Dunbar at the Mervin H. Sterne Memorial Library of the University of Alabama in Birmingham (UAB) was helpful not only in obtaining books from afar, but also in being perpetually

interested in my project. When I had lost my own enthusiasm—
after a day of fruitless library research or a long drive to an interview
turned up nothing—the enthusiasm of others, such as Malcolm
MacDonald, director of the University of Alabama Press, and Dr.
Tennant McWilliams of UAB, was important. Mrs. Emil Hess, a
strong supporter of the Alabama Symphony Orchestra, was also gen-
erous in her support of my fiddle research.

I am particularly grateful to the fiddlers (listed in the bibliography),
their families, and friends who so warmly shared their time, memories, photographs (and garden vegetables) with me. Several, including
Harmon and Evelyn Hicks, Guy Johnson, Vearl Cicero, Robert Stripling, and James Bryan accompanied me on trips to interview other
fiddlers. Fred Beckett, Ezra Quinn, and Russell McClanahan helped
me track down fiddlers in their areas. Temo and Marguerite Callahan of Tuscaloosa and "Dad" and Martha Hill of Pinson provided
much information, and their homes became mine on some research
trips.

My daughter Carey, since the age of nine, has been spending days
of her school vacations scanning county newspapers for the word
fiddle. My husband Jim, who inspired the book, was constantly sup-
portive and uncomplainingly stayed at work making his company's
computers run while I was out doing what he wanted to be doing—
listening to fiddlers. I hope that all the good people mentioned above
will be happy with their book.

About the Illustrations

I am fortunate that one of my good friends is a professional photographer with a knack for capturing the personalities of her subjects.
Kim McRae Appel, a travel photographer for Southern Living, did
all the original photographs and restored and copied the vintage photos that grace this book.

WITH FIDDLE AND
WELL-ROSINED BOW

1

THE FIDDLE IN
ALABAMA HISTORY

Fiddling in the Alabama Territory

In 1814, Tom Bailey and his family left southern Kentucky and headed for Alabama. Just inside the Alabama territory, they met the Acton family from Tennessee. "There were fiddles and good fiddlers in both families," wrote Bailey's great-grandson. "I might be safe in saying that one of the first fiddling sessions in the State of Alabama was held on the banks of the Tennessee River" that night.[1] The next morning the two families headed south together. They swelled the "mighty stream of emigration" that poured out of Virginia, the two Carolinas, Tennessee, Kentucky, and Georgia and spread over the entire Alabama territory.[2]

Now that General Andrew Jackson's army had forced the Creek nation to cede much of its land to the United States, white settlers entered Alabama on foot, on horseback, in wagons, and on flatboats, carrying with them the necessary items for turning the fresh land into homelands. Like the Baileys and Actons, many carried fiddles, carefully tucked among quilts and clothing, which they brought out after a long day of travel. Their playing brought music to the quiet nights and gave strangers a reason to gather.

The tunes played in those first Alabama fiddling sessions were kin to tunes originally brought from the British Isles. The Scotch-Irish, in particular, furnished the basis for the fiddling that came into Alabama, since they predominated in the early settlement of the Southern states. The Scotch-Irish had originally immigrated to Ireland from Scotland. Residing in the northern counties of Ireland, separated from Scotland only by the North Channel, they were able to maintain cultural ties with their homeland. Influenced more by the Highland bagpipe of Scotland than by the flutes and harps of

Ireland, their fiddlers tended to play undecorated melodies, enriched by rhythmic bowing and the use of drone strings.[3] Many southern American old-time fiddlers still retain those characteristics in their playing.

Scotch-Irish fiddling had become southern American fiddling before it reached Alabama, however. As the pioneers advanced westward along the frontier, differences in the types of social gatherings, dances, and accompanying instruments present in the new land caused changes in their music. Fiddlers from other ethnic groups contributed tunes and stylistic techniques to the music. One group of settlers, the Africans, contributed greatly to the development of a distinctive style of fiddling.

Africans had been in the American colonies since the early 1600s and had demonstrated their ability with the fiddle as early as 1700.[4] Slave owners who wished to provide dances for their families and friends were quick to notice and develop the musical interest and talents of their slaves. Some owners provided them with violins. Eileen Southern suggested that slaves in Charleston and other cities were taught to play by professional musicians just as some were taught bricklaying, carpentry, and other skills. In advertisments for slaves appearing in *The Virginia Gazette* between the years 1736–80, Southern noted more than sixty references to black musicans, forty-five being violinists or fiddlers. Some were fiddle makers.[5]

Thus, either by instruction or imitation, the African slave learned to play the reels, jigs, hornpipes, waltzes, polkas, marches, and other types of music required by dance masters for a proper "soiree." He also was allowed to play his fiddle to entertain his own people for various celebrations. It was in the slave quarters, during Saturday-night frolics, weddings, and Christmas dances, that southern fiddling gained much of its characteristic drive, the "hoedown" quality that differentiates it from the fiddle styles of New England and the British Isles. Accustomed to more complex and varied rhythms than those he heard in the British music, the African fiddler may have found the new music "childishly simple."[6] He played sedate tunes for his master's cotillions, then added bow shuffles and syncopations to the same tunes to power the rhythmic, emotional, leaping, hand-clapping dances of the slaves.

When "Alabama Fever" struck in 1814, more than a century of fiddling had gone on in America. The fiddlers who came into the Alabama territory were descended from pioneers who had moved through Virginia, the Carolinas, Georgia, Kentucky, and Tennessee, adapting their music to the conditions they found and adopting what they liked in the fiddling of others they came into contact with, whether African, French, Scandinavian, or British. By the time they reached Alabama, they were playing southern American music, which they carried across the length and breadth of the new land. Fiddle music in Alabama became not just "mountain music," but the music of the Black Belt, the Piedmont, the Wiregrass region, the river communities along the Tennessee and Tombigbee—the entire Alabama territory.

It is likely that fiddle repertoires and styles varied greatly from area to area within Alabama. In *The Formative Period in Alabama, 1814–1828*, Thomas P. Abernethy wrote that "most communities had their local color, and the state one came from was always a matter of significance." Abernethy found that, for the most part, the Tennessee River valley in northern Alabama was originally settled by Tennesseans, the southern counties by Georgians, and the cen-

Edgar K. Mixon and family at Little River in Seminole County, Oklahoma, ca. 1915. The Mixons had left Alabama for Oklahoma, but later returned to settle in Lamar County. Fiddlers like Mixon, who kept their instruments at hand as they traveled, aided in the movement of fiddle tunes from one area of the country to another. Photo courtesy of Mr. and Mrs. J. C. Brock.

tral Tombigbee-Warrior region by settlers from Virginia and the Carolinas.[7]

While neighboring states provided the bulk of settlers to Alabama, those from other countries also had some influence on fiddling in the state. In the fishing villages on the Gulf Coast, it is possible that the fiddling had a French or French-Caribbean flavor. Mobile historian François Diard related the local legend that one of Lafitte's pirates who settled at Coden "played on a reed-fife and fiddle and sang the folk-songs of the Creoles for the amusement of the settlers and fisher-folk of the vicinity."[8] Those settling in southeastern Alabama may have heard the music of the Scottish Highlands. A group of Scotsmen migrated to Barbour County in the 1820s, and that region still has a large proportion of families bearing the names of the Highland clans.[9] Irishmen fleeing the great famine of the mid-1800s brought their music to Alabama. Thomas Gibbons, a descendant of the fiddlers of Killacoma, Ireland, eventually settled in Birmingham in the 1880s, where he contributed such tunes as "Rory O'More," "Irish Washerwoman," "Garry Owen," and "Fisher's Hornpipe" to the local repertoire.[10]

For a time in Alabama, it may have been possible to tell the area a fiddler came from by the way he played. That is no longer the case. In this century, the automobile, radio, and phonograph have made it possible for fiddlers to step outside local boundaries. However, early recordings of Alabama fiddlers and the playing of older fiddlers reveal some regional differences. Fiddlers in the western part of the state, particularly the Tombigbee-Warrior region, tended to play descriptive, somewhat irregular pieces, like "Wolves A'Howling" and "Lost Child." They used a rolling bow, sliding fingers, and open, droning tunings. The playing of Charlie Stripling, which can be heard on County Recording 401, is representative of the type of fiddling done by many west Alabama–east Mississippi fiddlers. Those in the eastern counties, along the entire length of the state, had much more in common with the fiddlers of Georgia than with those of west Alabama. Their repertoires included melodic hornpipes and reels, played in a regular meter. They played with a strong, hoedown rhythm, but retained more of the "British" in their music than did their western counterparts. Recordings by Georgia fiddlers such as Lowe Stokes and Clayton McMichen are the most accessible examples we have of this style. This general east-west division indicates that fiddle styles within Alabama correspond more to the early territorial boundaries than to the political boundaries fixed by the government when Alabama became a state in 1819.

The Black Fiddler

During the first hundred years of Alabama's settlement and statehood, the black fiddler was enormously important. By the 1930s, fiddling was largely a white institution, and few of the fiddlers interviewed for this book recalled ever hearing or knowing black fiddlers. Because the institution of slavery has received the attention of scholars and journalists, however, more has been written about black fiddlers than about those of any other ethnic group in the state. Letters from visitors to Alabama, the writings of northern journalists, and the narratives of former slaves show the importance of the black fiddler during the antebellum period in Alabama.

In 1853, Jane M. and Marion Turnbull, two British visitors to a slave market in Montgomery, observed about sixty blacks "all dancing to the music of two violins and a banjo . . . a negro was standing on a chair, calling out what figures were to be performed in the Virginia Reel."[11] Frederick Law Olmsted, an observer from the North, noticed a large number of slaves on a steamboat passage from Mobile to New Orleans: "There was a fiddle or two among them, and they were very merry, dancing and singing. A few, however, refused to join in the amusement and looked very disconsolate."[12]

In both cases, all but the disconsolate few sought consolation in singing and dancing to the music of the fiddle. Many former slaves interviewed in the 1930s under the auspices of the Federal Writers' Project remembered the Saturday-night frolics and Christmas celebrations as some of the few good features of slave life. Fiddles were not present at all slave frolics, however. In Lee County, Lucindy Lawrence Jurdon and Frank Menefee recalled corn-shuckings where "somebody would clap hands, beat pans, blow quills or pick de banjer strings"[13] to provide music for the "buck-dance, sixteen-hand reel and cake walk."[14] More often fiddles were, according to Harold Courlander, "the essential requirement for a good-time dance."[15] Charlie Johnson, a slave on George Whitfield's plantation near Livingston, said,

When Christmas come, didn't get no present, just more meat and bread. Christmas and the fourth day of July was the times we was allowed to celebrate. Then we had fiddlin' dances. We had a old slave could fiddle, and a guitar and maybe a banjo, but anyhow a fiddle, and we do square dances and swing the partners.[16]

Around Florence, Alabama, the fiddlers for such frolics were likely to be W. C. Handy's grandfather or his uncle. Though Grandpa Brewer had "forsaken such sinful doing" before Handy was born, Uncle Whit Walker, "lively and unregenerate at eighty," was available to play for him. He showed Handy how to accompany him with a pair of knitting needles. Standing behind the fiddler, the youth "would reach around the fiddler's left shoulder and beat on the strings in the manner of a snare drummer." Handy wrote:

Uncle Whit fiddled and sang while I handled the needles.

> Sally got a meat skin laid away
> Sally got a meat skin laid away
> Sally got a meat skin laid away
> To grease her wooden leg every day.

Uncle Whit stomped his feet while singing. A less expert fiddler, I learned, would have stomped both heels simultaneously, but a fancy performer like Uncle Whit could stomp the left heel and the right forefoot and alternate this with the right heel and the left forefoot, making four beats to the bar. This was real stomping.[17]

The verse that Whit Walker sang as he played was a "floating stanza"[18] which could be sung to any tune whose meter was appropriate. Such stanzas were generally nonsensical, meant to add rhythm rather than meaning to the tune, and were sung at slave gatherings across Alabama. Hannah Jones, formerly a slave on the Gillium Place near Greensboro, still recalled the following stanza when she was interviewed in the 1930s:

> White folks says a nigger won't steal
> But I cotched six in my cawnfiel'
> If you want to see a nigger run
> Shoot at dat nigger wid a gattlin' gun.[19]

Frank Menefee remembered singing

> Dark cloud arising like gwine to rain
> Nothing but a black gal comin' down the lane
> Nigger stole a pumkin an' started outer town;
> Nigger heered it thunder, Lord, and throwed dat punkin down.[20]

Charlie Johnson, who lived near Livingston, said a favorite verse was

> Old Man Foster, settin on a log,
> Hand on trigger, and eyes on a hog

and another was

> Run, nigger, run
> Patroller catch you!
> Run, nigger, run
> Almost day![21]

Despite the fact that some of these verses are racially derogatory, former slaves recalled them fondly and willingly recited them to inteviewers of the Federal Writers' Project. The floating stanzas may have had the status of ethnic jokes: funny when told by a member of the group, but offensive when repeated by nonmembers. N. I. White of Duke University theorized that the stanzas were not of black origin. They came, instead, from the antebellum minstrel stage, from the "coon-song" writers of the 1890s and 1900s as well as the traditional songs of white people, and were learned by blacks who performed them for white audiences. Eventually, wrote White, blacks accepted the verses as their own.[22] However, it is probably the case that minstrel composers, who obtained their material by closely studying the music and manners of the slave, declared themselves the composers of verses that already existed or wrote new verses so close to the original ones that blacks were willing to claim them. Whatever their origin, verses chanted in accompaniment to the music of fiddles, banjos, and reed quills were a common part of a Saturday-night frolic in Alabama, as were showy buck-dancing and group dances like the Virginia reel.

Such festivities held off the master's property were not sanctioned, however. For instance, in 1846 John Kalaras of Mobile was charged with "entertaining Negroes in a variety of ways, among which was permitting them to assemble in a room to 'trip it on the light fantastic toe.'" He was arrested along with a number of slaves, the fiddler included.[23] Yet, under the master's watchful eye, "fiddling dances" were allowed, even encouraged. Hugh Davis, master of Beaver Bend on the Cahaba River in Perry County, held contests among the slaves to stimulate their productivity and rewarded the winners with parties. After a particularly successful cotton harvest, Davis described a celebration held on July 19, 1856, which featured a sumptuous supper followed by "dancing and music to the tune of 'Cotton is King,' all being merry & cheerful with a crop quite clean."[24]

Slave owners like Hugh Davis considered a good fiddler on the premises a necessity. Consequently the slave fiddler sometimes had a better life than that of his fellow slaves. His talent allowed him preferential treatment from his master and esteem from fellow slaves. For instance, W. C. Handy's grandfather was allowed to keep the money he made playing for dances.[25] Another fiddler allegedly escaped a great deal of labor because of his talent. Jake Green, who worked for Lam Whitehead on a plantation near Livingston, told Ruby Pickens Tartt the following tale:

> Dey had a darkey dere named Dick what claim he sick all de time. So de Massa man said, "Dick, dam it, go to de house. I can't get no work outten you." So Dick went on. He was a fiddler so dey jes' tuck his vittuls to him for seven years. Den one day, Old Massa say to de overseer man, "Let's slip up dere an' see what Dick doin'." So dey did an' dere sot Dick, fat as he could be a-playin' de fiddle an' a-singin,'
>
>> "Fool my Massa seben years.
>> Gwiner fool him seben mo.'
>> Hey diddle, de diddle, de diddle, de do."
>
> Bout dat time Ole Massa poked his head in de do' an' said 'Dam iffen you will. Come on outten dere, you black rascal, an go to work,' an I ain't never hyard of Dick complainin' no more.[26]

Bill, a young slave fiddler on Benjamin Fitzpatrick's Oak Grove Plantation in Autauga County, won the esteem of fellow slaves because of his ability. A reporter for the *New York Herald* who interviewed Fitzpatrick's slaves wrote that Bill the fiddler was "the musical celebrity and general favorite among the Negroes."[27]

The slave fiddler contributed not only to the happiness of his fellow slaves, but also to the social lives of the family and neighbors of the plantation owner. In matters of music and dance, there seems to have been much interaction between blacks and whites. Alfred Benners, author of *Slavery and Its Results*, described life at Arcola, a plantation on the Warrior River, six miles above Demopolis:

> Hospitality ruled supreme at the Big House, and kin, friends and strangers found constant welcome and lavish entertainment. At night Jim Pritchett with his fiddle, Mingo with his triangle, and Mose with his banjo came from the quarters and made music for the happy belles and beaux. They danced co-

tillions and the Lancers, winding up with the Virginia Reel. Sundry drams livened old Jim's fiddle, as the "Forked Deer," "Arkansas Traveler" and other old tunes of a like lilt and swing, quickened their flying feet. Jim was a noted mimic, as well as fiddler, and usually wound up with an improvisation of his own, which he called "The Dying Coon," in which his voice added to the witchery of his bow the shouts of the hunters, the baying of the dogs and the snarls and dying wail of the fighting coon.[28]

Like fiddler Pritchett, Charles Hayes's father, a slave at Day's Landing near Mobile, "usta play de fiddle for de white folks dances in de big house, an' he played it for de color frolics too."[29]

Often the "white folks" would follow the musicians to the slave quarters in order to watch the merriment. Mrs. Chandler of Guntersville remembered the fiddle tune "Sally Ann" being played on her father's plantation by a black family band that would play for dances, both white and black. Verses to the tune were made up to fit the occasion, and Mrs. Chandler recalled the amusement of the Negroes when the whites would sing it with them.[30] Former slaves also remembered the presence of whites at their dances, both as musicians and observers. Jim Gillard of Opelika observed that "Marster's brother would fiddle for us,"[31] and Hattie Clayton recalled, "Lots o' times ole Missus would come to de dances an' look on. An' when a brash nigger boy cut a cute bunch uv steps, de menfolks would give 'im a dime or so."[32]

Interaction between blacks and whites at antebellum festivities is best shown in a letter written by William Phineas Browne in 1859. Browne described the wedding of Sam Browne and Livey as it was taking place on his plantation near Montevallo:

> The yard is full of servants, their guests, and they are having a fine time of it and other white folks also are looking on. Mother gave them a fat turkey, a pig and a shoat . . . chicken and any quantity of cakes, etc., and they have got up a great supper. They are now dancing to the music of George's banjo and are in high glee. There are as many as fifty or sixty guests and all seem to be enjoying it greatly . . . Livey is dressed in white all nicely with her big hands covered with white gloves and mother has decorated her hair with a profusion of artificial flowers, making her look young and captivating no doubt to—old Sam.
>
> The table is sat in the yard and extends almost from the house to the kitchen. The supper is tastefully set out and looks inviting . . . The servants have just sent in for papa's fiddle—there

is amongst the guests one or two who play the fiddle and they want, they say, to have some cotillions now.[33]

After 1865 the slave fiddler continued his art as a free man. Ben Guyton, former slave of Daniel Hollis of Sulligent, became a servant who taught his master's son to play the fiddle.[34] His student, D. Dix Hollis, later became the first fiddler in Alabama to make commercial recordings. Other black fiddlers toured the country with troupes such as the Rabbit Foot Company and Mahara's Minstrels, while others became paid musicians at local dances. Gus Rhodes was a respected black fiddler in Clarke County. Rhodes, born in 1853 and living in Thomasville at the time of the 1900 census, could play classical and sacred music from written music as well as old-time breakdowns by ear.[35] He was described in the *Thomasville Argus* as "the city's master violinist." A report on "the crowning social fete of the season" (1897) noted that "Gus Rhodes wielded the bow on this occasion in his masterly way, to the tune of ten dollars."[36]

In St. Clair County, Gus Cochran was well compensated for his musical ability. His grandson, Ernest Mostella, a maker of hand-carved folk fiddles, recalled family stories about Cochran: "All these people knew him far and near. They'd go and get him and take him from one place to another to play for 'em"; he'd return "loaded down with gifts."[37] Cochran is remembered in a history of St. Clair County: "There were also the colored musicians, Gus Cockran [sic] and Pomp Montgomery, who made parties gay and lively with their fiddle and guitar dance tunes."[38]

By the early 1930s, however, black fiddlers were rare in Alabama. Perhaps traditional fiddle tunes of British ancestry lost their appeal to black musicians and dancers when blues and jazz, musical forms growing from African roots, came into vogue. Yet because of interaction between the races on antebellum plantations, white fiddlers were enriched by black fiddlers who turned the British reels into hoedowns and added the "hot" element[39] to southern fiddling.

Early Broadcasters:
Minstrels and Soldiers

The black fiddler's influence reached into areas of Alabama where there were few or no slaves, by means of a popular form of entertainment known as the minstrel show. Soon after minstrels began traversing the state with cork-blackened faces, the Civil War set young Alabamians on the road, as well. Traveling entertainers and soldiers both served to disseminate tunes and styles across the South, thus playing the role that phonographs and radios played in the following century.

The Minstrel Show. The fiddle entered show business in 1843 when Dan Emmett introduced The Virginia Minstrels, a quartet of Negro impersonators who played fiddle, banjo, bones, and tambourine. The group became popular immediately and spawned hundreds of all-male, all-white troupes, which traveled the country, "delineating" the Negro character and carrying his style of fiddling to areas where black fiddlers had never existed. In the early days of minstrelsy, many of the tunes performed on the stage were traditional ones. Dan Emmett, in particular, was careful that his tunes faithfully rendered the character and traditions of the southern slave.[40] He and other showmen collected folk tunes, such as "Jump, Jim Crow"[41] and "Possum Up a Gum Stump,"[42] on plantations and riverboats, added words, published them as sheet music, and performed them on the minstrel stage. They appropriated the British reels, jigs, and hornpipes that black musicians were playing at the time and used them during the finale of each performance, which, according to Carl Wittke, represented a " 'hoe-down' in which every member of the company did a a dance at the center of the stage, while the others sang and vigorously clapped their hands to emphasize the rhythm."[43] Hans Nathan, biographer of Dan Emmett, has traced several of Emmett's compositions to their Irish and Scottish antecedents, among them "Boatsman's Dance," "Turkey in the Straw" (formerly "Old Zip Coon"), "Jump, Jim Crow," and "Clare de Kitchen."[44] In fact, Emmett's most famous tune, "Dixie," may have come from traditional sources. Emmett maintained that he wrote and first performed "Dixie" in New York City in 1859, though some have attempted to prove that he wrote the South's "national anthem"[45] on the wall of the Montgomery Theater and first performed it in the capital of the Confederacy.[46] However, Henry Hotze, a reporter for the *Mobile Register* in 1861, may have been correct in writing that "its real origin is of much older date. Those who have travelled much on Western rivers must often have heard it, in various forms, among the firemen and deck-hands of the river steamers."[47]

"Buffalo Gals, (Won't You Come Out Tonight?)" is another tune that had folk origins though it was published in 1848 as a minstrel tune. It was already well known in Mobile in 1846, where a woman who had once been "a flower, innocent and beautiful but long since torn from its stem, trampled, soiled and desecrated" was arrested for drunkenly singing "Mobile Gals, Won't You Come Out To-night?" on the streets.[48]

Minstrel groups, most originating in northeastern cities such as New York, Buffalo, and Boston, traversed Alabama for nearly a century, beginning in the late 1840s and continuing at least until 1938 when Milt Tolbert's All-Star Minstrels performed in blackface in Cullman.[49] Many of the most famous companies made stops in Alabama. Mobile, being on the southern route to New Orleans, attracted minstrel troupes, among them the Buckley Serenaders and the Steamboat Minstrels.[50] The Mobile Theater, in the opinion of theatrical manager M. B. Leavett, was one of the nation's notable theaters of the late 1860s and 1870s.[51]

In 1855, Campbell's Minstrels pleased Montgomery audiences. Two favorite performers were Newcomb, "who played the banjo and delivered a lecture on 'Woman's Rights,' and Bryant, who gave the Nebraska Reel, 'a dance to make a negro's mouth water.' "[52] When Christy's Minstrels, or a group fraudulently using their name,[53] appeared in Montgomery the following year, a *Montgomery Advertiser* critic was unimpressed. "As delineators of the Negro character, they are failures . . . Their music is soso" (sic). Though the critic observed that many members of the audience enjoyed them, he concluded that "they are not good negroes, nor good musicians, nor good jesters."[54]

Minstrelsy continued throughout the Civil War, during which troops sometimes entertained themselves by putting on amateur minstrel shows.[55] After the war, professional minstrel troupes ventured outside Alabama's largest cities to smaller ones such as Selma, Eutaw, and Demopolis.[56] In north Alabama at the turn of the century, Al G. Field's minstrels were extremely popular. Enthusiastic audiences packed the Hayden-Pake Theater in Gadsden[57] and the Huntsville Opera House, where the balcony was reported to have had three sections: one for poor whites, one for Negroes, and one for harlots.[58]

Black minstrel companies also toured Alabama, usually under white management. W. C. Handy recalled that the Georgia Minstrels came to Florence and that Bill Felton, "a minstrel man and singing banjo player," organized a hometown minstrel show which played in Tennessee and northern Alabama, and got stranded in Jasper.[59] Handy, himself, toured with Mahara's Minstrels in 1896.[60] In the late 1920s, the professional Rabbit Foot Company, a group of "colored entertainers," took their tent show to small Alabama towns like Fayette.[61] At the same time, amateur minstrel shows were all the rage. Blackface performances by "the leading men of Chatom,"[62] the Eastern Star Chapter of Clanton,[63] the "Bessemer Shrine Minstrel,"[64] and thousands of elementary schoolchildren across the state brought howls of laughter from their neighbors and kin.

Thus citizens of Alabama's largest cities and tiniest communities became familiar with the popular tunes of the minstrel stage. Fiddlers learned them, not from the sheet music they were printed on but by hearing them sung and played frequently. Some minstrel tunes, such as "Arkansas Traveller," "Pop Goes the Weasel," and "Boatsman's Dance,"[65] came full circle: they had been played and sung as anonymous folk tunes, claimed and popularized by minstrel performers, then passed into the realm of folk music once more.[66] Others, of known composition, were claimed by fiddlers and passed down as authentic old-time tunes. Among them are "Oh! Dem Golden Slippers" (James A. Bland), "Listen to the Mockingbird" (Richard Milburn), "Climbing Up the Golden Stairs" (F. Heiser), "Little Brown Jug" (Eastburn, believed to be a pseudonym for Joseph E. Winner), "Yellow Rose of Texas" (composer only identified as J. K.),[67] and "Whistling Rufus" (Kerry Mills).[68] Such tunes became standards in the repertoires of fiddlers all across Alabama and the South.

The Civil War. Slavery, which had furnished the source of material for minstrelsy, soon became a cause for fighting. In the fall of 1861, Alabamians began gearing up for war. J. P. Cannon, a private in the Twenty-seventh Alabama Regiment, wrote,

> Parties were out drumming up companies. There were no examinations by Surgeons as to physical condition, nor were youth or old age a bar to eligibility; every man or boy capable of carrying a gun was gladly received, and no questions asked . . . The roll of the drum and the shrill note of the fife could be heard all over the land, while the work of collecting arms and other necessaries progressed.[69]

At such a time, it seems that men would lay down their fiddles for rifles, or at least take up instruments suitable for regimental bands. However, many did take their fiddles to war with them, thus contributing to the rapid dissemination of fiddle tunes across the South. For instance, Jack Gibson of the Perote Guards was one of "many superior fiddlers" who had brought their instruments when they joined the First Regiment of the Alabama Volunteer Infantry.

Joshua "Doc" Carpenter of Franklin County took his fiddle with him when he enlisted in 1863 in the Confederate Army, where he served as a private in Company E of the Fifth Regiment. Photo courtesy of Chuck Carpenter.

Edward McMorries, a fellow soldier, described the concerts that Gibson frequently gave in his tent after supper:

The first stroke of his bow never failed to be cheered enthusiastically by the regiment. After playing an hour or two he invariably closed with "O Lord Gals one Friday," which he would play, sing and dance at the same time. He was afterwards wounded . . . in the right arm just above the wrist resulting in a permanent deflection of the arm at that point; and being asked whether he could still use the bow replied: "Why, yes; my arm now has exactly the right crook for the business."[70]

The Twelfth Alabama Infantry also had a few fiddlers, but in the estimation of Robert Emory Park of Greenville, Georgia, the "most noted and skillful" one was Ben Smith, a fellow Georgian.

His skill with the fiddle was unequalled. I have heard many violinists since the war, in the great orchestras of Thomas and Sousa and Creatore, but none of their number could equal great Ben Smith. He had gifts, and his knowledge of distinctive Southern music, peculiar to country life, some of which I have heard our slaves often play with exquisite taste and great gusto on our Georgia plantations, was wonderful. Among the choicest in Smith's repertoire were "Hell broke loose in Georgia," "Billy in the Low Grounds," "Arkansas Traveller," "Dixie," "Money Musk," "The Goose Hangs High," "When I saw Sweet Nellie Home," "My Old Kentucky Home," "When This Cruel War is Over," "The Girl I Left Behind Me," etc. Crowds would gather around him and laugh and applaud and clap their hands, and joyously express their pleasure and appreciation.[71]

In the Twenty-seventh Alabama Regiment, fiddlers provided dance music. J. P. Cannon described a camp dance:

Nothing more than the regular routine during the day, but at night the lovely Spring weather and the bright light of the full moon infused into the boys a feeling of gayety, and someone proposed a dance. An old, battered fiddle was brought out and the fiddler struck up a lively tune. The cotillion was formed, and such another dance was hardly ever seen. The officers, from Colonel down, came out to witness it, and the dancers and spectators seemed to enjoy it equally.[72]

Because soldiers responded so enthusiastically to fiddle music, fiddles seem to have been in great demand. According to Bell Irvin Wiley, "an Alabama private [James Thrower] who must have been much better at music than he was at spelling, wrote proudly to his brother in 1861: 'Tobe I have got the best violent in the Regment Jo Jackson ses it is worth one Hundred dollars.' "[73] And when a fiddle was not available, a soldier handy with a pocketknife might make one, for J. P. Cannon wrote of "dancing by the light of torches and the music of a camp-made fiddle, til late in the night."[74]

The Civil War brought together men from diverse areas and economic backgrounds. For instance, Rode's Brigade consisted of three Alabama regiments, a Mississipi regiment, and a Virginia battalion. The three Alabama regiments were drawn from the entire state, from Henry County in the southeast to Marion County in the northwest. Mobile Cadets, composed of young aristocrats, fought beside Raccoon Roughs, backwoodsmen from the hilly counties of the north.[75] In the early, tedious days of the war, there must have been a good deal of tune swapping among the fiddlers of various regiments. Those who returned home at the war's end enriched local repertoires with traditional tunes from distant counties and states, like Ben Smith's version of "Hell Broke Loose in Georgia." Show tunes that had been popularized during the Civil War, such as "Bonnie Blue Flag," "Kingdom Coming," "The Girl I Left Behind Me," and "Dixie," also came with returning soldiers and took their places alongside older fiddle tunes.

The soldiers returned to communities in disarray. Even in areas untouched by fighting and unaffected by the release of slaves, there were problems arising from feuds, caused by differing loyalties, and farms that had been neglected while the men had been at war. Yet fiddling and dancing retained their popularity, and were even regarded as symbols of the return to normalcy. Thomas Robison of Wetumpka, who traveled the Black Belt as a dance master and fiddler, had become "a gallant officer during the war, sharing the sufferings and privations of Gen. Lee's army, and being several times badly wounded."[76] When he resumed his profession after the war, a newspaper editor explained:

> As a soldier and a gentleman, he did his duty to the land of his nativity, and now, re-echoing the language of our new President: "Let us have peace," he seeks, by the profession of which he is so bright an ornament, to do his share toward the promotion of that comfort and enjoyment which is so marked a characteristic of the people of the South.[77]

Fiddling Into the Jazz Age

Balls, country dances, and minstrel shows continued to entertain Alabamians through the remainder of the nineteenth century. During these years, black musicians, now free to pursue their own tastes, made further contributions to the South's music. In their hands, the old cakewalk tunes grew into ragtime, Negro spirituals developed into the "blues," and all of these, played on the brass instruments cast off by regimental bands after the war, became "jazz."[78] When jazz was brought to the dance floor early in the twentieth century, the new music captured the young people of the nation, influencing their manners, speech, and dress.

Many older people feared that jazz would lead to the demise of traditional fiddling, not to mention the breakdown of the entire moral structure of the nation. Newspaper readers across the state were informed that "the jazz spirit" was responsible for fifteen thousand suicides in 1923,[79] and were told that "Jazz Maniac's Mad Act Should Act as Warning to Parents" when a sixteen-year-old in San Francisco shot her mother and went out dancing.[80] They worried about joyriding—"They think when they get the Ford started, they are on their way to heaven. I am afraid they will run their Fords into Hell"[81]—and longed for a return to the "great moral age without short skirts and rolled stockings, snuggle dancing, hip pocket liquor and . . . bobbed hair."[82]

In such an age, it seemed likely that the tunes of yesteryear would be totally forgotten; however, just the opposite occurred. During the Jazz Age, the number of country musicians grew and their audiences expanded. Two inventions of this period, the phonograph and the radio, helped to increase the popularity of country fiddling; and as the minstrels and soldiers had done earlier, they rapidly disseminated fiddle tunes across widespread areas.

The Electronic Broadcasters

The Phonograph. In 1877, Thomas Edison began applying the principles of the newly developed telephone to another miraculous invention—the talking machine.[83] Years of experimentation followed, in which numerous inventors patented devices that recorded and reproduced sound with varying degrees of success, and by 1900 the Alabama fiddler could order from Sears, Roebuck "The Wonderful Home Graphophone" for $5. For twice that amount he could be the owner of "The Peerless Talking Machine," which was the same as the Home Graphophone with the addition of a carrying case and a recording diaphragm; thus it could make original records as well as reproduce those already made.[84]

Everis Campbell of Troy recalled that a device like the Peerless Talking Machine was used to settle a long-standing competition between his father and another fiddler in the early 1900s. A doctor named Stephens, who came from Chicago annually to treat the ills of the folks of south Alabama and north Florida, brought the hand-cranked machine to a dance and recorded the rivals on a beeswax cylinder. He then sent the cylinder to Chicago to be judged objectively, or "authenticated." According to Campbell, "Whenever it come down, Pa was the winner."[85]

The talking machine, wrote Roland Gelatt, was regarded as an "intruder or experiment" and was not assured a place in the home until about the year 1908.[86] By 1909 the Sears, Roebuck catalog was offering a variety of attractive "graphophones," now playing disks instead of cylinders, at prices that made them accessible to a farmer who had had a good year. Columbia Disk Graphophones with the "new Aluminum Tone Arm" ranged in price from $15 to $45, while "Harvard Talking Machines" came with forty-eight records and cost only $14.95.[87]

But the recorded selections available—mainly Sousa marches, cornet solos, operatic arias, presidential speeches—offered little for the fan of traditional fiddling. He may have listened to Columbia's recording of John Y. AtLee whistling "Listen to the Mockingbird"[88] and noticed its potential as a showy piece for fiddle contests, or laughed at "Arkansaw Traveler," which Sears, Roebuck offered in its 1905 catalog as "Descriptive of a native sitting in front of his hut scraping his fiddle and answering the interruptions of the stranger with witty sallies."[89] It was not until 1923 that he could buy a recording of old-time country fiddling, however. During that year, Polk Brockman, an Atlanta businessman who sold records in his family's furniture store, persuaded Okeh Records to set up a studio in Atlanta to record Southern artists.[90] The commercial success of Fiddlin' John Carson's recordings of "Little Old Log Cabin in the Lane" and "The Old Hen Cackled and the Rooster's Going to Crow" paved the way for the recording of traditional fiddle tunes by country artists such as Gid Tanner, Clayton McMichen, Uncle Bunt Stephens, Doc Roberts, and others. By the late 1920s the fan of old-time fiddling could listen to numerous recordings of fiddlers and fiddle bands.

For the rural fiddler, bringing home a new fiddle record was akin to having a new fiddler move into the community. In the past, new tunes and playing styles had been learned when fiddle-playing relatives came from Texas to visit the old Alabama home, or when a soldier brought back tunes he had learned in the Civil War from a Georgia fiddler camped near him, or when a fiddling coal miner from West Virginia had moved to an Alabama mining camp. Now the local musician could get records by mail order, buy them at the furniture store in town, or select one from those that agents brought out to the mining-camp commissaries on Saturday mornings. Once the record was on the turntable, he could play it on the hand-cranked machine as slowly as necessary in order to learn the new tune.

Arlin Moon of Holly Pond had an uncle who bought a hand-cranked Edison record player in 1927. According to Moon, his uncle

> was able to buy stuff like that, where we wasn't. He heard a good record somewhere, why he'd just buy it. And that's where I got a lot of these old tunes that I know now, 'cause I'd . . . sit and play that old record player half the day or half the night at a time . . . And then a lot of times somebody lived eight or ten miles over there; why they'd get a new record and we'd get on the mule and ride over there and play that record 'til we learn't it.[91]

Not only did the phonograph provide a new source of tunes for the country fiddler, it also gave him an opportunity to learn new styles. He could break away from the predominant fiddle style of his community or incorporate new techniques into that style. For instance, some fiddlers who played in the "shuffle bow" style became intrigued by the longer, smoother bow strokes they heard on some recordings and attempted to play in that style. According to many Alabama fiddlers who learned to play during the middle 1920s, the most influential recording artist was Clayton McMichen of Georgia, whose playing represented a more modern, smoother sound than they were accustomed to hearing. In the following decade, the phonograph made it possible for fiddlers across the nation to admire and imitate the "rolling bow" of Tennessee fiddler Arthur Smith.

Though the phonograph was a source of inspiration to many Alabama fiddlers, few of them had much success as recording artists themselves. Chapter 3 relates the careers of three Alabama recording artists: D. Dix Hollis, Charlie Stripling, and Y. Z. Hamilton. Other fiddlers had rather dismal experiences like those related by Olen Mayes, who recorded with the Short Creek Trio in 1927. Mayes recalled that Gennett Records, owned by the Starr Piano Company of Richmond, Indiana, had set up a temporary recording studio in its Birmingham store. One night while performing at a local theater, the trio members were approached by Martin Ringleberg, assistant manager for Starr, who invited them to record at the studio. On July 11, 1927,[92] the group, consisting of Mayes on fiddle, Charlie Ross on guitar, and Reuben "Red" Burns on banjo, made their first recording. Mayes recalled that the recording equipment was set up in a large room and that the musicans arranged themselves around two microphones. The music was recorded on a soft wax disc which could be scraped off, if necessary. This happened twice during their recording sessions. According to Mayes, "The manager knew music. He said, 'Y'all made one mistake, maybe two.' He scraped it off and we tried it over till we got it right, the way he wanted it."

The first fruit of their labor was "Hand Me Down My Walking Cane," which was issued as the reverse of Y. Z. Hamilton's "Old Sefus Brown." Later in July they recorded four tunes on which Reuben Burns sang the lead. Two of these, "The Burglar Man" and "Nobody's Business," were released. In August they returned to the studio with Cliff Click, a powerful hoedown fiddler who was living at Short Creek at the time, and recorded "The Buckin' Mule" and "Old Hen Cackled and the Rooster Crowed." Gennett later leased all of the Short Creek Trio recordings to other record companies who issued them as the reverse of recordings by artists such as Ben Jarrell, Frank Jenkins, and Doc Roberts. On these labels the name Short Creek Trio was replaced by pseudonyms, the "Logan County Trio" and the "Henry County Trio."[93]

For his participation in three recording sessions, Olen Mayes received $63. Mayes recalled that he had a lengthy wait for the check. "I went to the mailbox one day and had a envelope from Richmond, Indiana. It was a check for $63 and something—that's all . . . I figured that time I got that little old check they was cheating us out." The Short Creek Trio continued playing for radio and theater performances, but gave up the idea of being recording artists. Until recently Mayes's daughter was unaware that her father had once made records.[94]

Fiddler James W. "Jack" Jackson, born in Morgan County in 1897, traveled to Chicago in 1927 to record for Paramount with the Hugh Gibbs String Band of Huntsville. According to Jackson, a businessman from Birmingham and one of the band members had arranged the recording session and had been offered a $20 guarantee and a 2¢ royalty on every record sold; however, they had shown the rest of the band a false contract offering less. When Jackson discovered the discrepancy, he left the group and did not listen to the recordings until the author gave him a tape recording of two of the tunes fifty-seven years later.

Other fiddlers were disappointed when their recordings remained unissued. J. C. Glasscock, a champion fiddler from Steppville who had been a finalist in the state-wide fiddlers' convention in Birmingham in 1925, returned to the city in 1927 to record "Hop Light Lady" and "Peek-A-Boo Waltz" for Gennett.[95] J. C. Price of Clanton, who was selected by voters in twenty states as the winner of a radio fiddle contest in Atlanta, also recorded with the Dixie String Band while in that city for the contest.[96] Neither fiddler had the pleasure of seeing his recordings released.

In 1928 the Johnson Brothers of Sand Mountain traveled to Atlanta to record on the Okeh label. The failure of that company to release the records disppointed their many fans on Sand Mountain, who had read the following article in the *Sand Mountain Banner*:

JOHNSON BROTHERS STRING BAND
MAKING PHONOGRAPH RECORDS

The well known string band of Sand Mountain, "The Johnson String Band," are now in Atlanta, Ga., making a "record" for themselves as well as for Old Sandy, for they are in that city for the purpose of making phonograph records for the Okeh Record company, and these new records producing the music of our own Sand Mountain and Albertville boys will soon be placed on the market for sale. Everyone on Sand Mountain will probably want one or more of these records which will reproduce their fine music . . . These records made by them for the Okeh Record Company will be placed on the market on or about Sept 1st.

We will surely want some of these records which reproduces [*sic*] the music made by our own boys.[97]

Many Alabama fiddlers went unrecorded because they were unaware of recording sessions. Others declined the opportunity. Ed Rickard, the blind fiddler of Russellville, whose fiddling was his main source of income, refused to play for 1¢ a record.[98] "Monkey" and Charlie Brown, well-known Tuscaloosa fiddlers, were asked to make records for a company in New York. "Monkey" recalled, "I turned them down on the grounds that we were green country boys and might get killed or lost up there."[99]

Thus the number of old-time fiddlers of Alabama who were commercially recorded is small, and most of those who actually made records found the experience unrewarding. Fortunately, at the same time another medium was developing that furnished a more satisfactory outlet for their talents.

The Radio. On November 2, 1920, ham operators listening on home-made equipment heard the world's first scheduled radio broadcast from Station KDKA in Pittsburgh, Pennsylvania. Two years later the Alabama Power Company was granted a license to operate a 500-watt station, WSY, in Birmingham, and during that same year, radio station WMAV began to broadcast from Alabama Polytechnic Institute in Auburn. Broadcasts by both stations were infrequent, however, and in 1925 WSY was dismantled, shipped to Auburn, and combined with WMAV. The call letters were changed to WAPI in reference to the institution at which the station was located.[100] First broadcasts from the station were heard in February 1926, and in the following month a trustee of the institution extended invitations to performers across the state, "thereby encouraging and developing these talents and giving them a wide field for expression."[101]

At the end of March, the Johnson String Band drove two-hundred miles in their Model T Ford to represent Marshall County on the radio, their travel expenses contributed by the businessmen of Guntersville and Albertville.[102] In April, the Sulligent Commercial Club sent its "brag" fiddler, Dr. D. Dix Hollis, to Auburn to issue a challenge "To the World."[103] He was to play for two nights to give potential challengers "an idea of what they will have to compete with" should they challenge him in a contest to be held in the fall.[104]

Dr. Hollis's challenge to the world is not as unrealistic as it may seem, for in 1926 it is possible that the broadcast reached foreign countries. In January of that year only 536 stations were active in the United States,[105] and transmissions could travel long distances with little interference from other stations. For instance, William C. Davis, Jr., of Jasper, won a *Radio Digest* contest in March 1926 by identifying twenty-seven foreign stations including those in Vienna, Prague, Stockholm, and Buenos Aires.[106] On April 9 of that year, WAPI reported that its signals had been picked up in the state of Washington and on Vancouver Island, British Columbia, more than 2500 miles by air from Auburn.[107]

We do not know what became of Dr. Hollis's challenge, because WAPI did not release a follow-up story on it. A similar contest was broadcast over Atlanta's WSB the following October. J. C. Price of Clanton, Alabama, "received first honors in the fiddling melee by a vote cast by radio listeners in 20 states." To win the $50 prize, he received more postcard votes than "twenty-two of the most prominent fiddlers in the southeast."[108]

Though few people in rural Alabama owned radio sets in the 1920s, fans of the Johnsons, Hollis, Price, and other "brag" fiddlers usually knew at least one amateur "wireless" operator who would open his home to them. After listening to the program, they would send someone into town to wire congratulations to the performers and praise the station for its good taste in programming.

One radio critic in Bristow, Oklahoma, bemoaned this practice, noting that the radio audience seemed to prefer novelty stunts—"something that is lively and stirs up fun, action, and smiles"—to more serious music. In a wire-service article appearing in the *Birmingham News* in 1925, the critic explained:

> For example, a group of artists from Ada is giving a three-hour program. It is some of the best music—singing, violin, piano, cello, opera, quartet, duet, band—that can be had anywhere. After each number goes on the air the folks back home keep the wires hot to tell the players to keep it up, great stuff, congratulations to all, and so forth. The applause comes chiefly from the home town and persons in the other towns who are personally acquainted with the artists. But right in the midst of one of these high class programs let someone step up to the microphone, play "Arkansas Traveler" or "Yankee Doodle" on a fiddle—not a violin—and the cheering comes thundering in from all over these United States.[109]

By mail and telegraph, listeners of WAPI (Auburn) were quick to register their opinions of the new radio station's programming. Alabama Cooperative Extension Service Photo, courtesy Auburn University Archives.

While the critic ventured that "the old time stuff" was popular because it battled the static better, a letter to WAPI from C. Kirkpatrick of Sprottsville, in 1928, suggested another reason:

The other day when you had those old fashion fiddlers pulling the bow to the tune of "Bully of the Town" you came very near making me lose my dinner. The Madam kept on ringing the dinner bell, and sent the cook in two or three times to tell me dinner was ready, that if I did not come on everything would be cold, etc., but I sent her back word to "let her freeze," the boys at Auburn have "Billy in the Low Ground" now and that I was going to stay here until they get out on the other side and "Raise Hell Among the Yearlings." But the boys did not play that inspiring piece. The ones you played, however, kept my feet shuffling around on the floor until I got stiff in the "jints." Boy, that was great; it carried me back to the days when we had old time dances . . . If you expect me to make any pecans this year you had better cut out that kind of tantalizing stuff at Auburn.[110]

Whatever the listeners' preferences and reasons for them, WAPI insisted on giving them a wide variety of programs. By October 1926, the station was on the air six days a week with two daily programs, one starting at 12:30 p.m. and continuing about thirty minutes and the second beginning at 8 p.m. and lasting an hour or more.[111] At those times one could hear lectures on egg production, crop rotation, and family nutrition, as well as classical piano pieces, "Miss Laurie McKerley rendering several selections on a handsaw with studio orchestra,"[112] new releases of popular records from Victor played on the station's Electric Victrola,[113] and groups like the Goss Brothers String Band of Fairfax[114] or the string trio made up of J. B. Ellis, Jr, banjo, Bob McKinnon, guitar, and Sam Mosley, violin.[115]

While WAPI had been expanding in Auburn, two other radio stations—WBRC and WKBC (later WSGN)—had been established in Birmingham. By the time that WAPI moved to that city and set up its new "Cathedral" studio on the fourteenth floor of the Protective Life Building in 1929,[116] Birmingham had become a radio mecca. Rural musicians seeking to expand their audiences and to achieve fame among the folks at home could travel to the city, play at one station, then walk to another station and play again. Whereas making records had been a frustrating experience for many fiddlers, playing on the radio for little or no money seems to have been a gratifying one.

These Birmingham musicians called themselves the Plow Pushers when they broadcast from the Hood-McPherson furniture store on Saturdays in 1930. From left to right: Louis Marston, better known as "Uncle Bud" of the Boll Weevils; "Dud" Connolly, radio announcer; "Zeke" Herman Phillips, E. E. "Silas" Akins, and Johnny Motlow. Photo courtesy of Hood-McPherson Furniture Company.

The Flat Creek Boys, 1932: Wallace Tuggle, guitar; Dan Shealey, mandolin; Gaines Arnold, fiddle; and Vearl Cicero, guitar. Photo courtesy Vearl Cicero.

Vearl Cicero, now of Ensley, recalled the discomforts that his band, the Flat Creek Boys, were willing to endure to play on the radio in the early thirties. The band was composed of Gaines Arnold, Dan Shealey, Wallace Tuggle, Paul Tuck, and Cicero. All were miners at Flat Creek, twenty-five miles northwest of Birmingham. Flat Creek Mine was open only three days a week, and the miners had little to do on the other days. Each Thursday at 4 a.m. they would pile into the open touring car that belonged to one of the members, cover themselves with quilts, and be in Birmingham in time to play over the radio on the 6 o'clock sunrise program. "One day," Cicero recalled,

we broke down by the Industrial School on 8th Avenue. As we went around that curve, we had a puncture. So we had to get out and walk from there—or run—to get there on time. We was about five minutes late and old Chad Bridges was there just jumping up and down and said, "Where you boys been?" And we said, "We've been coming over here. We broke down." He got a good laugh out of it but we went on and played. We'd play about an hour.[117]

For their efforts they shared about $25 a performance. From time to time, they would travel to the fourteenth floor of the Protective Life Building to perform on WAPI's "Saturday Barn Dance," on which bands played without pay. Cicero remembered that the main problem was that the elevators would break down and "you might get up there and have to walk down, or you might not get up there without you walked up. . . . There was several other musicians walked up there, carrying their instruments and groaning and grunting about it."[118]

Sam Busby also became familiar with the fourteen flights of stairs that led to WAPI's Cathedral studio. Around 1932, while a student in high school, Busby had formed a string band with Dick Mains and Gene Sullivan.[119] They played old-time tunes they learned from fiddler "Uncle" Walt Pearson, as well as popular tunes like "Nola" and "Goofus" that they learned from records. During the summer and on Saturdays they lingered at the radio station and eventually were invited to participate on WAPI's weekday program which began at 6 a.m.:

We had to catch the streetcar at Wylam at 4:30 and we got to Loveman's at 5:15 and we would be on the air—I guess it was 6. Back then the elevators didn't operate and we had to walk up fourteen stories of the Protective Life Building. It was too early for the elevator operators. They wouldn't bring an operator down for that. The air was practically free of other radio stations back then. There was maybe one or two. WAPI had more power than WBRC. We'd get mail from I guess as many as eight or ten states because the air was perfectly clear at that time and it would just reach and reach and reach. It was a big-time show.

Gene and I would get up and catch the streetcar in Wylam; Dick would meet us in Ensley. We'd get off in Birmingham; we'd play the show, let's say from 6 to 7. There was other bands there, too. We wasn't the entire show at all. Then we'd have to hustle to get our instruments, get back down to catch a streetcar and be at Ensley High School at 8. The boys' advisor liked us real well and kept our instruments in his office. The principal, Dr. Sechriest, would take us to play at the Rotary Club at Ensley. We was the principal's pet. And also one of the music teachers— oh, she thought that was marvelous. So we would play on the

Young musicians on Station WAPI (Birmingham), 1932: Sam Busby, guitar; Dick Mains, fiddle; and Gene Sullivan, guitar. Photo courtesy Sam Busby.

stage every so often during "auditorium." Uncle Bud [whose band, the Boll Weevils, played professionally around Birmingham] would come by and pick us up and take us on show dates. Say, we'd play at WAPI, we'd go to school, then long about 1 p.m. on certain days, when Uncle Bud wanted us, he'd come by and pick us up and we'd go out to, say, Empire or Alden and play. Get back home about 9 or 10 o'clock, and by the time you got in bed, it was time to get up, 'cause we had to be in Wylam, you see. Loved every minute of it.

Finally, we went up and told 'em we couldn't play for nothing no more, and we figured up the carfare at $3.75 each and cheated them because we included strings and I think carfare was two-for-a-nickel for student fare. So we were just cheating the stew out of WAPI, getting $3.75 a week—apiece, mind you.[120]

In the early 1930s radio stations were founded in Montgomery, Gadsden, and other Alabama cities. Bill Harrison, discussing fiddling in Limestone County, recalled that the radio stations in nearby Huntsville, Florence, and Decatur were eager for fill-in talent:

Saturday quickly became the day for local musicians within commuting distance of these radio stations to pool their money for gasoline and in most cases hire someone with an automobile to drive them to the places where they could experience the glamour of "playing over the radio."

The station managers welcomed all talent, good or bad, to play. From early morning until late afternoon, listeners "out there in radio land" could hear old-time music in profusion. The quality of the music ranged from bad to excellent. But within time limitations, the station managers denied no one the opportunity to play over the radio.[121]

Radio, besides offering a large audience for the fiddler, also provided him another source of tunes. Few fiddlers active in the twenties and thirties who had access to a radio failed to tune to WSM in Nashville for the "Grand Ole Opry" on Saturday nights. Arlin Moon remembered that the same tune would be played often enough on the program that a talented fiddler could learn it.[122]

The development of the phonograph and the radio, which perhaps could have been perceived as rivals to the fiddler's popularity, were instead boons. The fiddler embraced the new media as rich sources of tunes and as means to a wider audience. And indeed, the audience widened. Even the big, sophisticated city of Birmingham, whose

Fiddlers Make Debut

"The Short Creek Barn Dancers" will make their stage debut in Birmingham next week. This group of musicians and dancers have worked out a program of old-fashioned cavorting that is expected to be "something really different" in vaudeville entertainment. The Short Creek folks will be an added attraction at the Lyric during the coming week.

The popularity of old-time music in the mid-1920s led managers of vaudeville theaters in Birmingham to book groups like the Short Creek Trio and Barn Dancers. This article appeared in the *Birmingham Age-Herald*, February 19, 1926. Photo courtesy of the *Birmingham Post-Herald*.

newspapers had previously ignored country music and reported only on classical and jazz performances, suddenly, in 1925, began to cover fiddle conventions and country performers like Uncle Dave Macon, who was setting unprecedented attendance records at the Loew's Bijou Theater.[123] Early in 1926 when Olen Mayes walked into Birmingham's Temple Theater to try to book his Short Creek Trio as a vaudeville act, the manager listened to two fiddle tunes and said, "You're just what I've been looking for."[124] And though the large city newspapers and theaters soon lost interest in such matters, the county weeklies continued to report regularly on square dances, country music performances, and fiddle conventions. Two of them assessed the effects of the phonograph and radio upon fiddling. The *Northwest Alabamian* of Fayette stated:

> Although the lines of the older heros of the fiddle and bow have been thinned from time to time, the music which they have brought to each succeeding generation is being perpetuated by the younger generation and also through the medium of Victrola and radio.[125]

The *Fort Payne Journal* observed, "With the invention of the radio, the perpetuation of the old-time music on the fiddle and the bow has been doubly assured."[126]

Henry Ford's Influence on the Alabama Fiddler

The creator of a third modern device also influenced old-time fiddling. By the late thirties, the Ford automobile, which had been accused of carrying young men to Hell, was carrying fiddlers to conventions. W. V. Jacoway, organizer of the annual conventions in Fort Payne, wrote in 1938 that

> it was unlike a quarter of a century ago, when the fiddlers came to town on horseback or in buggies, spending the night with friends and getting back to their homes in the afternoon of the following day. The network of magnificent highways and the high-powered car annihilates distance in a safe speed of more than a mile per minute, thus the old ways of travel will soon be forgotten.[127]

Henry Ford, whose production methods made the car financially accessible for many country people, provided the fiddler with more than a means of transportation to fiddle conventions. He was in part responsible for the survival of old-time fiddling during the Jazz Age. Ford was attracted to the fiddle and to country dancing because they harked back to a simpler age. Believing that old-time music and dance could serve as antidotes to the jazz dancing that was currently so popular, he had his agents seek out traditional dances, fiddle tunes, and musicians; invited fiddlers to his home, where he bestowed gifts on them; sponsored fiddle contests at Ford dealerships;

and published a dance manual entitled *Good Morning: After a lapse of 25 years, old-fashioned dancing is being revived by Mr. and Mrs. Henry Ford.*[128] Few fiddlers of Alabama were able to take part in Ford's contests, which were held in the East and Midwest, the nearest taking place in Tennessee, yet they were made aware of his interest in old-time music and dance by the enormous amount of publicity that Ford's favorite fiddlers received. Mellie Dunham of Maine was constantly in popular magazines, and photos of him occasionally appeared in the county weeklies of Alabama. John Baltzell, a champion fiddler from Gambier, Ohio, was described in Alabama newspapers as one who "pulls a mighty mean bow and wouldn't mind at all crossing bows with Henry's pet," Mellie Dunham.[129] Uncle Bunt Stephens of Tennessee, winner of Ford's grand championship contest in Detroit, made records, broadcast on the "Grand Ole Opry,"[130] and toured western Alabama as Ford's champion fiddler.

Some Alabamians sought Ford's attention. The Sulligent Commercial Club reported that Dr. D. Dix Hollis had a fiddle made in 1717 that Henry Ford was interested in buying,[131] and W. V. Jacoway wrote in 1932:

> Even one of the wealthiest men of this day and generation is doing what he can to perpetuate the tunes and the barn dance of the old time fiddler.
>
> There is some correspondence going on now to interest Mr. Ford in a movement to erect a Fiddlers' Auditorium at this place because of the unparalleled record of a quarter of a century of Fiddlers Conventions held at Fort Payne without a break in time or place.[132]

Though Hollis's fiddle stayed in the family and Fiddler's Auditorium was never built in Fort Payne, Ford's interest in old-time fiddling helped bring the art to the attention of the nation and contributed to the upsurge in its popularity which was already being aided by the phonograph and the radio.

Thus old-time fiddling survived the Jazz Age heartily, yet it was touched by it. In the thirties, fiddlers like Bob Wills in Texas were beginning to play the old tunes with a jazz beat and adding jazz instruments to their bands. The resulting music, now termed "Texas (or Western) Swing," attracted many young Alabama fiddlers. Some, such as Wiley Walker and Carl Stewart, joined professional swing bands, while others stayed at home and added the tunes they heard

At Ye Sign Of Mellie's Fiddle

REMEMBER readin' about Mellie Dunham, the veteran Maine fiddler whom Henry Ford brought to Detroit to fiddle for him? Well—Mellie's back home again. Taking life easy. He made enough on his stage tour after leaving Detroit to both pay the mortgage on his dwelling at Norway, Maine, and to keep the home fires burning for the rest of his days. Photo above shows his home—with a large fiddle over the door—and Mellie and "Gram" on the doorstep.

Readers of county newspapers like the *Union Banner* in Clanton (January 13, 1927) were aware of the success of one of Henry Ford's champion fiddlers, Mellie Dunham of Maine.

on the radio—"Milk Cow Blues," "San Antonio Rose," and "Faded Love," among others—to their repertoires.

A Fire in the Sawdust Pile

Old-time fiddling flourished during the Depression. Square dances and fiddlers' conventions were merry and affordable ways to forget, at least temporarily, economic woes. World War II caused a slight pause in fiddle activities; some annual conventions were postponed; dances were canceled; but most got under way with the soldiers' return.

In 1946 an unknown, inexperienced politician, James E. Folsom, began "to fiddle himself into the Governor's office."[133] Though not a fiddler himself, Folsom was familiar with the musical tastes of rural Alabamians and with the rhythms of farm life. He put together a string band of Cullman County musicians, named them the Strawberry Pickers after one of the county's principal crops, and in the depths of winter began his campaign. Carl Grafton wrote, "Folsom's logic was that people in rural areas had few sources of entertainment

The Strawberry Pickers were an important part of Jim Folsom's successful 1946 campaign to become Governor of Alabama. This photograph appeared in *Life*, June 3, 1946. Used by permission of Charles Preston, Jr.

and little to do in January and February; so they would welcome a good string band (and the Strawberry Pickers were first rate) even if it was accompanied by a politican."[134]

The Strawberry Pickers would drive into a small town and burst into tunes like "Oh Susanna," "Down Yonder," and "Yellow Rose of Texas." Bob Kyle described them as "snappy fiddling tunes that would make grandma take on hepcat ways, mixed with lonesome numbers that moaned of trouble between a gal and her man."[135] When the musicians had drawn a sizable crowd, Folsom would begin. Critics said that Folsom "emphasizes music instead of a program for the state," and contended that most people attended Folsom's rallies to hear the Strawberry Pickers;[136] yet Folsom's strategy was successful. He captured the attention and loyalty of country people, convincing them that he understood their needs and, as governor, could fulfill them.

While old-time fiddling had thrived during the Great Depression, it barely survived the economic prosperity of the 1950s. Prior to that era, the lives of Alabamians centered on their own communities, within which they produced their own food, educational system, medical and spiritual care, entertainment and recreation. After World War II, however, such communities gradually became less isolated, less self-sufficient. Rural electrification brought light and music into homes; telephone lines brought the voices of friends and neighbors closer. People were able to afford automobiles and trucks, and during the Folsom administration great numbers of county roads were paved. One effect of these improvements was shown by Mattie Lou Teague Crow as she recalled earlier days in Ashville, Alabama:

> Never an Autumn passed without a fiddler's convention and a spelling bee. On many a summer afternoon the court square would be alive with people, young and old, enjoying a strawberry festival or an ice cream supper. There were square dances throughout the year . . . Today, except for small gatherings of friends, people seek entertainment outside the town. With modern means of transportation, Ashville folks drive or fly to attend concerts, parties, and sports events.[137]

Others began to leave the small towns permanently. Inexpensive power provided by the TVA attracted industry to the northern third of the state and, according to George Sims, it was not long before "northern Alabama farmers and hillbillies would move to the cities, learn new skills, and begin new lives as industrial and clerical workers."[138] Soldiers returning to rural communities at the end of World

War II often found they had to move to the city to make a living. These moves disrupted family musical traditions. For example, when the sons of two musical families, the Striplings of west Alabama and the Johnsons of Sand Mountain, moved to Birmingham to find jobs, they left rich musical communities that they were unable to reestablish in the city. These and many other transplanted country musicians put their instruments away, thus raising their children in musical environments very different from those of their own childhood.

The development of rock 'n' roll in the 1950s contributed to fiddling's decline. Fiddlers had survived other musical fads by adapting to them and adding contemporary tunes to their repertoires. Dance fiddlers usually knew a few Charlestons, fox-trots, rags, and swing tunes that they could play in addition to square-dance numbers. However, fiddlers were uninterested in learning to play rock 'n' roll, with its minimal melodies and emphasis on the beat, and audiences were less interested in hearing them try. Dance halls that had formerly provided string-band music for round and square dancing were now turning their stages over to all-electric rock bands. Radio stations began to use only recorded music, many employing all-rock formats. Some fiddlers held Elvis Presley, in particular, responsible for the sad state of affairs. Al Lester, who was playing professionally at the time, recalled, "Elvis Presley came out and everybody done away with their fiddles."[139]

During the 1950s, fiddlers who did not put their instruments away found their best outlet to be in bluegrass, a style of music that Bill Monroe had begun to derive from old-time music in the late 1930s. It was performance-oriented, with rapid and showy instrumentals and close-harmony singing. The fiddler was not the most important performer in a bluegrass band. He would step forward and play fancy variations upon the melody, then step back to play a chordal accompaniment to other instruments and to the vocalists as they took the lead. While young fiddlers enthusiastically adopted the style, many older fiddlers found themselves unable or unwilling to master it.

With little demand for their talents, old-time fiddlers continued to play at home with a few friends or, as Gene Dunlap recalled, "to these four walls,"[140] or they stopped playing entirely. Alvin Horn of Clay County said, "It made me sick because I went into lots of homes where the daddy was a good fiddler and maybe I'd find the fiddle, with the back of it planed off and it glued to a plaque hanging up on the wall—never another note played on it."[141]

Of course, this was not the first time that interest in old-time fiddling had declined. The rash of fiddle conventions and commercial recordings of fiddlers in the mid-twenties were part of a revival after a period in which many worried that fiddling had become extinct. A similar period may have occurred in the 1800s. In 1858, Jasper E. James of Bibb County wrote in his diary, "Who would believe that fiddling and dancing are becoming fashionable again?"[142] Bob Kyle, a fiddler and a columnist for the *Tuscaloosa News*, recognized the cyclical nature of such revivals when, in 1957, he assured readers that "fiddle music will never die":

Old-time music on the fiddle is like a fire in a sawdust pile. You can snuff it out in one spot and it breaks out in another. Modern guitar thumpers with tousled hair and a plowstick wiggle are in the saddle right now. But the old fiddlers will wear them down. . . .

A fiddler never loses his touch. He can set himself back by taking violin lessons and learning how to read the notes, or he can get married. But the fiddling urge outlives schooling or a ma-in-law.

Down through the years fiddling in Alabama has ridden along in up or down fashion. It had its heyday in Hoover days, rose to its glory in W.P.A. days and rested up when the wars brought on income taxes. A fiddler is more appreciated when meat is scarce.[143]

Kyle's words proved true. About ten years later, while a revival of interest in folk music was taking place across the nation, a group of fiddlers and fans in Limestone County decided to hold a fiddlers' convention. Its success spawned a flurry of contests across the state. Old fiddlers were encouraged to limber stiffened fingers, put new strings on their fiddles, and try again. Others took up the instrument for the first time. Fiddlers who had played in the isolation of their homes found others to play with. Old-time musicians began to meet in community centers, shopping centers, and barns and warehouses that had been converted into music halls. In some areas, square-dance callers of the old school were encouraged to organize a set or two at each gathering.

Old-time fiddling today is wildly diverse. It is made up of senior fiddlers who took up the instrument after years of silence and thus play in an older style than those who never stopped. Beside them are fiddlers who joined bluegrass bands in the fifties, then honed their skills to win fiddlers' conventions in the sixties. There are young fiddlers, attracted to the music by the new round of fiddlers' conventions, playing in the "super-smooth" style currently in vogue among contest fiddlers. Other young fiddlers play in an entirely different style learned from fiddle recordings made in the 1920s and from visits to old masters. Some, having grown up listening to rock 'n' roll, have managed to incorporate those rhythms into their music, as earlier fiddlers mingled ragtime and blues with theirs.

All of these fiddlers differ from their predecessors in one way. Their music is not rooted in their geographical communities; they do not play with and at the insistence of their families and neighbors. They now form musical communities, traveling great distances to conventions and festivals, where they can play with those who share their musical styles and preferences. In between such gatherings, record albums and cassette recordings maintain the various communities.

Fiddling is alive in Alabama. The tunes shared by the Bailey and Acton families on the banks of the Tennessee River in 1814 are being played today. Though there are differences in style and circumstances, the fiddler's pleasure in drawing music from the fine wooden instrument and making people merry with it remains the same.

CHAPTER

2

MODEST MASTERS OF
FIDDLE AND BOW

The "Particulars"
of Old-Time Fiddling

In earlier days, those writing about fiddlers' conventions sometimes
waxed eloquent. Fiddlers became "bow wielders," "fiddle 'n' bow
artists," "followers of Stradivari," "modest masters," and "heroes
of fiddle and bow." One contest in Fayette (1907) was described
completely in verse:

FIDDLERS' JUBILEE

It's not often the people have a chance to see
The fun that was had at the Fiddlers' Jubilee,
But they were there, notwithstanding the weather,
And seemed to enjoy it, all together.

Fifteen fiddlers had signed an agreement to play,
Why eleven failed to show up, I cannot say;
But there were four who stood by their word,
And played some of the best music that was ever heard.

There was old man Peters, whose given name is Bob,
Showed to all, at once, that he was on to his job,
With his brand new fiddle, and a great long bow,
He played on all the strings, both high and low.

Then came Tom Johnson, with his preacher coat,
Who sawed on his box, and made quite a note.
Also, Charley Stanley, with his fiddle in tune,
Played, "Come out girls and dance by the light of the moon."

There was Dr. Young, who opened the Jubilee,
With one of the best fiddles you ever did see,

As he played his first tune he was somewhat excited,
But before he got through the folks were all delighted.

There was Mr. Goodwin, whose title is Judge—
Try him ever so hard, he would not budge.
And W. W. Harkins, whose office is our Post,
Went home to supper as white as a ghost.

R. T. Hamner—his business was so brisk,[1]
Under no circumstance would he take the risk
So he remained at his business selling the boys rum,
While the faithful at the court house
     played "Lexington on a Bum."

Mr. Belk was present with his fiddle and his bow,
And the audience called for him loud and low—
They waited and watched, but at last did observe
That Mr. Darling Belk was minus a nerve.

Mr. J. B. Mace said he forgot the night,
But it's the opinion of many it was due to stage fright.
And Mr. W. A. Anderson was sorry to say
That his dear wife would not allow him to play.

Mr. A. C. Nichols, who lives in Oldtown,
Was one of the number who had put his name down;
But when the time came he did not appear;
So it's an evident fact he had taken a "skear."

Of W. R. Enis we have nothing to say;
As he was sick and could not play.
He would have been there if he had been well.
And of one more faithful we would have something to tell.

H. C. Enis, who is commonly known as "Red,"
Wanted to get sick so he could go to bed,
For he very much feared Young, Stanley, Tom and Bob,
And like Dick, his employer, he stayed at his job.

Of A. A. Gentry there isn't much to say;
For there are only two tunes that he can play.
And when he gets down he plays one of them first,
And if there is any difference, the last is the worst.

Now comes Dr. Blackburn, a great big man,
Who plays "Great Big 'Taters' on Sandy Land,"

And he, with the other ten, as you will observe,
Is lacking that necessity known as nerve.

Now a word to the people who live around here:
When you want some good music you need not fear;
Just call on us four—we agree to act manly.
Our names are known as Young, Peters, Johnson and Stanley.[2]

"Fiddlers' Jubilee" reveals that in 1908 there were at least fifteen fiddlers in or near the town of Fayette, population 636.[3] Its jesting tone indicates that the fiddlers were friends, familiar with each other's repertoires and talents, having played together at fiddlers' conventions, square dances, and other community gatherings over the years. Most of them were leading citizens of the county—an attorney, six businessmen, two saloonkeepers, two medical doctors, a postmaster, sheriff, and probate judge.[4]

Until the early 1950s, when other sources of entertainment became available to even the most remote communities of Alabama, such clusters of musicians could be found all over the state. Alvin Horn of Clay County in eastern Alabama remembered his boyhood in the 1920s:

At that time, shoot, there was a fiddle in every other house, you might say, through this part of the country. You take a walk to Uncle Bill Brown's up here; his granddad Pete Robertson, he was a fiddler and had a boy who made a fiddler. And Uncle Bill, he was a good fiddler. He had one he ordered from Sears, Roebuck. He didn't have a case and carried it in a flour sack when he went to play for a dance. But he had some boys that were banjo pickers out of this world. And they'd back Uncle Bill up with banjos.[5]

In south Alabama near Andalusia, the situation was the same, according to Osey Kersey: "There was music every two or three miles. You could start off on Sunday morning and go, and you'd see folks out on the porch playing music. There'd be a couple of guitars and a fiddle a'going. Every community, just about, had a bunch of musicians."[6]

Among the abundance of Alabama fiddlers were "plain everyday set-in-a-rocker-and-scratch-aways"[7] who played a few simple hymns and parlor tunes to entertain themselves. There were also fiddlers like A. A. Gentry of "Fiddlers' Jubilee" who reputedly knew only two tunes. Such fiddlers could hold a square dance together, if necessary, and could help fill out the program at a fiddlers' contest.

And every county had one or more "brag" fiddlers, the first to be mailed invitations to fiddle conventions, the ones driven to square dances by whoever owned a good buggy or automobile. A good number of fiddlers were women. Alabama's fiddlers represented all social classes, from backwoods moonshiners like "Doc" Bigham of Northport who was hanged in 1919 for shooting the county sheriff,[8] to the solidly middle-class fiddlers of Fayette, to the aristocratic D. Dix Hollis of Sulligent, medical doctor, and son of a slave-holding planter.

Despite the plenitude of old-time fiddlers in Alabama prior to World War II, it is difficult to find detailed information about them. Until recently, the fact that fiddling was commonplace kept it from being a topic of interest to scholars. Fiddlers and their kin contributed to the scarcity of information on the subject. Learning tunes without the aid of written music, fiddlers did not often rely on writing for other purposes, either. In general, they did not keep lists of tunes or newspaper clippings about contests, nor did they write descriptive letters or journals about their music. When they died, it was seldom thought necessary to mention in obituaries the fact that the departed were fiddlers. For instance, Bob Peters, probably the author of "Fiddlers' Jubilee," was described at his death in 1941 as the "dean of local lawyers" and "a student of literature," with no mention of the fact that he delighted in playing the fiddle and was the organizer and judge of many conventions in the region.[9] When Y. Z. Hamilton was killed in a car accident in 1936, newspaper accounts did not include the fact that he was one of Alabama's champion fiddlers.

Yet information about early fiddling in Alabama does exist. Details reside in the memories of fiddlers across the state, now in their seventies and eighties, descendents of fiddlers who have made music in Alabama since the 1800s. There is Mack Blalock of Mentone, whose family brought fiddles to Alabama in 1813 and who still plays tunes he learned from his great-uncle, J. M. Blalock, born in 1854. There is Everis Campbell of Troy, born in 1909, who learned to play from his great-grandmother, father, and older brother. There is Thomas "Dad" Hill of Pinson, born in 1910, whose father, grandfather, uncles, and great-uncles, as far back as any Hill can remember, were fiddlers. As children and young adults, today's senior fiddlers led lives very much like those of their ancestors, plowing with mules, traveling by foot, horse and buggy, or train, all their music self-made. Now they are no strangers to air-conditioned automobiles, stereophonic record and tape players, and color television, yet they remember the "old days" of fiddling and can describe the conditions under which it flourished.

Valuable information about old-time fiddling also rests in the pages of weekly newspapers of rural counties and in the county and personal histories that Alabamians have lovingly collected and published over the years. The following quiltlike description of the old-time fiddler pieces together the words of journalists, local historians, and old-time fiddlers across the state of Alabama.

It Runs in Families

In earlier days, by the time a child was old enough to hold a fiddle, it is likely that he could already hum or whistle a number of fiddle

William C. Durham moved from the coal mines of West Virginia to the mining community of Straven in Shelby County, where he raised a family of musicians. From left to right: William and his sons Charles, Terry, and John Durham. A younger daughter, Juanita, not pictured, also played the fiddle. Photo ca. 1920, courtesy of the Harrison Collection, Birmingham Public Library Archives.

tunes. If he was part of a musical family, he had heard the tunes all of his life. Barney Dickerson of Houston County recalled family gatherings in the 1920s before he was old enough to play an instrument himself:

My daddy [Alto Dickerson] fiddled; his brother [Aley] fiddled; I had an uncle that fiddled and his brother fiddled, and Buster Dickerson, old man Aley's boy, he played a good fiddle. We'd just gather up . . . one played fiddle awhile and they had two or three changing a guitar, and all of it was in the family. And boy, they'd just play and play. And a fellow wouldn't [want to keep playing] and he'd just pass his fiddle on. And if he didn't want to use the one that the other fellow was playing, he'd just get up and get his. Most of the time that's what they done—it's like plowing with a plow. You know if you ever get one set, you can't plow with the other fellow's . . . They'd just play and play and they'd just change over and change over. And we'd just be listening.[10]

Three of Alto Dickerson's nine children—Coley, Carley, and Barney—became fiddlers, and the others learned to play a variety of stringed instruments, as have their children and grandchildren. Today, when one hears old-time and bluegrass music in Houston County, it is likely that a Dickerson has something to do with it.

In Cullman County, Arlin Moon heard old-time music played by his elders as he slept:

They played fiddles, five-strings, guitars, what have you . . . We'd go to the neighbors' houses . . . 'course we was little fellers, too small to play. They'd carry us a quilt and make us a pallet on the ground, and they'd get together outside in the yard. It was 10 or 11 o'clock at night and we'd go off to sleep, and I remember just how sleepy I was when they'd get me up to go home and go to bed.[11]

In such a setting, when a child was ready, he had no problem finding encouragement and opportunities to play. As a child in Brown's Valley, fifteen miles south of Guntersville, Tom Hill was surrounded by musicians:

There was a full band there at the house. We played at picnics and square dances. I was kind of a spoiled brat, you know, everybody made over me—a kid goes out and does something, you know. I was kindly embarrassed a lot of time at the attention

I got . . . My dad played fiddle, my sister Avor played guitar and organ and piano. One of my brothers picked the banjo; Buck, we called him. My oldest brother, Pete—he was a fiddler and a pretty good fiddler at that. He was kind of popular all around the community, at parties. He used to carry me around a lot.[12]

Jim Robertson was raised in Pickens County playing music with his father, W. C. "Bud" Robertson, eight brothers, and three sisters. In the Robertson family each child taught the next one down the line to play the fiddle. Jim, as did many fiddlers, learned to play when he was so small his feet could not touch the floor when he was sitting down.[13]

Even if they were not born into musical families, children had many opportunities to hear traditional fiddling and observe how it was done. From family and community members, they received the encouragement they needed to master the instrument. Webster Colburn of McCalla learned to play around 1910 after he and his father went to Selma to peddle the chairs and porch swings that the senior Colburn had made. There they listened to a left-handed black fiddler playing "Hen Cackle" on a street corner. His father liked the music so well that he told Web on the way home, "I'll buy you a fiddle if you'll learn to play that 'Hen Cackle.' " According to Web's son Howard, who also became a fiddler, Web Colburn learned to play "Hen Cackle" better than anyone he ever heard play it, and continued to play the fiddle until shortly before his death at age 85.[14]

Alvin Horn of Ashland, in Clay County, took up the fiddle after hearing it played with a guitar accompaniment:

Old man Custis Smith was one of the best fiddlers in this part of the country. I attended a dance over at his grandmother's, and his granddaddy and his daddy made music, and that was the first time that I had got to sit in on a guitar playing rhythm for a fiddle. I didn't care nothing about the dance; I just got me a chair over there near the musicians, and after old Brother Custis Smith had him a couple of shots, he really got with that fiddle. He was wonderful. They had some stuff that they played there that night that just fascinated me when they'd go from one chord to another on that guitar, old Bill backing him up on that fiddle . . . They wound the dance up at 12 o'clock, but they must have played for two, two and a half hours after it was over . . . just Mr. Smith and Bill. I came home that night and the music was on my mind. I didn't sleep a wink the rest of the night; I was just going over and over them changes they was making . . . it was so beautiful.[15]

Having received such inspiration, a young person could easily find the other elements needed to nourish his development as a musician. A fiddle could be borrowed from a family member or neighbor. There was time in the evening to practice. According to Vearl Cicero, who grew up in Coal Valley (Jefferson County), "None of the people had entertainment. No radios. You just went home and sat down and looked at the stars or something like that," if you didn't play an instrument.[16]

In such a setting the fiddler had an appreciative audience. Gaines Arnold of Quinton remembers that the people of his mining camp felt "really hungry for music. We were glad to hear anyone sing just any kind of song even by theirself without any kind of music. So fiddle music really sounded good to us." When Arnold started playing the fiddle as a child, "all the boys and girls about my age would come over to my house and get a stick and imitate me. In a year or two, they was inviting me over to their house to play for parties and things."[17]

The Lure of the Forbidden

Had families forced their children to play and practice the fiddle in order to uphold a family tradition or to provide music for the community, the art of fiddling would have died out long ago. They did the opposite, placing the family violin just out of reach—on the wall, in a drawer, or under a bed—giving the child firm instructions to leave it alone. However, as if it were an initiation rite for fiddlers, the child would manage to obtain and practice the instrument surreptitiously until he proved himself worthy of playing it publicly. Fiddlers recounted many charming variations of this event. Tom Hill recalled learning to play when he was a seven-year-old in Brown's Valley:

> We were cotton farmers. Everybody worked in the fields except the very young. There was a set of twins just under me and one sister, and I had to watch after these younger ones. A lot of times I'd spread a pallet out on the front porch where it was cool and get them to sleep. My dad had his fiddle hanging up there on a nail with a string, and he didn't allow nobody to touch that. I sneaked it down and I went to making little sounds

on it, you know. Finally some of his old tunes—I learned to play some of 'em—without any teacher. He came to the house one day after a drink of water and heard that fiddle and slipped off in there and caught me and liked to scared me to death. And he says, "Aw, don't be afraid, I'm not goin' to whip you. Go ahead and play me something." I did. I was kind of nervous. That night he got his fiddle down and let me play it. My sister played the guitar and organ . . . and she backed me up on guitar. That was my first experience with the fiddle.[18]

J. C. Brock of Crossville in Fayette County learned to play when he was about nine years old:

Now you know I had four brothers and I was the middle boy— two older and two younger. And the oldest one, he could play a fiddle a little. He had a fiddle and he'd hang it just as high as he could so I couldn't reach it. And I knew I'd get a little kicking if I did. But he couldn't tune his fiddle and he'd walk three or four miles to a neighbor's house where the guy could play a little and tune his fiddle. And he'd bring it back and give us good orders to leave that fiddle alone. Well, I got it down one day and I thought I was learning to do what he was doing. And I hit one of those pegs and it got out of tune and I couldn't tune it. We had an organ and I went over to it and took a pencil and marked the note and got that string back in tune.

And then his fiddle got out of tune one day, and it was about two or three days before he'd go get it tuned, and I was wanting it tuned. So I tuned his fiddle and played what I could and then I put it up tuned. And he come and he wanted to know who tuned his fiddle. And you know, I owned up to it and that calmed him down. I could get it down from then on.[19]

Monk Daniels was a well-known fiddler of Sand Mountain who took up the fiddle when he was about seven:

Along about that time I'd hook my daddy's fiddle out and hide and try to play it. Course he'd catch up with me and he'd give me a little jacking up. He was afraid I'd break it or something. So he'd make me put it up and he'd leave again and I'd get it out again. Finally he told me, "If you learn to play one tune, I'll give you this fiddle." Well, boy, I sat on the floor with that fiddle and I sawed and sawed and sawed and finally I learned all of "Casey Jones" . . . played on one string. So from that I learned another and kept on. Seven years old and I played fair. When I was ten years old I won the first fiddle prize.[20]

Because variants of this story are told so often by fiddlers, interviewers sometimes regard it with skepticism. However, given the environment in which fiddling was done, it seems logical that the incident of the forbidden fiddle would occur again and again. The fiddle was a fragile, cherished family possession. An unsupervised child could easily break or soil its strings, lose the bridge, and damage the hairs on the bow. It was sensible to forbid small children to touch the instrument. It was also understandable that children who had seen their elders get such joy from playing and listening to the instrument would feel compelled to disobey those who forbade it.

The least believable part of the story is that the children secretly taught themselves to play what is considered a very difficult instrument. Most of those who tell the story admit, however, that their first tunes were simple, familiar songs like "Nellie Gray," "The Preacher and the Bear," "Monkey Wrapped His Tail Around a Flag Pole," and "Casey Jones." As Osey Kersey admits of his first tune: "It wasn't like it ought to be. It was on a string or two, but I could play it."[21] Similarly, Jimmie Porter said, "I probably didn't make too good a music, but I was playing it."[22] And though the piece may have been played out of tune, with a scratchy bow and very simple style, the parents' anger at seeing the child with the forbidden fiddle would melt upon hearing him coax a recognizable melody from the instrument. When the family saw that the child "had an ear for music," he would be welcomed to join their music-making and to sit at the center of attention for a while.

Homemade Fiddles

Even after proving his ability and gentleness with the fiddle, a small child often had to wait until he was bigger and more mature before being given a real instrument. Alvin Horn recalled how his nephew Dewey Bryant became a fiddler:

He wanted his daddy's fiddle. He slipped it out one day and his mother missed the fiddle out of the trunk. She got out and got to walking down across the field . . . and he was down behind the terrace. Had that fiddle and bow out there playing it. She took that fiddle away from him and carried him to the house and just wore him out for getting Uncle Bill's fiddle 'cause money was hard to come by back then. Later on, she missed it again. And that time she whipped that boy something scandalous. And Uncle Bill told him, says, "Dewey, you leave my fiddle alone. I'll get you a fiddle some way or other. Meantime I'll make you one that you can play on." He got an old long-handle gourd and made a fingerboard to go on it, cut it out some way or another and cleaned the seeds and stripped that old gourd out, strung it up. And Dewey Bryant learned to play the fiddle with a homemade fiddle bow. Uncle Bill had made him that gourd fiddle.[23]

Other would-be fiddlers had to make do with cornstalk fiddles. Osey Kersey's mother showed him how to make and play one. In the fall of the year, just after the corn had been gathered, they would find two dry cornstalks, one for the fiddle and one for the bow. They created fiddle strings by carving below the outer layer of one stalk, inserting a bridge, and making four slits in the upraised layer. They haired the bow in the same fashion, making a longer hollow and inserting wedges at the top and botton to separate the "hair" from the rest of the stalk. With a little rosin on the bow, said Kersey, "I'd play 'I went down to my pea field, black snake bit me on my heel.' It would just grunt like the dickens . . . I could hear it; I don't know if anyone else could or not. So I tell people I learned to play off a cornstalk fiddle."[24]

About 1878, when D. A. Cole, later a champion fiddler of Limestone County, began learning to play, he made himself an instrument from an axle-grease tin. His horse provided hair for a homemade bow. After Cole played an identifiable tune on this device, he was given a fiddle by an older brother who had despaired of ever learning to play the instrument himself.[25] Another well-known Limestone County fiddler, Ruff McGlockin, learned to play on a cigar-box fiddle made for him by his older brother.[26]

Vearl Cicero of Coal Valley, a mining camp in Jefferson County, was so impressed after hearing "Uncle" Billy Gray's fiddling at an ice-cream social that he went home and tried to duplicate the instrument:

I just imagined a fiddle and took a board and began to whittle. I made the neck and all together and I just made it out of a piece of pine board, about two inches thick, I guess. Then I cut out the inside of it to hollow it out and then I took pieces of an orange crate, put it on there, and then got my strings. I used

A cornstalk fiddle with a shoestring bow, as played by a Blount County youth. Others, such as Osey Kersey, made both the fiddle and bow from cornstalks. Photo by Kim McRae Appel.

Stanley Bailey of Nashville, Georgia, first learned to play on a cigar-box fiddle.
Photo ca. 1924, courtesy of Mary and Stanley Bailey.

some of my daddy's guitar strings. I cut 'em off and put 'em on. That left his guitar without any strings on it. You can just figure out what happened from there.

Best as I remember, we had some peach trees and some of them had been cut down, and I busted open one and made a bridge for that fiddle so it would hold the strings up on the neck, and I made me a fingerboard and put it up under there and I drilled some holes in it, and I made the pegs out of some of that peach wood that I had busted out of there because it was hard, kind of like maple when it gets dry. And I made those pegs and instead of having holes in the pegs, I just looped the strings around them and hooked them on a little nail in the back. And I've said to myself many times, "How did I tune that thing?" Seems like I carried it over and got Mr. Gray to tune it for me. He kind of laughed about it and said that was a good job. Everybody thought it sounded real good. I wish I would've kept it. That would have been a talking piece now.[27]

Eventually Cicero "got ashamed" of his homemade fiddle and earned enough to go into Jasper with his uncle and pay $9 for a fiddle and bow.

Lacking cash and living far from towns, however, many fiddlers found it necessary to make their own instruments, even as adults. Using a maple tree, a pocketknife, and a pot of glue, fiddlers, such as John Chambers of Limestone County, Young White of Cullman County, Adous Johnson of Albertville, and Professor Hawkins of Rocky Ridge[28] were able to produce fiddles that served them well.

Arlin Moon, whose family farmed for a living, was one of many fiddlers who began making instruments as a necessity: "We just couldn't buy one, you know. If you play, you play someone else's instrument; then you go home and you don't have one to play. You've either got to make one or do without; you don't have money to buy one."[29]

Moon continues to make and repair instruments today, obtaining curly maple from family land in Morgan County and walnut from a tree his grandfather planted in the middle 1800s. Black-heart persimmon trees provide wood for his fingerboards, as do dogwood trees.

Accustomed to making whatever they needed, many rural fiddlers were undaunted by the delicacy of fiddlemaking. Every region of the state has had its share of fiddlemakers, producing instruments from native woods for themselves, their children, and neighbors, with varying degrees of skill.

Acquiring the "Strad"

To many fiddlers, acquiring an instrument of their own was a memorable experience, whether it involved making it themselves, buying it at the local jewelry store or pawnshop, or getting it as a result of clever negotiations.

Osey Kersey's first fiddle was a "seed fiddle": "Book come out, advertising book, you know. You'd sell so many seeds and they'd give you a fiddle—it was three-quarter sized. There wasn't much to it. After a few years of playing it, he sent $10 to Montgomery Ward to buy a $19 fiddle on sale. Every day he "met the mail carrier" and when the fiddle finally arrived, he "sat down under a tree and tuned that thing up and went to fiddling. I could play a tune where you could tell what it was."[30]

Similarly, Chester Allen of Scottsboro ordered a fiddle from Sears, Roebuck: "It come in on a Saturday and I sat down right there at that mailbox and tuned that fiddle up the way Herbert McComb's fiddle sounded to me . . . By the time I got to the house I could play 'Great Big Tater in Sandy Land.' "[31]

Fifty years after arduously paying for his first fiddle, J. C. Brock of Crossville (Fayette County) is still playing it. The fiddle was brought to the county in the sack of a tramp who spent the night with one of Brock's neighbors, the owner of a country store. The merchant could play the fiddle, and when the tramp left, he said, "Since you won't charge me anything to spend the night, I'm just going to give you this fiddle." Knowing that Brock was learning to play his brother's fiddle, the merchant offered to sell the new fiddle to Brock. When Brock replied that he had no money, he was asked, "What have you got at home?"

> I said, "There's a little old calf they say is mine." I claimed it. He says, "Well, I tell you what. Give me that bull calf and $5 and I'll let you have this fiddle."
>
> O.K., I paid him a dime at a time, because that was what we'd get—30 cents or 33 cents at a dance. And my part would be a third. A string cost a nickel, too. I'd go down there and pay that guy a dime. He had a big old ledger and my name was listed.

Violin made in 1925 by Adous Johnson of Albertville. Maple and pine
from the Johnson land were shaped with a pocketknife, and thinned
with a chisel and a broken pane of glass. The purfling (inlay) was
mail-ordered. Photo by Kim McRae Appel.

The most I'd pay was a quarter and the least was a dime . . . Ten years later my brother said that calf wasn't mine to sell, but by then I had $5, so I just paid my brother off.[32]

Alvin Horn was not as successful in the purchase of his first fiddle:

My father had a masterpiece of a fiddle. He sort of sawed around on it. He wasn't a fiddler, but he loved it. He let me keep it. And when Arthur Wesley left over here—he went back to Kentucky—and he had a Stainer, which is a good brand of fiddle, a Stainer is, and I asked Daddy, I said, "Daddy, he's selling everything that he can get any money out of to pay his moving expense. Will you get me that fiddle?"
He went down there. Says, "Arthur, will you sell me that fiddle there for Alvin?"
He said, "Yes, sir, I sure will."
"How much you want for it?"
He says, "I'll practically give it to you. I'll take $5 for it."
Daddy got his pocketbook out and says, "Arthur, I haven't got but three."
He says, "I ain't taking less than five for it. So I'll take your three and throw in the other two." So I got it and it was the sorriest fiddle I ever had. It was no good. I did everything in the world that I knew how to, to make the fiddle come out, but it just wouldn't get there.[33]

Horn's disappointing violin was probably a copy of an instrument made by Jacob Stainer, who produced violins between 1640 and 1700 and was considered the greatest German luthier.[34] His violins were more highly arched than those of Stradivari and were capable of producing a sweet, rich tone, yet lacked carrying power.[35] While favored by chamber musicians, they certainly were not the ideal instrument for a country fiddler attempting to be heard at a square dance—especially a Stainer made to be sold for $5 or $6 by Sears, Roebuck, the likely origin of Horn's fiddle.

For rural fiddlers, mail-order catalogs were the most accessible source of instruments. In the first three decades of this century, each Sears, Roebuck catalog contained several beautifully illustrated pages of violins. In 1900, a fiddler could send $1 to the company and receive any violin C.O.D., subject to inspection. For $2.50 he could get a "Genuine Stradivarius Model" with "extra strings, a nice bow and a valuable instruction book." For $4.75 a Maggini model with double inlaid purfling could be his. A Stainer model cost $6.25, a

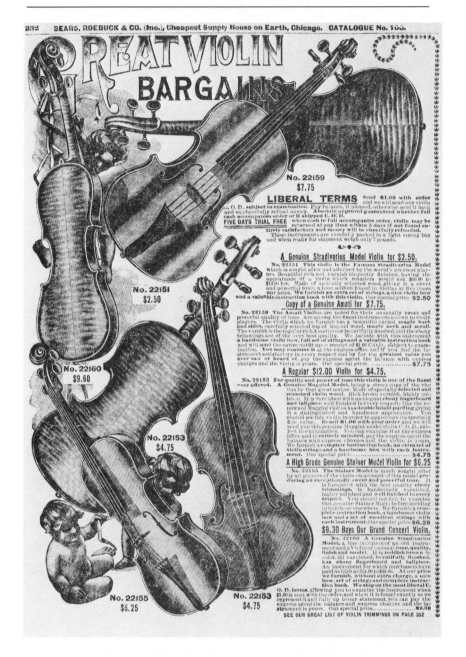

One of several pages of violins offered for sale in the Spring 1899 catalog of Sears, Roebuck & Company. Photo courtesy of Sears.

copy of a genuine Amati could be gotten for $7.75, and for $9.60 he could purchase "A Genuine Stradivarius Model, a fine imitation of an old instrument." By 1909 the selection range had widened, and the fiddler could pay from $1.95 for a Stradivarius model (with ten weekly lessons) up to $22.45 for the Ludwig Concert violin.[36] Few of the instruments came in cases, which caused country fiddlers like Uncle Bill Brown to carry them in flour sacks.

Mail-order fiddles were all clearly described as "genuine" copies or models, yet many of them, as their shiny varnishes acquired a patina of age, became genuine Stradivaris in the eyes of their owners. An attempt by Herbert Goodkind to document the whereabouts of all existing Stradivarian instruments resulted in the identification of 700 of the 1,100 believed to have been created by the master. The rest, concluded Goodkind in 1972, had been lost or destroyed.[37] It seems, however, that the missing instruments are all under beds and behind sofas in rural Alabama. Many fiddlers believe they are playing the genuine article, and few will be disappointed by appraisers, as most insist they would never attempt to sell the instrument. When, after much searching, swapping, and saving, a fiddler finds an instrument that pleases him, he remains steadfastly loyal to it.

Building a Repertoire

Young fiddlers, secretly scraping music out of purloined fiddles, chose tunes that they had sung many times, whose melodies were fixed firmly in their memories. They experimented with their fingers on the strings, until the sounds coming from the fiddle matched those in the mind. As they continued to play, they would move on to more complex tunes, such as the breakdowns needed for dances and fiddle contests, continuously adding to their repertoires. By the time that most of them had reached their peak as fiddlers, they could "play all night without repeating a single tune," knowing at least a hundred fiddle tunes—all learned in basically the same way they learned the first.

Everis Campbell of Troy said that there are two types of fiddlers: the "noted" and the "gifted." "Noted" fiddlers learn their music from the printed page; "gifted" ones play by ear.[38] All the fiddlers discussed in this book are "gifted." Though some had mothers and sisters who had taken piano lessons or played the family pump organ with the aid of written notes, though some had attended "singing school" and could read "shape notes," few found the printed note

Olen Mayes of Sand Mountain displays his new fiddle from Sears, Roebuck &
Company, ca. 1920. Photo courtesy of Olen Mayes.

useful in learning fiddle tunes. They learned in a number of other ways.

First, a fiddler might listen to the tune being played and try to fix it in his memory for future reference just as Web Colburn listened to the fiddler on a corner playing "Hen Cackle." According to Carl Stewart, a Jefferson County fiddler who played professionally with Hank Penny:

> I'd say that 90 percent of the hoedown fiddlers, when they start, have a tune in mind they want to learn. They don't start out with no scales. I think it's just a gift to people that can play like that. They hear somebody play a tune, then they get off and they practice and they play that same tune.[39]

J. C. Brock recalled that Charlie Stripling once learned a tune by listening to the calliope music of a merry-go-round in a traveling road show, and asking a companion to help him remember it until he got home to his fiddle. But memory is imperfect, and Stripling's son Robert remembered being awakened by fiddle music: "Daddy had thought of a tune . . . and had got up and got that fiddle about 2:30 in the morning, and he was up walking the floor playing it. He said if he didn't get up and play it then, he'd never remember it."[40]

J. C. Brock told a similar story: "I went to a fiddler's convention one night, and next morning I was plowing and there was a tune bothering me bad, trying to think of it and I couldn't. You know, I thought of it, tied my mule to a peach tree, went into the house and fiddled the heck out of it."[41]

The fact that our earliest fiddlers had to rely solely on memory in learning tunes accounts for the great variety of names and variations one fiddle tune may have. When the fiddler played at musical gatherings, he had the opportunity to relearn a tune that he had "misremembered" or to pass it on in its altered state to others. According to Harmon Hicks of Bibb County, such gatherings were the best source of new tunes:

> If your bunch gets around to playing, some know some pieces and you might know some they don't. If he plays a good fiddle piece, you'll say, "Hey, I want to learn that." He might play it three or four or five times, but probably before you left from there, you could play that piece of music. That's the way a lot of it got to moving around. Maybe I was playing one or two he liked, and he'd pick out one. And by doing that, why, you can just have all kinds of good fiddle music.[42]

Another way to learn a new tune was to seek out a fiddler who played it well. In that way, the fiddler could get tips on tuning, bowing, and style as well as learn the basic melody. Osey Kersey spoke of a neighbor who taught him tunes: "Old man Tom Jackson, who lived on our place down there. He was 84 and I'd just gotten my fiddle. All his boys could fiddle, and they say his first wife could beat him on a fiddle when she was alive. He had a girl who was good on guitar. I'd plow around his house and he'd have that old fiddle out there . . . that's all he done. I learned 'Cotton-eyed Joe' from him."[43]

J. C. Brock described how he sought Charlie Stripling as a teacher in the early thirties:

> We learned to play during the "brush arbor" time. lt was all beginners and carried their fiddles in a flour sack with the bow sticking out the end, and if you sat it down on the bed, somebody'd lay a baby on it or cover it up with a coat. We all come along and was all interested and didn't have really anyone to listen at but the Skillet Lickers on recordings and Dave Macon on the radio. And Mr. Stripling was an old country fiddler and he and his brother made some records, and we were eager to get ahold of them. And then he and his family—his two sons—were playing, and I'd get the road hot going down to try to learn one of their tunes. In fact, what I learned, I learned from Mr. Stripling. He was the closest and handiest and had more patience with me. Course, we didn't have no conveyance, but we could catch a train at Fayette and go to Kennedy and spend the night with Mr. Stripling, and more than one night, as far as that was concerned. It was something to board a train and see the gang get on and then get off at a little town like that. It was a lot of fun.[44]

With the commercial recording of fiddle music in the midtwenties, another method of learning tunes became possible. If a fiddler had a record player, he could learn "Hen Cackle" from Fiddling John Carson or "Bully of the Town" from the Skillet Lickers. Harmon Hicks recalled learning fiddle tunes from the record player:

> Back when we were young, we had one of these wind-up Graphinolas . . . old Riley Puckett and Gid Tanner, they were the ones that put out the records mostly in those days. Well, that Graphinola was geared up some different from what the stereos and things are today. You could just slow that thing down to

just like you wanted it, and you could get your instrument and play along with it. And so I learned a lots of records from back in those days . . . "Big Eyed Rabbit," "Flop-eared Mule," "Old Joe Clark," and things like that.[45]

By the middle thirties, the radio and record player were beginning to modernize the tastes of rural audiences. At country dances, couples began doing "round dances"—fox-trots, two-steps, and waltzes—between square dances. A fiddler who wanted to stay up-to-date and in favor with the dancers learned tunes like "Three O'Clock in the Morning" and "Love Letters in the Sand," with no recourse to sheet music. A. D. Hamner, whose family band furnished music for many dances around Northport and Tuscaloosa, learned such tunes from a jukebox:

> Back then, when we was playing, we'd go to town to the WocoPep. We all had to have a bowl of chili; we'd go there and get us a bowl of chili; I don't care if we just ate supper. Then'd we'd go on and play for the dances and come back there and have to have another bowl of chili. It wasn't but a dime back then. They had a record player in there: we'd stick a nickel in it and learn a new tune. You can play it about three times, and if you want to learn it you can play it. That's the way I learn. If I listen to it, but not another one, I can play it, but I can't listen to anything in between. But if I ever play it, get it down, I won't forget it, unless I stay off it so long. If you play five tunes, I'll only learn one of them—that'll be the last one; I lost the first one when you played the second one.[46]

Vearl Cicero learned popular tunes from the radio, though his family didn't own one: "The only way I had to learn a tune when I was first coming up at Coal Valley—I remember it very well—I'd hear the radios playing as I'd walk to school. I had to walk two miles to school, and I'd walk down through the residential section. And if I heard a tune that I wanted to learn, I stopped and listened to it. Didn't have a radio at home or Graphinola or nothing. But when I'd hear that tune, I'd start humming or whistling it. By the time I got to school, which might have been half a mile on down there, I'd be able to go back home and play it on the fiddle."[47]

Popular tunes produced in big cities found their way into the repertoires of the rural fiddler of the thirties in the same manner that once-modern tunes like "Dixie" and "Red Wing" and old traditional tunes had entered: Fiddlers listened to a tune being played or sung, then experimented with it on their own instruments until they had reproduced it to their satisfaction. Upon finding their rendition pleasing to listeners, they retained it in their repertoires, regardless of its source.

A "Peculiar Wiggling of the Bow"

"As variety is the spice of life," noted the organizer of a Fayette County fiddle convention, "everybody seems to enjoy the peculiar wiggling of the bow passing across the fiddle."[48] *Peculiar* is used here in its oldest sense, meaning "particular," "unique," or "private property." It is an apt term, expressing the individuality of the old-time fiddler who delights in adding subtle variations that make a tune his own. Charlie Stripling, whose 1928 recording of "The Lost Child" is regarded as an old-time fiddle classic, explained to interviewer Bob Pinson that he had heard the tune played by Pleas Carroll at dances, "but I added some more to what he had. Nobody wouldn't pay much attention to it the way he played it, but what I added to it, why it made it more entertaining."[49] Fiddlers retain the basic melodic line and structure of a tune, but few attempt to play it exactly as another fiddler plays it. Barney Dickerson explained:

> Every bit I got—and it's not much—but I learned it by listening . . . you pick up a lot of good turns and a lot of good things in a tune by listening at the other fellow . . . Of course there is tunes that I play that I make up little bypasses in, because it'd be easier for me to play it like that than it would to play it like the other fellow played it all the way through. Like I told my brother. He told me, says, "You don't play 'Billy in the Low Ground.' " And I says, "Listen, let me tell you something. You didn't hear the fellow that wrote 'Billy in the Low Ground.' " I said that was before mine and your day. And I said it passed right on down, right on down, right on down. I said my daddy played it. You don't play it like my daddy does. I don't play it like my daddy does. I just picked it up and played it, and I put parts in that you won't never know weren't originally put in there.[50]

Even if a fiddler wished to play a tune exactly as another fiddler played it, he would have trouble doing so unless he had learned to play from that fiddler. With some fiddlers holding their instruments down on their chests, others under their chins; with some using four fingers, placing them precisely where they are wanted, and others using two fingers which they slide from note to note; some grasping their bows close to the middle, leaving room only for short, choppy strokes, and others holding them close to the frog, allowing space for long swooping strokes, there is little likelihood that a group of old-time fiddlers could play in true unison. The most to be hoped for is compatibility. This was especially true in older days, before recording equipment brought a degree of standardization to fiddle tunes, and before the greater availablity of accompanying instruments narrowed the range of keys and tunings that the fiddler used.

Of course, other instruments had been available in Alabama since its settlement. The banjo, an instrument of African origin, had been brought to the state by slaves.[51] By the 1850s it was being carried into areas without slavery by minstrel troupes. Being fairly simple to construct from native materials, banjos were played across the state, not only in the slave quarters but at community gatherings such as the 1858 Fourth of July festivities in Bibb County at which Captain T. W. Gantt's reading of the Declaration of Independence and John Pratt's oration were followed by the music of fiddles, banjos, and accordions.[52] The accordions may have been brought by immigrants or could have been purchased in Alabama. Isaac Bryan advertised accordions for sale at his Comb and Variety Store in Mobile in 1846. Monied citizens could purchase pianos, violins, guitars, bass viols, flutes, and flageolets from Bruno and Virgin's shop in Montgomery in 1849.[53] Guitars were especially popular in the 1850s, and according to Alabama historian Marie Bankhead Owen, "no young lady was considered 'accomplished' unless she could play The Spanish Fandango and one or two other pieces."[54]

While the merchants and planters may have been able to afford a variety of fine imported instruments advertised in Montgomery and Mobile papers, plain folk made most of their music on fiddles and banjos until the early 1900s when less expensive, factory-made instruments became available, largely through mail-order catalogs. Between the years 1900 and 1930, cellos, which in 1900 could be purchased from Sears for $11.20, found their way into the Green family band of Sand Mountain and the Stripling family of Lamar County; the ten-button accordion became part of Matthew Hill's family gatherings in Pinson; and the guitar and mandolin joined the twin fiddles of the Langston Brothers of Six Mile (Bibb County). Pump organs, which could be purchased in installments of $1 a month, decorated country parlors across the state. As a child, Tom Hill recalled seeing them in many Brown's Valley homes, where they frequently became part of string bands: "They might just be

Classical violinists are taught to hold the violin between the shoulder and chin so that the hand, not having to support the instrument, will be free to reach all positions on the fingerboard rapidly and precisely. Fiddlers develop their own methods of supporting the instrument. Above, Mrs. Mary McLean of Skyline Farms (Farm Security Administration photo by Ben Shahn, 1937. Courtesy of the Library of Congress); opposite, Pat Harris of west Jefferson County; and on page 68, Tom Hill of Pinson. Photos by Kim McRae Appel.

The Covin String Band of Fayette County had no lack of guitars when they posed for this photograph around 1905. Front: Maude A. Swanson and Jala Nichols. Back: Stacy Cargile, Autie Raley, and Lilla Nichols. Photo courtesy of Charles J. Swanson.

playing chords to a fast tune, but they are a good second to a fiddle."[55] Another common instrument was the "mouth harp," or "French Harp." Sears, Roebuck called them harmonicas and sold them for 19¢ apiece in 1909. Every musical family had a member who excelled on the "harp," and in Elmore County the instrument was so respected that fiddle contests were often called "Fiddlers' and Harpers' Conventions."

Prior to the growth of old-time bands, however, fiddlers alone provided most of the music for rural activities. Descriptions of dances in Madison County in the early 1800s, Talladega County in the 1850s, and Lamar County (1889) mentioned only fiddlers.[56] Betsy Hamilton, who wrote local color stories of life around Talladega, described a party where "they kep' two fiddlers playin' constant. Ef one got tired he'd pass the fiddle over to another, an' the same tune went on."[57] Several fiddlers interviewed for this book recalled that their elders always played unaccompanied. They tuned the strings to whatever pitch sounded pleasing on their instruments. Attempts to accompany the old fiddlers with a guitar or other musical instrument often failed, not only because of unorthodox tunings but

The Langston Brothers of Six Mile [Bibb County] had a full complement of instruments in their string band, ca. 1900. From left to right: Obediah "Obe" Langston, Edward "Doc" Langston, James Columbus "Lum" Langston, and William J. "Willie" Langston. Photo

because, according to Aubrey Phillips of Robertsdale, "they cut corners in some places and added some in others to suit themselves."[58]

A lively backup rhythm for the fiddler and dancers could be provided by a good strawbeater, however. "That was a band back in those days," said A. D. Hamner, "a fiddle and someone beating straws."[59] The straws were thin stalks of broom sedge plucked from fields or, in the midst of the fun, from a homemade broom. The strawbeater might use two straws "in the manner of a snare drummer," as W. C. Handy's grandfather used knitting needles. One straw would suffice, however. Marcus Bailey described "beating the straw" as it was done by an expert in Rocky Ridge: "He used a broom corn reed or a small cane reed, holding it between thumb and finger of the left hand. Forming a mitt with his right hand, the thumb of the right hand would be below the back end of the straw (about 1/4 of it) and the back of thumb and finger of his left hand. The palm of the right hand would be above the straw and above thumb and finger of the left hand. He could beat out a double rhythm I have not heard since."[60]

For strawbeating, the fiddle was generally played in a tuning called "high bass and counter," a departure from the classical tuning of the four strings: E, A, D, G. In such a tuning the third, or "counter," string is raised from a D to an E, and the fourth, or "bass," string from a G to an A, resulting in an AEAE tuning. Mack Blalock of Lookout Mountain called this tuning the "round key of A": "That's where you want to beat your straws; you can beat strings that you're not a'noting—two of them." Blalock explained that as the fiddler played on the bass, or "coarse," strings, the strawbeater would beat on the high, or "fine," strings. Then, for variety, the two could just "swap out," with the fiddler noting the high strings and the strawbeater tapping out rhythms on the bass and counter strings.[61]

In homes and communities where strawbeating was a popular fiddle accompaniment, fiddlers employed a variety of "cross-key" tunings which left open or unnoted strings in the strawbeater's domain. Blalock, for instance, knew a special "round" tuning for each of the keys in which fiddle tunes are commonly played. Such tunings were used, also, because they made fingering easier. By raising or lowering the pitch of a string, the fiddler could bring into easy reach a note that otherwise would require a tricky stretch. Moreover, the cross tunings usually enriched the sound of the instrument. Strings were tuned so that the unplayed strings served as "drones" to the noted ones, creating sympathetic vibrations and increasing the vol-

John McDougal beat straws while Charlie Sellers fiddled in west Jefferson County, ca. 1890. Photo courtesy of Francis and Howard Colburn.

ume of the instrument. And, if the fiddler had a banjoist to accompany him, he was likely to use cross tunings. The five-string banjo employs a drone string, and is retuned whenever one desires to play in a different key, as is the cross-tuned fiddle.

As string bands grew in popularity, however, the use of straw-beaters and cross-tuned fiddles decreased. Fiddling became less "peculiar." The fiddler no longer needed to leave open strings for the straws, and when accompanied by other instruments, the additional volume provided by the open tunings was not essential. More fiddlers began to use the standard EADG tuning, from which they could play most tunes without the nuisance of retuning frequently. "I tune with these fingers," said Ed Rickard of Russellville,[62] implying that a variety of tunings was not important to a skillful fiddler. Carl Stewart of Jefferson County recalled learning to play as a child with his fiddle tuned AEAE, until another fiddler, Clarence Pounds, told him, "All right, boy, if you're going to learn to play the fiddle, you're going to do it right . . . He sat me on his knee and made me play until I learned to play EADG."[63]

Women Fiddlers

In 1928, Bud Silvey, promoter of fiddle conventions in north Georgia and Alabama, directed a fiddlers' convention in Huntsville. According to the *Huntsville Daily Times*, the contest attracted more than forty fiddlers from four states. "Among the surprises of the whole affair, " said Silvey, "is the women artists listed as old-time fiddlers."[64] The winner was Mrs. Emma Crabtree of Merrimack, and second place was won by an unidentified woman, most likely Mrs. Delia Mullins, a champion fiddler of Madison County.

Silvey's surprise is understandable. It was much more common to see a woman seated at a piano or pump organ in church, than playing onstage at a fiddlers' convention. In musical families, daughters might play stringed instruments at home after supper or for square dances in the homes of neighbors; yet after they married, their responsibilities as wives and mothers made it difficult to continue as musicians. A number of talented women did play, however, and are remembered as popular community fiddlers. The following women, active in the 1920s and '30s, were vigorous, confident fiddlers who played for dances and won their share of prizes in the "man's world" of the fiddlers' convention.

Annie Blalock Cooper was one of the many Blalock fiddlers on Lookout Mountain. Mack Blalock recalled that his aunt "could get that bow to going . . . I never seen anybody who could use a fiddle bow like she did . . . She could beat us so bad."[65] He remembered her winning over well-known fiddlers, such as Joe Lee (see Chapter 3), at area fiddlers' conventions during the twenties and thirties.

In west Alabama, Pearl Duncan Morgan defeated her share of

Mary McLean of Skyline Farms, Alabama, in 1937. Farm Security Administration photo by Ben Shahn, courtesy of the Library of Congress.

champions. As a child in Lowndes County, Mississippi, she beat straws while her father, Andrew Duncan, fiddled. After she began playing, she went with him to fiddlers' conventions, which he stopped entering when she started winning. Morgan married at age 16, but her young husband encouraged her to participate in conventions, and when their child was born, he cared for the infant while his wife fiddled at dances and contests. At 18, she won first place over Charlie Stripling in Vernon, Alabama, and in following years was often among the finalists in contests at Fayette, Sulligent, and other west Alabama communities.[66]

Eula Spivey Rushing of Troy made fiddlers' contests in Pike County exciting. They would turn into "shoot-outs" between her and several excellent fiddlers in the area.[67] Everis Campbell, one of her top competitors, described her as "a crack-shot fiddler."[68] Her admirers often requested a breakdown called "Old Slow." As she played, Ellis Spivey remembered, "she'd pitch her voice to the tune and holler."[69]

She was also a popular dance fiddler, usually accompanied by one or more of her twelve children. She insisted that the band play well. "If you'd drag on her or if the G string of the guitar was out," said Carter Rushing, "she'd reach over and peck you with the bow." He recalled that she would play for a dance any night of the week, but on Saturday night, she would set out a little clock. When midnight arrived, "She'd put a shave and a haircut" to the tune.[70] Eula Rushing was not one to lead people into dancing on Sunday.

In Madison County, "if you won a contest, you had to beat Delia Mullins to do it," said Tom Sutton.[71] He remembered one time when he did:

> One of the judges was a man who just loved her fiddling. She walked out on the stage and he'd holler just like a drunk man. You could hear him two or three city blocks. And boy—she'd get out there—she always played "Tom and Jerry." So one Friday night I said, "I'm going up there and I'm going to do the very best I can. I'm going to do my best to win second prize 'cause Mrs. Mullins is going to win first prize."
>
> And so when we got up there, we was in classrooms, tuning. I saw her and walked over and said, "Mrs. Mullins, you're going to get it tonight, ain't you?"
>
> She said, "Naw, you know you'll get it."
>
> I said, "I'm playing for second because you're going to get first. It's a certain thing." Lo and behold, that's the night they give me first. Like to killed her.[72]

While Mrs. Mullins (1883–1935) did not win every contest she entered, she had an impressive record of victories. When she entered the fiddlers' contest at Athens Agricultural School in 1924, the *Alabama Courier* reported that her "wonderful ability has won for her first prize in every contest she has entered prior to this." It noted that she played left-handed, "and it is said by some that left-handed music is not so easily understood, but she disproved this as she was heartily applauded and encored time and time again." At the conclusion of the evening, Mrs. Mullins was awarded fourth place, though "it was believed by many prior to the awarding of the prizes that she would easily take first place."[73] When she did win the Athens contest in 1926, the *Courier* reported:

> Several lady fiddlers were present and it was one of these, Mrs. Mullins, who was here a year ago [actually two years ago] and to whom it was thought should have gone the first prize, that was given the first prize this year. This is the fourth contest this year she has been in and won the first prize. She is both an artistic and graceful handler of the bow.[74]

James Cole of Athens said that Mrs. Mullins, "a left-handed lady playing over the bass strings," was fascinating to watch. A left-handed fiddler usually restrings the instrument so that the strings most often played are within easy reach of the bow. Mrs. Mullins did not do that. She arched her bowing arm over the instrument to reach the higher strings, thus giving a very dynamic appearance to her playing. Audiences enjoyed watching her play with her brother, Robert Reynolds, also an excellent fiddler. The two would face each other. As Reynolds was a right-handed fiddler, their bows seemed to form mirror images.[75]

In 1928 another Madison County woman, Mrs. Emma Smith Crabtree, won the prestigious fiddlers' convention at Athens. That year she also won first place in Bud Silvey's contest in Huntsville, receiving a new violin for the prize. Born in 1898 in Franklin County, Tennessee, she was raised in Merrimack, near Huntsville, where her family was employed by Merrimack Mills. Her father was a fiddler, and all of his seven children, except one, played music. She married a mill worker and worked in the mill herself, forming a string band with three fellow workers. The Merrimack Band was an important part of life in the mill village, a community with its own stores, school, hospital, theater, and recreation facilities. During rehearsals, the Crabtree home would fill with listeners.[76] E. F. DuBose, principal of Joe Bradley School in Merrimack, remembered the fiddlers' conventions held there two or three times a year, when audiences would overflow the thousand-seat auditorium. DuBose considered "Miss Emma" the drawing card of the convention, "the Elvis Presley of her time."[77]

Crabtree, who died in 1977, lived through a period in which few were playing old-time music. When fiddlers' conventions began to be held in the late 1960s, however, friends encouraged her to start practicing again. She found herself onstage once more, winning prizes as a senior fiddler.

Old Fiddlers Remembered

Few fiddlers manage to persist at the art throughout their lives. They have "spells," some lasting decades, when they do not take their fiddles from their cases. Barney Dickerson hated the times when his father lost interest in fiddling:

> You could beg him sometime for two hours and a half and he wouldn't play the fiddle at all. The best way we found, later in years, after a long time, to get him to play when he'd be on a spell like that was just to get to bragging on a tune that so-and-so played that we knowed Pa played. Directly he'd start moving around in his chair. In the summertime, everybody sat out on the front porch. He'd look in the house. "Boy," he says, "go in there and get your fiddle and bring it out. I believe I can play that tune." And that'd get him started. Sometimes then he'd fiddle right by himself, not even no guitar with him . . . sometimes two hours. He'd throw his head back on his shoulder where he could hear that fiddle. He was a great musician and he learned it just on his own. After the boys got up to where they could work and he got up in age, he didn't have nothing to do and he'd just practice on that fiddle.[78]

Vearl Cicero explained a long interruption in his fiddle-playing that coincided with the period in which few fiddlers were playing: "You don't have time when you are a'raising a family. You come in so tired, you don't want to practice. You don't feel like going out and playing at some party, and naturally, they'll quit inviting you when you don't feel like coming. Then more entertainment comes along . . . like Elvis Presley, and all the younger generation would rather listen to that than some old fiddlers' convention."[79]

But the folk-music revival of the late 1960s found Cicero, Crabtree, and many others retired and ready to play again. Old tunes, surprisingly, came back to them. Playing after a thirty-five year break, Harmon Hicks said, "You won't ever forget. I don't believe that anybody who plays music in his younger days will ever forget all of them, if he's a natural."[80] Should he forget, there are recordings to jog his memory.

"A fiddler never loses his touch," wrote Bob Kyle. "He can set himself back by taking violin lessons and learning how to read the notes, or he can get married. But the fiddling urge outlives schooling or a ma-in-law."[81] In later years he is more likely to be set back by

Fiddler Johnny Hamner, accustomed in earlier days to playing for large crowds without the aid of microphones, now uses an electric pickup for his fiddle when playing at the Northport Community Center. Photo by Kim McRae Appel.

arthritis and loss of hearing than by wives and violin lessons. Older fiddlers do not play with their former rapidity and preciseness. They begin to prefer waltzes and hymns to hoedowns. Yet they do not lose their "touch." One who listens carefully can detect in their playing the unique harmonies, special bow strokes, and personal renditions of tunes that delighted listeners in earlier days.

After old age or death has silenced their music, fiddlers who once played for community dances, conventions, picnics, and other gatherings are not quickly forgotten. They have been a part of the good times that people want to remember. Thus a number of fiddlers who were active at the turn of the century have been written into local history books. Among them is J. C. Carroll, the herb doctor, who settled in Ider (De Kalb County) in 1889: "He was very fond of his violin and kept up his practice. He attended the conventions and won many prizes."[82] In Suggsville (Clarke County) was Benjamin S. Barnes, a medical doctor, who had "the wizard's touch" on the violin: "In the last years of his life, with a penknife he carved a beautiful violin and completed the instrument in every particular, and the writer of this sketch never enjoyed a musical number more than the one he produced after completion of the instrument."[83]

In Monroe and Conecuh counties there was "Uncle" Van Harris, "who knew all the tunes and all the dancers wanted to dance to his music."[84] In Etowah County, Lee Phillips frequently played his fiddle for young people who stopped by his house after hay rides.[85] In Fayette, "Dandy" Hendon served the community by "making caskets, building houses, doing shop work, and making music for school and social functions. Many times he won prizes at Fiddlers' Conventions at Fayette Court House."[86] In the Hatchet Creek community (Clay County), where dancing was "denounced as a cardinal sin," was Jasper Campbell:

> Jasper was a middle-aged farmer, shy and modest in his comportment, who accepted invitations to parties only under heavy pressure. His repertory was extensive, but "Arkansas Traveller" was his favorite piece. While playing this piece, he would stay his hand at intervals and, in a drawling voice, speak what purported to be the words of the song. Thus: "Old ummern (woman), look under the bed and get fully half that squirrel and cook it." Then he would resume his sawing as if he were playing the tune that fitted the words. How we laughed at that![87]

Other fiddlers have not yet made it into history books, but some have achieved legendary status among younger fiddlers who heard

them play. Early in this century, John Chambers was the most respected fiddler in Limestone County. Tom Sutton recalled, "Just
nobody played like him. Course we have better all-round fiddlers
today. But on them old tunes that he played—he could sit down and
play half a day without playing the same tune—it's just hard to find
a man who could beat him."[88]

Limestone County was also the home of Sam McCracken, who is
considered the "granddaddy" of the Tennessee Valley Old Time Fiddlers' Convention in Athens, and Ruff (pronounced "Rufe") Mc-
Glocklin, an itinerant fiddler noted for his ability to play and sing
at the same time.

In west Alabama, fiddlers remember Henry Ledlow. A. K. Callahan
first saw him at a contest at the courthouse in Tuscaloosa in the
early 1920s: "It was going on pretty strong. This old fellow with the
dirtiest sawmill 'overhauls' came in there with a fiddle in a flour
sack and says, 'Is this thing open to anybody?' . . . That's the first
time I ever saw Henry Ledlow, now. He got up there and played. He
stole the show . . . He was as smooth as silk. He played all over the
thing. And he won the money that night. He was the most impressive fiddler you ever saw, and he didn't look like he'd washed in six
months."[89]

Webster Colburn liked to tell about a convention (possibly the
same one) when Ledlow came late, after some contestants thought
"they had first place wrapped up." He won with his rendition of
"Screech Owl Froze to Death in the Summertime."[90]

People in the vicinity of Sand Mountain remember Monk Daniels
(1904–1971). W. A. Bryan wrote that Daniels "could get a lot of
action and enthusiasm out of a group of square dancers. He was
always ready to use his fiddle and ability in helping out at civic and
charity benefits, and never failed to respond when called upon."[91]
During the folk revival of the late 1960s, Daniels opened his door
to many young musicians who wished to learn the old tunes as he
played them.

In rural areas across the state when people recall the celebrations
and entertainments of earlier days, these fiddlers and many more
are remembered.

A "Gifted" Fiddler

William Everis Campbell of Troy was one of many fiddlers who
furnished information for this book. His interview took place in an

Monk Daniels of Sand Mountain (1904–1971). Photo courtesy of Bill Harrison.

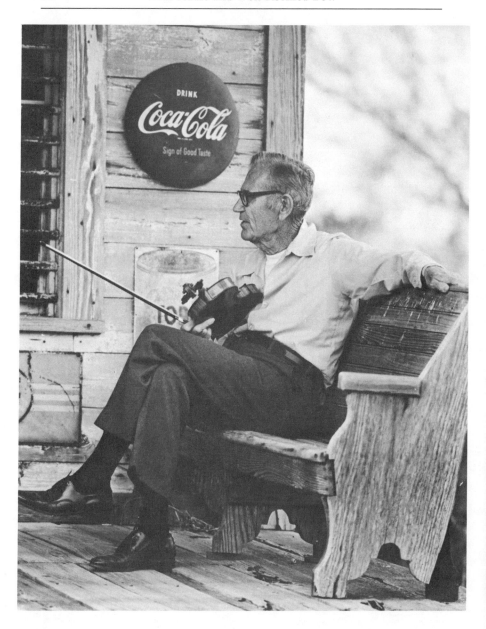

Everis Campbell of Troy, Alabama, at the Pike Pioneer Museum. Photo by Kim McRae Appel.

old schoolhouse of the Henderson community in southeastern Pike County. When consolidation closed that school in the late 1930s, the Locklar family purchased the building for use as a community center, and since that time it has been the site of country fairs, square dances, and bluegrass festivals. On the day of the interview, Rex Locklar, a devotee of fiddle music and a long-time friend of the Campbell family, pulled Mr. Campbell from a cluster of musicians at the bluegrass festival that was in progress and ushered him to a small office. He introduced himself as Everis Campbell ("E-V-E-R-I-S . . .That's the reason I look so puny and bad—from them a'hanging that name on me.") Campbell recounted his stories with great animation, frequently changing his voice to imitate other characters involved. He needed little prompting from the interviewer; thus his words are presented here as a continuous narrative rather than an interview.

Born in Laurel Hill, Florida (ten miles below the Alabama-Florida state line), on May 9, 1909, Campbell moved with his family to Pike County, Alabama, around 1918.[92] He began playing the fiddle when he was six years old and played for the next seventy years. During that time, said Campbell, "I done everything from raise cotton to peanuts and then I went and toted a rifle for three year too long for my Uncle Sam. And I come back home and I joined a construction outfit and I stayed in that until I got so old they wouldn't have me, I reckon. But in all the meantimes I was playing for square dances." He spoke first of his great-grandmother, Caroline Steele Johnson:

I would set on the porch a lot of nights in the summer and she would fiddle and tell tall tales. She would play such as "Billy in the Low Land" and like that and she'd sing a verse and play a verse on her fiddle. She'd play "Soldier's Joy," "Arkansas Traveller," "Leather Breeches," "Paddy on the Turnpike," "The Devil's Dream," and just a number of them that skip my mind.

My daddy's daddy were a fiddler, and his people on his mother's side was fiddlers and I just guess he inherited it. Naturally his grandmother a'fiddling all around—you know he'd be like me. He couldn't help it.

You know my daddy, he was kindly funny about his fiddle strings and his fiddle. He didn't want any grease, anybody with greasy hands to pick it up, being that bow had rosum on it. He didn't want any grease and he told me. He come in on me one time. I had went in the closet and sneaked his fiddle out and tested it out. It was tuned and I began, and from that time on I was playing the fiddle.

And so I thought that he had gone to Orion to the Woodmen meeting, and I was in the closet playing up a storm. And so I heard him a'coming in and I didn't think it was him. He come in and opened up the door and he told me, he says, "Now, son, I've heard of a lot of people going into the closet to pray, but people don't go into the closet to play the fiddle. Come out here and take a chair and play some." Naturally, it was his orders; I went out there and done what I could. And he said, "Well, anytime you get ready for that fiddle . . ." Said, "Always wash your hands when you get up from the table," and he says, "Go get it when you want to." Says, "If it's out of tune, come to me."

Then old Sandy Claus, a little after that—I reckon it was when I was about eight year—he brought me a three-quarter-sized fiddle. And so I was always used to my orange and my apple and my two or three sticks of peppermint candy. My [great-]grandmother—she had done got up, built a fire, and was a'preparing breakfast—so I went in and she says, "You didn't look, 'cause something's wrong." I says, "This is all." And she says, "No, it's not." She says, "Take that lamp." We didn't have no 'lectricity back then. She says, "Take that lamp and go in there and look at the head of your bed." I went there and looked and I seen my fiddle bow sticking out, and I messed around there and I pulled out a little three-quarter-sized fiddle. So I got in at the fireside and I tuned that fiddle up like I wanted to and I woke the rest of them up.

Then from then on I played for square dances. I started whenever my daddy would let me go without a chaperone, and that was about twelve year old, and I've been playing for square dances ever since. The last square dance I ever played for was right in yonder, and I'd say that was two or three year ago. I don't know a thing in the world [about calling a square dance]; all I know is I'd go in there with black eyebrows, and whenever I'd come out of there they'd be so much fiddle rosum on my eyebrows, until they'll be as gray as a possum.

I'd play until they'd get a set out. I played for some that I thought lasted an hour and fifteen minutes. It was according to how many couples was out there, and just generally, I would say forty-five minutes. He [the caller] would come back—I didn't know when they was out—he'd come back and say that was it. He'd say, "Kiss the fiddler," or something like that. Then they'd have intermission and then come back and say, "Get your partners for the next set." So I knowed what to do.

I would change [tunes during a long dance]. I'd give them the key of G and I'd go on, and then I'd trail the guitar players over on D to wake my fingers up. And I'd play on D awhile and then I would go on in A and then probably C. If I had some guitar players that was used to playing with me, I would go on from one key to the other key on the count of my fingers wouldn't go to sleep. That's what they wanted. They wanted somebody that would stay there and play and not rest all the time. And that's what I done. And I played for square dances until I was just about getting too old to even leave home. And then I used to go to every fiddling contest I could hear of, far or near. I've even hitchhiked to them.

I've went into Milton, Florida, and I've went into Pensacola, Florida. I've went into Laurel Hill, Florida. I went up to Atlanta, Georgia. And I've been back out over into Lowndes County—it was in Lowndesboro, Alabama, and I been back down, way on down below Luverne to what you would call Highland Home, and Rutledge and all like that. I just—I went to fiddling contests, and I don't care what they was.

I hitchhiked to a many one of them and then I have got on a model T Ford and went to some of them. I used to come to Henderson. They had an annual fiddlers' contest right at this place, and I had on knee pants, ribbed stockings, button shoes—I looked like a grasshopper, I imagine. All the schools had fiddling contests.

I went to one in Milton, Florida—now, this here is just a little too much on the boasting side. [The interviewer assured him that boasting was allowed.] Well, I went down there and there was a little boy and his name was Bennon Peek. He moved close to us, and his brother Bob Peek was a fiddler and his daddy was. And Bennon always played the guitar, and I got with him and I taught that boy how to play the guitar. Well, I'll tell you why I done that— because I used to go up around High Ridge and some kind of Oak— Postoak, Alabama, up in Bullock County or on the line of Pike and Bullock. And so my crowd had got rich, they thought, off what we was getting up there, and so they made a resolution one New Year's Day to never play for another square dance. And I loved the square dances and so I could not.

I reckon they thought they was too good to play for a square dance or thought it was old-fashioned or something. I enjoyed them better than I did the round dancing. Well, they swore off. None of 'em wouldn't come. So I began training me some guitars. I trained up a boy, that Bennon Peek I was telling you about, and I trained up a feller here close to Henderson, and his name was James Sunday, and he would help me down here, and so whenever we'd get all down this way, we'd have our Brogan Rallies.

[Laughing] I'll tell you . . . the Star Brand Shoe Manufacturing Company just kept my mailbox full of thank-you cards because people wore out so many—back then they didn't have nothing but a leather sole on a shoe, and people wore out so many of the shoe soles until they was always agoin' and getting another pair of Star Brand. They had dress shoes and also the brogans—that's what you plowed in and cut logs in and like that. So they kept my mailboxes full of thank-you cards. So that's the reason that I had two outfits that I played with, around Highland Home, Henderson, Glenwood, and that place below Highland Home—what is it? Rutledge, Alabama.

One of the band names was "William E. Campbell and his Swingers." That was for that "Hold to What You Got" dance [Campbell's term for "round dance"]. They didn't care who he was, whether he was Stringbeans or Grandpappy Jones, just so I come in and played for the square dance. I don't know what it was I had, but everybody wanted me to play. I played square dances down below Spring Hill on down into Elba, Alabama, and around down that way and coming back around this way. I had me a book. I'd tell them when I was booked up, up back the other way. [In a later conversation Campbell said that he made $5 to $7 per dance, which he considered good pay for those days. When he found himself without an accompaniment, he provided one himself: "Well, I took a corset rib which was made of a whale bone and stuck it between the sole of my shoe and the top, and I propped a guitar up on two brogan shoes and just patted my foot. It'd be tuned open in G."]

At Christmas time they'd have what I called "protracted" dances. You know, in the summer they'd have protracted meetings—and I said that was protracted dancing. I would go into Bullock County and they'd have one over at Mr. Jones's, one over at Mr. Henderson's, and one over at Mr. Adams's, and then come back over into China Grove to the annual New Year's dance and we'd tend to that.

In that day and time, you'd move your furniture out of one room and get in there and strow sand. They'd scour the floor—it'd be the cleanest thing you ever saw the next day. So that's the way we would square dance. And I played for a number of square dances—more than a number, I reckon—I don't know—I couldn't count—where I enjoyed myself and had a bigger time than them people out there swinging their partners. I just loved it—loved the square dances and I loved the fiddling contests!

Whenever I'd hear of a fiddling—I'd generally get a postcard from the fiddling contest, where they was going to have it, and I would go. I didn't even miss them nowhere.

About the biggest fiddling contest I was ever at was at Atlanta, Georgia. And they would kindly audition you. There would be two men or two ladies a'setting behind the desk there, and you would walk in and tell 'em your name and where you was from, and they'd say, "Say you play a fiddle?" "Yes." Says, "Let's hear a cut of old 'Arkansas Traveller' or 'Leather Breeches' or something like that." And I would cut it off and they'd say, "You go down this hall, and go on in there and you'll see where to go." I'd go in there and there'd be some more in there, you know. Well, some would go to the left. I think it was the good'ens would go to the right, and them that would go to the left would come in and just—they didn't pay nothing—they'd get in the contest—they could attend, you know, and hear. I reckon I was lucky. I went to the right.

I got up there and there was several fiddle tunes just coming out—you know, fiddles used to be famous. God knows, anybody in the state I was borned in, you'd go possum hunting and the dogs would tree—and if you shook the tree, a fiddle or a five-string banjo would drop on your head. I heard fiddling—I reckon I heard fiddling the night or the morning I was born—I don't know what it was— because my daddy was a fiddler and so that's all I knowed was to fiddle, or that's what I thought. But anyhow, getting back to this fiddling contest, I got up there, and none of the guitar players— seemed like they wanted to just pass me as just a castoff or something. And there was one big old heavyset fellow, and I taked his name down and I never will forget it. His name was Tex Forman and he slapped a bass fiddle, and he said, "Looky here, Piney Woods." He said, "Let me tell you, this here bass fiddle is just as good as any guitar. Come on back here in this anteroom." We went back into this little room, liken to this, and we tuned together. He'd pat that bass fiddle with me, you know, and to my good luck, I singled out what they called "The Devil's Dream," and boy, he could do it perfect. Oh, my Lord, he could do it. And so, the tune of "Up Jumped the Devil," it had come around, and it was very popular and I done heard two or three play "Up Jumped the Devil." So whenever it come my time to play in the contest, I said, "Well, I've heard this 'Up Jumped the Devil' out here. It's very popular and everything. But I can't figure why the devil jumped up. Unless he had a dream." I said, "He could have had a bad dream. That could have rousted him. Or he could have had a good dream." So I says, "I'm going to play 'The Devil's Dream.'" So I played "The Devil's Dream." And so they sent me away with the first place there.

I'll tell you. Whenever I'd walk out that way, you've seen a mule's kneecap jump? Well, mine probably was that way. But if that fiddle ever hit under my chin, I was as calm—just as calm. So I tore down and done the best I could.

I would say it was in the thirties . . . about '38, because I went into the Army in the first part of '40. And I quit my contestin' then.

And then the next 'un I went to was—a big one—was in Pensacola, Florida. Well, the champion fiddler's name down there was Bryant Parsell, and I reckon he had a mean guitar player—I don't know. In other words, they had—we started one morning at 10 o'clock and by 4 o'clock I'd seen one-legged fiddlers, female fiddlers, young-'un fiddlers, old-men fiddlers with beards there ain't no telling how long, and they'd eliminated everybody but me and Mr. Bryant Parsell and Brack Hudson. Brack Hudson was from over there around Niceville, Florida. But he was a good fiddler and they'd eliminated, and they called us all back there. Well, whenever they called me out—they wouldn't even let us have a guitar player—we soloed. Well, my guitar player told me—that was Mr. Peek, Mr. Bennon Peek—he told me, says, "Don't get your bow." Says, "Get Mr. Hudson's bow." And so I think, "Well, he always tells me right," so I just went over there and asked Mr. Hudson could I borrow his bow, and he said, "Yes, take it." So I got his bow and we went on through, and so that night they still didn't have enough. And I called it "grudge fiddling." Nobody wasn't mad or nothing, but we went to a place—they had a filling station in the front of it and a store and another part—and so I reckon the ladies got tired and went to bed, but we fiddled all night long.

I got a little bit fast there. What I wanted to tell you was why Peek told me to not use my bow. Because back then times, the people used brilliantine—the men—on their hair, and this gentleman had got my bow and sawed it across his head. That was Mr. Bryant Parsell's guitar player that did that; now, Mr. Parsell didn't do it. And so after the contest I asked him, I says, "Bennon, why didn't you want me to get my bow?" And he said, "Because that there fellow sawed it on his old greasy head, and it wouldn't even have made a sound." And so I put Mr. Parsell—now excuse me for my boasting—but I put him behind—I put him out in the second place. Now, I wouldn't say he put his guitar player up to something like that—I wouldn't do that way—but I'll tell you, some of them fiddling contests I'd go to—I had a younger brother [Gene]; he was my baby brother. There was about four years difference in mine and his age, but he wanted to fiddle and I didn't think he could fiddle so good. And they would show him up, and when they'd try to do that, they just waved a red flag ahead of a bull. They'd get old "Fiddling Pappy" all roused up. Now, one we went to down in the old country, I call it, that'us where I was born—Laurel Hill, Florida. When we left there we was just small kids when we moved to Alabama.

Naturally, when we went in there, I was standing up there with my little pullover sweater on and my shoddy pants; 'course everybody else was dressed up. And they'd been telling a tale about the champion fiddler from Florala, Alabama. His name was Obie Adams, and they'd said he'd got in a car wreck. And you could see them fiddlers, their faces would light up—oh, their faces would just light up like everything. I was still a'standing over there and I never had said nothing to nobody, you know. So they'd go to fiddling— tuning up their fiddles and everything and just a'fiddling up a storm. Well, directly Mr. Obie Adams popped in at the door. He says, "Oh, it was a mistake. There's nothing to it." Says, "It was the other people." And them fiddlers' feathers fell. You could see 'um. They looked like they had a bad night.

I never will forget the piece of music that my younger brother played on the fiddle. I was going to play the guitar and him the fiddle. And he played a tune called "Katy Johnson." And Mr. Adams, whenever it come his time, he said, "I think this feller needs to hear 'Katy Johnson.' Somehow I believe it would help him." And so, he played "Katy Johnson." And so naturally around I come in my time and I said, "I heard those two gentlemens play 'Katy Johnson' and I believe to my soul I learnt it and I want to play it before I forget it." And excuse me, I don't mean to be boastful or nothing like that. But it just turned the old man on—that's all—and so I played "Katy Johnson."

I won, and what tickled me was Mr. Adams says, "Who is that hoboist that played that fiddle?" He referred to me as a "hoboist." Mr. Johnson was my cousin and he was introducing me around. And Mr. Adams was late and missed the introduction. And so he says, "Charlie, who in the world is that hobo out there?" And he says, "That's one of old Bud's boys." And he says, "God's bones, why didn't you tell me?" And my cousin said, "I didn't have time."

Then I went to one here in Troy, Alabama. The Kiwanis Club put this on. That was in the late thirties, I'd say. But there was a good old feller; his name was Mr. Herman Moll. Taught violin in the high school in Troy. He had a big hand in the contest. In fact of the business, he was one of the judges. Well, my older brother, he challenged Mr. Moll, and he says, "Mr. Moll, you reckon this long-haired stuff you play and teach, do you reckon you know anything about fiddling? Do you reckon you could really judge a fiddler?"

And he says, "Hand me your fiddle, Newt." And my brother Newt handed him his fiddle. And he said, "Everis, is that guitar tuned up with this fiddle?" And I says, "If it ain't, I can tune it." He says, "Get it." And he said, "Newt, what do you call 'Chicken Reel'?" And Newt says, "I'd call it a good old fiddle tune." And he tore out and he played the mischief out of that "Chicken Reel." And he says, "What do you think now, Mr. Newt?" And he says, "I'll tell you." Says, "I think you could judge anything you want to." And he says, "Here's your fiddle." And Newt says, "No, I've decided to give you that fiddle." And Mr. Moll says, "No, Newt, I want you to take that and practice 'Chicken Reel.' " He was rough, I tell you.

Well, I come out [first], but if the contest judging would have been left to the audience that night, my youngest brother Gene would have carried home the first prize because he got more [claps to indicate applause] that night. But to tell you the truth, I'll tell you what the old man said just before the contest. He said, "We've heard the mockingbird sing, the old hen cackle, and the rooster crow, and we've always heard the old train blow, but tonight, folks, all that's going to be judged is fiddling!"

Now, Newt, I'm not throwing off on him, because, I'll tell you one thing, whenever he'd lay that head down on that fiddle and play his "Soldier's Joy," and his "Arkansas Traveller," I've never heard nobody beat him. There ain't nobody could beat him. I can't do it and there ain't never any other brag fiddler in the world who could. Now, he was just what I'd call an old hoedown fiddler, but he was one of the best fiddlers that ever put a shoe in Alabama or Florida or anywhere. Now, he wasn't no violinist.

The contest I previously mentioned in Troy, Alabama, was about the biggest prize. It was an instrument. It was sponsored by the Kiwanis Club. This instrument, Mr. Moll went and picked it out

Everis Campbell with the fiddle he won at a Pike County fiddlers' convention.
Photo by Kim McRae Appel.

*himself, and it would have retailed at about $130; that's consisting
of the bow and the case and the fiddle. God knows, the $35, $75,
and $50 prizes, there was so many I can't count them.*

*Around here it [the prize money] was $10, $15. I remember that
in Perote, Alabama, I went one time and they had $15 in gold for
the first prize, and that was a lot back in the thirties. And my daddy
was yet a'living. So I throwed down corn middles until about the
middle of the evening and I said, "I'm taking out." I left my brother
to finish, and I went and I thumbed me a ride down to Perote,
Alabama, and naturally my old buddy Arthur Brown that I talked
about, he had sold two or three dozen eggs and got on his model
T Ford and he come down there. There he was, and I was so glad
to see him because he could play with me. But I captured that $15
and so they give me paper money, and it was a ten and a five. And
I come back to my daddy's little house out in the pecan orchard,
and he says, "Well, how'd you come out?" Well, I says, I'd always
tell him, "They got sorry for me and give me first prize." I says,
"But it was not in gold. It was in paper. They said it would be in*

gold." He says, "Son, let me see it." And I handed it to him. He says, "If you want gold, go down to the Farmer's and Merchant's Bank and tell them this is a gold certificate, both of these." Says, "You can get gold for them." I went down there and got my gold— but I didn't know that.

[Rex Locklar encouraged him to tell about his father's last tunes, and Campbell responded with the following story.]

Well, it was some kind of a lung trouble he had. I don't know what it was. It was something that cooking fumes would—would just get him. We built him a little house in the pecan orchard, not too far from our house and where we could see to him, you know, and that's where he lived. And he stayed there until his last days. And one evening, just about 3 o'clock, he asked to be propped up in the bed. He asked for his fiddle and he laid back there and played two pieces which was "Billy in the Low Ground" and a piece that they call "Hell Broke Loose in Georgia" or "There's No Hell in Georgia"—either name. He played them two and then he says, "Newt, put this up and take it home with you." He says, "I won't be needing it anymore." He says, "I bought Everis a good fiddle and he likes it," and he says, "You like this one." And so he give him the old Stainer fiddle. That was the one Newt handed to Mr. Moll I was telling you about. They are a famous fiddle—German made. But he died about the same time the evening after he played the fiddle. Just about 3 o'clock—that was whenever he passed on. But he was a good fiddler, and a serious fiddler, and I'll tell you one thing, he taken his fiddling just like some people would giving the children the wrong thing to eat. Boy, you'd better fiddle if you'd sit down to play with Pop. He'd crack you on the head with the bow if you messed with him.

I didn't tell you about one of my brothers. [Campbell had three brothers and four sisters, but in the interview he talks only about the family fiddlers.] He [Thomas] was always the feller who fixed up fiddles. He would just fix up whatever was done wrong with the fiddles—he would fix it up. He never entered but one contest in his life, and he got as good as any that night. That was at Inverness, Alabama. They wouldn't decide on which was first place. They took first and second and combined it, and fifty percented, and give it one to Mr. Hickman and one to Thomas Campbell. I call him my middle brother—he was between me and Gene. But Gene he was the dancer, the ladies' man, the guitar player—he could dance, he could play the fiddle some. He never did win no first prize, but he has won several seconds and third prizes.

Now, me and Newt was friendly about this. We never did have no grudge. He was my oldest brother, but boy, me and him has had a many, a many of a tear-down. And there's some other people that I will not mention on account of we've had some tear-downs.

There was a lot of good fiddlers. Webster Youngblood. The hottest thing I ever met in Alabama was Mr. Webster Youngblood because Mr. Webster Youngblood played the ragtime and popular music. In other words, he played by ear and he played by notes, on the 'count of his daughter. Now, Mr. Web didn't know, to start with, about playing by note, but he had a daughter. Her name was Margaret Youngblood. She went to Troy over there when it was State Normal. She would get on the train at Youngblood, Alabama, and she'd ride to Troy and she'd catch a train back that evening, and she'd hitch up and harrow peanuts until the next morning. But she finished up and he was such a fiddler, and so he put her under Mr. Herman Moll, the teacher I was telling you about previously, and so she went on, and being turned that way, she learned everything and she come home and she learned her pappy how to read. So him and Margaret were really good.

They were both fiddle, but I'm going to tell you, back in those early days . . . back then when you would get in competition, you didn't have any accompaniment all the way. You had to come out and solo. Well, Mr. Web played some kind of a hornpipe whenever he would solo. Oh, he'd just fiddle up a storm. I know he was on an odd key—it was on the key of B flat, was where it was. Well, my oldest brother, whenever he would solo, he had one called "Tom and Jerry" and it was kindly an odd key—well, it was in the key of A. Oh, he'd give Mr. Youngblood a lot of trouble. He'd take home the first prize a lot of the time. And to show you, that's what I was talking about the noted fiddlers.

And too, there was two fellers that knowed what it was all about. There was one feller, I don't know why he left Oklahoma and come to Alabama. His name was John Turner. But he could take it off the sheet and could play it, or he could do anyway. I stayed with him a lots. I played a guitar whenever they would do this round dance—I called it "hold to what you got." You never changed partners. You just got out there and hold to what you got. And I'd call the square dance, "You swing Sal and I'll Swing Sue." Well, whenever it would get to the square dance, I taken the fiddle and Mr. Turner taken the guitar. There was some people loved to square dance and some loved to round dance.

Then there was another feller, I would call him a noted fiddler, or violinist. But he wanted to turn fiddle. His name was Charlie Winter and he knew what it was all about. He lived in Hagerstown, Maryland, and he just come down here and he met me at Cardwell's Barber Shop and he met Newt there and everything, and by God, he stayed. He said he wanted to pick up some of that hillbilly—he called it hillbilly—fiddling. And he did.

When we lived in Laurel Hill, Florida, a Doctor Stephens come down and he played a five-string banjer, mostly, and he would doctor the people all around through there until he would be good and tired. And he'd hear of a hoedown somewhere and he'd go out there and the first thing he'd do is come in there with that five-string banjer. He'd sit down and then he'd get up and he'd change shoes, and he'd get out there and he'd say, "I want the dancingest girl in the community." You know they faced their partners then, and you could just cut up. But there was a feller, Cauthen, down there, and they couldn't figure which was the best—Hutch Cauthen or my daddy.

This Doctor Stephens—I reckon he'd turn it with his hand—but it was a beeswax record and was a cylinder, and so he taken that record down of them a'playing and he sent it to Chicago, Illinois, and I reckon you'd call it "authenticated" or something like that. It was judged in Chicago, Illinois. Nobody down there didn't judge it. They sent the recording to some—Dr. Stephens, him a'being an educated feller, he knowed where to. Whenever it come down, Pa was the winner.

And Mr. Arthur Brown—when they laid that old feller to rest there wasn't many equal to him because he was a musician to his toes. He knowed about all of it. He played string, he played reed, he played bass, he played guitar, he played everything. He was a way older than I was. He played a good fiddle. He played a fine guitar. I'll tell you one thing—he taught me a lot. He could take his old glasses and get over by the window and take a songbook and put it down there and play it on the fiddle just exactly like it should be played. You take a feller like that, it's very handy to have around a bunch of just old—I would say "gifted"—musicians; I don't know just what you would call them. That's what I was. I don't know one note. What I know is what I heard.

Now I have trouble with this wrist. This is very sensitive and I almost drop the fiddle. I have to put a padding on there to even play the fiddle. If I make it, which I hope I will, until May the ninth of '85, I will be 76. And now I'd love to say you a little something on there [the recorder] if it's all right.

My name, it is Old Fiddling Pap
I've fiddled around a lot of places on this U.S. map.
You can round you up one-hundred fiddles and align them
*   down the wall,*
And I'll bet you one-hundred fiddle tunes, that I'll play
*   some of them all.*
I played with ninety-eight before I stopped on the 'count
*   of the fingers on my left hand had done run most red-*
*   hot.*
So I went out through Rex's kitchen and I got a order of
*   camp stew*
And I come back through and I played with the other two.

That evening Everis Campbell joined a conglomeration of musicians thrashing out lively tunes on the stage. As he fiddled along with a honky-tonk piano, steel guitar, upright bass, and several guitars and fiddles, Campbell would not confine himself to the range of a microphone. Finally a friend who wanted Campbell to be heard grabbed a microphone from its stand and followed him as he danced about, playing a swingy tune for a "hold on to what you got" dance.

3

ALABAMA'S
BRAG FIDDLERS

Like politicians, fiddlers have constituencies—followers who enjoy their playing above all others. The followers may be like Mrs. Mullins's fan who "hollered like a drunk man" whenever she walked out on the stage;[1] they may be the regulars at the local community center who spring from their chairs to dance whenever a particular fiddler comes to the microphone, or they may simply be the family members and neighbors who gather to hear their favorite on the front porch after supper. Alabama has had many excellent fiddlers with constituencies of the latter sort, those who, because of geographical isolation or personal modesty, were never widely known. Among them may have been Alabama's best fiddler, but we shall never know. After viewing a Nashville fiddlers' convention in 1927, a reporter for *Outlook* concluded, "The man proclaimed champion of the South is no better fiddler than another, away up at the head of some hollow, who could not neglect his corn planting long enough to make the trip—and who was too modest to do it anyway."[2]

Alabama has also had a good number of "brag fiddlers." This term often appeared in news accounts of fiddlers' conventions in the 1920s and '30s and described fiddlers who were sources of community pride. Such fiddlers achieved fame by performing on radio, making records, and winning numerous fiddlers' conventions across the state. Among this state's brag fiddlers were D. Dix Hollis, Y. Z. Hamilton, and Charlie Stripling, who made commercial recordings and played on radio; Joe Lee, who influenced some of the nation's best-known fiddlers; "Fiddling Tom" Freeman and "Monkey" Brown, flamboyant fiddlers who caught the attention of state and national journalists; and the Johnson brothers of Sand Mountain, entertainers for three generations of North Alabamians.[3]

D. Dix Hollis
Early Paramount Recording Artist
(1861–1927)

D. Dix Hollis was born on the eve of the Civil War, learned to play the fiddle at age 10 from a family servant, traveled to New York to be Alabama's first commercially recorded fiddler, and later broadcast a challenge to the world from the first radio station in the state.

Hollis's family was prominent in Lamar County. His grandfather, Darrell Upright Hollis, had established a 1500-acre plantation with 125 slaves at Moscow, Alabama, and had fought in Alabama's Indian

D. Dix Hollis of Sulligent, in a photo probably made in 1926 at Station WAPI, Auburn, Alabama. Photo courtesy of Mrs. Chloe Weaver.

wars, most notably at the battle of Horseshoe Bend. His father, Daniel William Hollis, born in 1829, served as a state legislator.[4] Hollis, himself, became a respected medical doctor.

In 1926, at the request of Mrs. Edward McGhee, Hollis sent his "history as a fiddler and musician . . . to be used in the book to be published by the University of North Carolina."[5] While such a book has not been found, a copy of the letter provides information about his early days as a fiddler. Hollis learned to play with the help of a family servant and from other fiddlers of the Old Moscow community:

> Ben Guyton . . . one of our slaves noticed my great talent and love for the fiddle and taught me all he could about it. When 10 years old I could play all his tunes. John Tucker, Dirk Holms, Dr. R. J. Redden, Marion and Levy Gibbs, B. H. Holliday lived near me and were all good old time Fiddlers . . . my love and attitude for music was wonderful. I pushed my talent with great vehemence . . . Am sure the creator gave me a talent for music and have been with me. It was music that moved the Evil Spirit from King Saul. Samuel 23.[6]

In 1884, Hollis traveled to Baltimore and studied at the University of Physicians and Surgeons for five months. At the same time he studied violin with an Italian violinist from whom he learned "some of the most beautiful and opporatic [sic] and most classical tunes ever played on the Fiddle."[7] After five months, in which "he alternated between reading medical books and playing his fiddle until midnight each night,"[8] Hollis returned to Alabama possessing a medical diploma.

He set up his practice in Sulligent, a small town (named for two Frisco Railroad officials, Sullivan and Sargent)[9] not far from Old Moscow. Engraved on his letterhead was the following:

Dr. D. Dix Hollis

Dealer in

Drugs and Perfumery

Hollis' Chill Tonic and Spike Oil Liniment

City Health Officer

Though to modern readers those words may evoke the image of a snake-oil dealer, residents of Sulligent remember his making house calls and delivering babies. Hollis developed a tonic that was considered effective against malaria. He also married, raised a family, played cornet at the Methodist Church, and continued to play his fiddle, entering and winning many of the small fiddle contests held in schoolhouses all over Lamar County.[10]

In 1924, at age 63, he traveled with Mr. E. E. Forbes, president of Alabama's largest music store, to New York City. There he became one of the first country fiddlers to record for the Paramount Recording Company. In his letter to Mrs. McGhee, Hollis wrote, "The Paramount Recording Co. made me 12 record [sic] some of which you will see above. They are for sale by the doz. at Port Washington, Min. by Paramount Recording Co." Unfortunately, a copy of the list did not accompany Hollis's letter. Today, only four of the twelve titles are documented. "Turkey in De Straw" and "Walking in the Parlor" appeared as Paramount recording #33153, while "Dixie"/ "Yankee Doodle" and "The Girl Slipped Down" were issued on the Silvertone label of the Sears, Roebuck Company.[11]

Paramount 33153 is in the archives of the Country Music Foundation in Nashville. Recorded acoustically and unaccompanied, Hollis's music seems distant. The listener feels as if he were standing on the street outside a house where some lively fiddling is taking place. He cannot see the source of the music, but from the sound of it he can imagine that the fiddler is bearing down on the bow, and rosin is flying about the fiddler's head. The recording indicates that Hollis was what some call a "jig" fiddler, one who uses short bow strokes, one stroke for each note, no matter how rapidly played. He played "Turkey in De Straw" in a clear, vigorous, staccato fashion much as it is played today except that he reversed the parts, playing the chorus first each time. On the third and fifth times through, he replaced the "verse" with a third part which seems rather like a cakewalk or humorous allusion to a turkey strut.

Hollis's "Walking in the Parlor" begins with a smooth cascade of sixteenth notes. His version of the tune bears little resemblance to that played today, being much more complex. However, the second part, which Hollis played with great drive and virtuosity, is more familiar. The recordings make it clear that Hollis was truly a country fiddler, less influenced by the classical Italian violinist than by the family servant who taught him.

According to the *Lamar Democrat*, Hollis's recordings were still selling well in 1926 when he was ready to involve himself with the recording industry's newly emerging rival. Under the auspices of the Sulligent Commercial Club, Hollis traversed the state to initiate a fiddlers' contest on Alabama's first radio station, WAPI, in Auburn. The journey was probably inspired by Henry Ford's contests, which had given three fiddlers—Mellie Dunham of Maine, Uncle Bunt Stephens of Tennessee, and John Baltzell of Ohio—enormous amounts of publicity.

Articles appearing in the *Opelika Daily News* and the *Lamar Democrat* announced that "preparatory to a big fiddlers' contest over radio, Dr. D. Dix Hollis, famous fiddler of Sulligent, will give challenge programs from Station WAPI in Auburn, Alabama, April 23 and 24." Declaring Hollis to be "one of the most widely known fiddlers in Alabama," the articles gave detailed information about the approaching event:

> The Commercial Club of Sulligent . . . is backing Dr. Hollis and has issued the challenge for him. Fiddlers everywhere are invited to tune in on Station WAPI during either or both of his challenge programs in order to get an idea of what they will have to compete with when they meet him in contest some time next fall, either October or November.
>
> The challenge is issued "To the World" and arrangements will be made for the radio audience to decide the winner in the fall contest.[12]

Before allowing his name to be used by the Sulligent Commercial Club, Dr. Hollis had insisted that all fiddlers be restricted to "the good old tunes of long ago":

> Among them he named: Billie in the Lowground, Turkey in the Straw, Leather Breeches, Gray Eagle, Dixie, Bonnie Blue Flag, Hoplight Ladies, None Greater Than Lincoln, Lone Indian, Sallie in the Wildwood, and Mocking Bird.[13]

In a second announcement, *The Opelika Daily News* wrote, "The people of Sulligent declare that no better fiddler can be found than Dr. Hollis, and that they are expecting him to become the champion radio fiddler as a result of the contest next fall." It quoted Hollis as saying that "he can play all night if necessary."

Hollis's actual performance was not described in either newspaper, but it is likely that the accompanying photograph was taken at the WAPI studio as he played. The contest promised in October or November appears never to have taken place. Hollis remained the champion fiddler in his hometown, however. Mrs. Inez Gibbs described a local event that took place a year after the radio contest was to have occurred:

> On August 20, 1927, S. J. Gibbs, a Master Degree man in vocational agriculture from Auburn bringing his bride, was sent

to this western Alabama town, by the State Department to establish the teaching of Agriculture to the men and boys of this community.

Immediately we met the town Doctor, Dr. Dixie Hollis. He had served this community all his years and was still doctoring mostly from his office. Being an elderly man his days of house calls and the delivering of babies were about over.

In late October it was suddenly announced there would be a fiddlers' convention at the school on Friday night. Preparations began at once and the place was packed with listeners, some wearing legging boots. The fiddlers made a complete circle on the stage. Near the center sat Dr. Hollis. He stole the show, first with "Turkey in the Straw." He arose and with the fiddlers' dance he received the cheers of the crowd by his rendition of "Put on Your Old Gray Bonnet."[14]

D. Dix Hollis died the following December at age 66. He did not become as famous as Henry Ford's favorites, but his importance extends beyond Lamar County, Alabama. His enthusiasm for old-time fiddling and his desire that it be preserved led him to put his music on record, to write down a personal fiddling history which included names of tunes and fiddlers, and to see that the old tunes were brought to the public on radio. In doing so he left a valuable record of old-time fiddling for those who still seek to preserve it.

Y. Z. Hamilton
A Legend Among Fiddlers
(1888–1936)

When Bob Kyle entered his first fiddlers' contest in Tuscaloosa County in the late 1920s, young boys gathered around him and asked, "You going to play against Y. Z. Hamilton?"

"I reckon so. Who's Y. Z. Hamilton?"

"You'll find out," answered the children.

Kyle did find out. "He was a stocky man and didn't have a hair on his head. And he laid that fiddle under his chin and laid his head over it and commenced stroking it, and I said, 'My gosh.' He commenced playing that 'Fifty Years Ago.' Just mesmerized me."[15]

Hamilton's playing often had that effect on listeners. A. D. Hamner remembered Hamilton's as "the best-sounding music I ever heard."[16] A. K. Callahan said, "Hamilton was to fiddling what Fritz Kreisler was to violins."[17]

Hamilton also played guitar and piano, despite the fact that an

Y. Z. Hamilton in 1926. Photo courtesy
of Olen Mayes.

early accident had left him three nubs instead of fingers on his right
hand. With them he could hold a fiddle bow or a guitar pick, and
could "play the stew" out of Scott Joplin piano rags.[18] In addition
to his musical talents, Hamilton was a colorful character. Witty and
sociable, he was also a heavy drinker, whose unruly conduct often
got him in trouble with the law and his wife.

While many remember Hamilton's musical exploits and his es-
capades involving liquor, few know factual details about his life;
thus the following biographical data come from public documents.
According to census records, Hamilton was born in 1888, the youngest of ten children. Prior to his birth, the 1880 census found his
parents, Cisero J. and Sarah Adcock Hamilton, living with their
seven children in Randolph County where Cisero, age 33, was a
farmer. In the next extant census (1900), 11-year-old Y. Z. lived with
his father (now listed as a physician), mother, and two older sisters
in Anniston. All documents indicate that his given name consisted
of nothing more than the final two letters of the alphabet. Perhaps
the initials were his parents' way of giving notice that their tenth
child, born when the mother was 42, was to be the last. Whatever
the origin of the name, it took several forms over the years: on
recordings it became "Wyzee"; on the radio it was "X.Y.Z.,"[19] and
in one newspaper account of a fiddlers' convention it was "Wise
E."[20]

At the time of the 1910 census, Hamilton was living in Gadsden
where he was a theater musician. He may have played at a vaudeville

house called the Onawanda Theater or at the Hayden-Pake Theatre, which housed musical extravanganzas, Shakespearean dramas, and minstrel shows.[21] At either theater Hamilton could have gained experience that served him well in later years as a country performer.

By 1912, Hamilton had moved to Bessemer, where he married Mollie Tucker.[22] Hamilton worked as a molder in a foundry but continued to play for dances and contests. After a convention in Birmingham in 1925, sponsored by the Nathan Bedford Forrest Klan, he began to be called the champion fiddler of Alabama. To win the title he overcame A. A. Gray, one of Georgia's champion fiddlers; Earl Johnson of Georgia, a well-known trick fiddler and recording artist; and many of Alabama's best fiddlers.[23] Thereafter his name began to appear in the daily papers of Birmingham in announcements of theater performances and square dances. Such advertisements pointed out that Hamilton was "the winner of the championship of the latest contest among fiddlers of Georgia, Alabama and Tennessee and Mississippi."[24]

It is likely that talent scouts from Paramount Records were in the audience of the Birmingham convention, for the following year, Hamilton recorded "Hamilton's Special Breakdown" and "Fifty Years Ago" for that company. He was accompanied by "Tucker" (possibly a brother-in-law) and "Lecroy," one playing tenor banjo, the other playing an inaudible instrument. The recording reveals Hamilton as a virtuoso performer with clear, fluid fingering, strong, smooth bowing, and graceful ascent into high ranges.

Released on the Paramount and Herwin labels, both numbers were influential. "Fifty Years Ago," a romantic waltz, is still a favorite among Alabama fiddlers. "Hamilton's Special Breakdown" is thought to have influenced recordings by other well-known fiddlers. The tune may have floated around for years under various names before Hamilton recorded it, adding fanciful variations to the second part. It was later recorded as "G Rag" by Earl Johnson and by the Afro-Cherokee fiddler Andrew Baxter with the Georgia Yellow Hammers. J. E. Mainer recorded the tune under the title of "Concord Rag."[25]

In 1927, Hamilton assembled a different group of local musicians to record at Gennett's temporary recording studio in Birmingham. Hamilton's Harmonians consisted of Y. Z. Hamilton, fiddle; Art Frazier, tenor banjo; Frank Nichols, second fiddle; and Luther Patrick, guitar.[26] Patrick was an attorney, humorist, and radio announcer. He later became a U.S. congressman; wrote a poem entitled "Sleeping at the Foot of the Bed," which became a country-music hit in the 1940s; and published several volumes of what he termed "old-timie" writings.[27] Luther Patrick is remembered as the "Will Rogers of the South," not as a musician. Company records suggest, however, that he was the guitar player, and a photo of the group on the cover of a Gennett catalog shows him holding that instrument. The collaboration produced four sides that were actually released: "Because He Was Only a Tramp," "Old Sefus Brown," "Grandfather's Liver (Ain't What It Used to Was)" and "Cornbread." The latter two were musical arrangements of country poetry, recited by Patrick.[28] Released on various labels as the reverse of recordings by other performers and given the pseudonym of "Davie Meek and His Boys" on some issues and "Reuben White" on others, the Gennett recordings did little to enhance Hamilton's fame.

About 1928, Hamilton moved to the small town of Holt (Tuscaloosa County) to work at the Central Foundry Company. There he joined a flourishing community of good fiddlers such as Web Colburn, Charlie Sellers, "Monkey" and Charlie Brown, and Bob Kyle. He may have found the fiddlers of west Alabama more difficult to beat in local contests than the famous Georgia fiddlers he had conquered in Birmingham. Bob Kyle, who was impressed by Hamilton's "Fifty Years Ago," captured the prize from him in one competition by playing "Listen to the Mockingbird." Kyle remarked, "I didn't beat him. I got the prize."[29] Several other fiddlers laid claim to having won over Hamilton during this period.

Oscar Riley, a square-dance caller, recalled that Hamilton, being state champion of Alabama and a recording artist, was sometimes not allowed to compete in contests, but was a popular fiddler at home dances. Said Riley, "I'd give a dance one week, and somebody else the next and somebody else the next. Y. Z. would always play and we just passed the hat around and gave it to Y. Z."[30] At such dances, recalled A. K. Callahan, Hamilton "could wear out the hair in a fiddle bow in one night. He'd bear down on it." Riley remembered that as Hamilton played, he would call out to the dancers such incitements as, "Kill yo'self. You ain't going to heaven anyway."[31]

Hamilton returned to Birmingham in the 1930s and joined "Uncle Bud and his Boll Weevils." "Uncle Bud" was Louis Marston, guitarist and mouth-harp champion. A steamfitter by trade, Marston formed the group as a means of earning money during the Depression. By playing on Luther Patrick's "Farmer's Sunrise Hour" and filling fifteen-minute radio slots during the day, the Boll Weevils were able to get paying jobs at square dances and company picnics. They were invited to perform at schoolhouses and movie theaters in many communities surrounding Birmingham.[32]

At such performances, the Boll Weevils did comedy skits with their music. Hamilton was the rube. Dressed in baggy trousers held up by suspenders and wearing a comic wig, he could draw hearty laughter from the audience. With his bald head uncovered, false teeth removed, and cheeks sucked in, he could become a hundred-year-old fiddler.[33] Shows often began with the band onstage, waiting for Hamilton's appearance. The audience would begin to shout, "Come out, Y. Z." After he had yelled out several mangled reasons for not doing so, Hamilton would enter to great applause.[34]

During this period, Hamilton may have played professionally. The 1934 City Directory of Birmingham listed him as a musician. The following year, however, he was listed as a molder once again. Yet he was an active fiddler, doing square dances and joining informal sessions at Johnson's Barber Shop in downtown Birmingham, where local musicians traded tunes with performers such as Clayton McMichen, Gid Tanner, and young Curly Fox when they came to town.

One Sunday afternoon in 1936, Hamilton was struck by a car as he crossed the street on which he lived. According to newspaper accounts, his body was hurled seventy-four feet. His skull was fractured and he died in a hospital the following day at the age of 47.[35] Because Hamilton is a legend among fiddlers, however, the story has been embellished, and his agent of death is more often said to have been a streetcar or a speeding train.

Hamilton died more than fifty years ago, yet his name is still familiar. When older fiddlers play "Hamilton's Special Breakdown" (often called the "Y. Z. Special") or "Fifty Years Ago," they are likely to share stories about Hamilton's extraordinary playing, his drinking, his missing fingers, his violent death or the time they beat him in a contest. Tales about Y. Z. Hamilton stay alive with his tunes.

Charlie Stripling
Alabama's Most Recorded Fiddler
(1896–1966)

Charlie Melvin Stripling and his guitar-playing brother Ira "climbed to the heights of music fame from a beginning as inauspicious as the human mind can imagine," reported the *Commercial Dispatch*

To get a laugh from the crowd, Y. Z. Hamilton would transform himself into a very old fiddler (1926). Photo courtesy of Olen Mayes.

Charlie Stripling flanked on the left by the Freeman brothers of Pickens County and on the right by his brother Ira, who usually played guitar rather than the cello pictured here, ca. 1927. Photo courtesy of Robert Stripling.

(Columbus, Mississippi) in 1929, on the occasion of the brothers' first recording trip to Chicago:

> Born twelve miles east of Kennedy in North Pickens County, a region whose only claim to fame lies in the great number of fiddlers which it has sent out into the world, the Striplings grew up among those sturdy self-reliant Pickens Countians, unassuming young men. Musical instruments did not have a place in the early years of the Stripling boys lives, as would be supposed, and it was through sheer accident that Charlie discovered his talent for music. At the age of eighteen years he ordered a toy violin costing forty-seven cents for a Christmas present for a nephew. The toy arrived several days before Christmas and Charlie, giving over to childish instincts, used the miniature violin while awaiting the proper time for its disposal, finding that he could "strike tunes" easily.[36]

In 1963, Bob Pinson, a record collector with a deep interest in country music, interviewed the Striplings. Charlie Stripling recalled the toy fiddle that began his long fiddling career:

> Well, I ordered a little toy fiddle from Roebuck for my nephew. It came in about four or five days before Christmas and I opened into it and set it up and tuned it up. The fiddle was about a foot long, a little tin fiddle, and the bow was about a foot long. And I tuned it up. I'd learnt how to tune one—there was an old man by the name of, they called him Old Uncle Pleas Carroll [pronouced "Plez"] that lived in our community. He played for dances and I'd been to—I was just a lad of a boy, but I'd been to a few dances and heard him play, and I remembered some of the tunes he played. And I got to sawing on that fiddle after I tuned it up and got to where I remembered one of the tunes he played was "Lexington on the Boom"; that's what he called it,[37] and I remembered that tune and I got to where I could start it. After I gave my nephew the toy fiddle, that kind of got me interested. I decided if I could start a tune in that length of time, maybe I could learn to play. So I bought me a fiddle and bow— it cost a dollar—from one of my neighbors.[38]

Ira ordered a $6 guitar from the Baltimore Wholesale House and soon was backing his brother's playing.

A Series of Triumphs. The two practiced together for almost a year before entering a fiddle contest at Kennedy. At that contest, Charlie was surprised to take first place over a large number of fiddlers. Thereafter, said the *Commercial Dispatch*, it was "about as easy to win first prize over Stripling at a fiddlers convention as for the proverbial camel to gallop through the eye of a very small needle."[39] After winning that contest, said Stripling:

> I really got interested in it and I went to practicing . . . And I got to going to fiddlers' conventions, then, going to Fayette and Millport for awhile and then I got to getting invitations further off away from home. And I kindly felt like I couldn't go off, you know, to communities I wasn't known, in a strange place, and win a prize. But it looked like it was easy to get them—the further off away from home, the easier it was to win it! I went to Parrish, between here and Birmingham, four times at the high school. They'd have a fiddlers' convention every year, and I went

up there four times and got the first prize every time. And then I went to Birmingham.

The 1925 fiddlers' convention in Birmingham has already been described. At it, Charlie was surprised to learn that "they wouldn't allow a guitar accompanist. You had to play the fiddle by yourself . . . and it didn't sound as good to me. I was used to having a guitar second for me, you know." Despite this handicap, the *Birmingham Age-Herald* listed "C. M. Stibrbling" [Stripling] of "Kentucky" [Kennedy] as one of the $25 winners.[40]

In 1926 he learned of a major contest to be held in Memphis. That May, a half-page advertisement in the *Lamar Democrat* had announced that Uncle Bunt Stephens, "Henry Ford's Champion Fiddler," would perform in Sulligent, Millport, and Vernon.[41] Stripling told Bob Pinson: "I'd heard of old Uncle Bunt Stephens. I think I remember reading where Henry Ford had picked him up in the mountains of Kentucky [actually, Tennessee] and he liked his fiddling. And he made him famous. And after he give him his start, he got to going around on tours, putting on musical concerts."

Like many other fiddlers of that area, Stripling attended one of Stephens' performances and was unimpressed, perhaps feeling that Henry Ford should have listened to the fiddlers of Pickens, Lamar, and Tuscaloosa counties before choosing his champion. Said Stripling: "He played this old-timey 'Leather Breeches,' you know, and these old-timey fiddle pieces. And I didn't fancy he was so good. Some of them asked me, 'Charlie, why didn't you bring your fiddle down here? You'd show that old man how to play the fiddle.' I said, 'Well, I was expecting to hear some real fiddling,' but he wasn't as good as what I expected him to be."

During the performance, someone from Memphis called Will Waldrop, the local Ford dealer, to invite Stephens to take part in a convention to be held on Henry Ford's Day, June 2. According to Stripling, Stephens already had an engagement on that date, so Waldrop told the Memphis promoter, "I've got a man here that can beat him a'playing the fiddle." The reply was: "Just bring him on over there."

The Memphis contest, entitled the Dixie Fiddlers' Convention, took place on June 2, 3, and 4, and was sponsored by the Dixie Fiddlers' Association, the Shelby Council of Parent-Teacher Associations, and "the Ford enterprises of Memphis."[42] It was well publicized, and according to the *Memphis News-Scimitar*, "The convention has created so much interest that [the] manager of the auditorium is making arrangements to use the large north hall for the sessions at which the contests will be staged."[43] This hall reportedly seated 8,000. During the days preceding the contest, groups of fiddlers gathered to play at Court Square, and some were taken to the Ford plant "to serenade the manager and employees, in recognition of the part Henry Ford has taken in popularizing old-time tunes." The *Memphis Commercial Appeal* on Thursday, June 3, announced that "more than a score of contestants have already arrived and others are arriving on every train. . . . Charles E. Stribling [*sic*], who claims the Alabama championship, accompanied by his brother, I. L. Stribling [*sic*], guitar picker, arrived yesterday and was entered in the contests by W. W. Waldrop, automobile dealer of Millport, Ala., as the representatives of the Millport Motor Co."[44]

Stripling recalled that, as in Birmingham, fiddlers were required to play unaccompanied. He felt he could not win; he told Bob Pinson:

> Of course, the first two nights they didn't give prizes out. They'd have large crowds, though. But the third night, on Saturday night, was the final contest, and that's when they'd give the prizes out. I know there was a bunch of fiddlers there— there was a large number . . . And I realized I had competition. And I was talking with Lester Howell that moved from Kennedy and had a clothing store in Memphis . . . I told him, "I won't win no prize. I got too big a competition. There's too many up agin me." Well, he said, "Don't get scared. You just sit down there and play that fiddle and just imagine you was home by yourself." And that's what I done.

After the rosin had settled at the end of three nights' playing, "Sawmill" Tom Smith, of Harrison, Tennessee, was declared champion fiddler of the Dixie Old Fiddlers' Association. The *Commercial Appeal* reported that "the contest was so close that the judges called back five of the best for a second trial. Second prize went to Charles Stripling, of Millport, Ala." Stripling was awarded $25 in gold.[45]

A year later Stripling won another important competition in Tuscaloosa. This contest, held on March 3, 1927, at the Casino Theater, was unusual in that only well-known fiddlers were asked to participate. The *Tuscaloosa News* reported: "Plans are being made to bring eight of the select fiddlers of the southern states to Tuscaloosa for a fiddlers contest," though it did not name them.[46] Stripling recalled the contest:

> They didn't invite all the fiddlers; they just selected eight of the best fiddlers. And the champion fiddler of Alabama, then,

was Y. Z. Hamilton. And he was down there that night . . . all the seats was full and [people were] standing around on the edges.

They arranged that a little different to what they'd been, all that I'd been to before . . . That time they let the audience judge. They just had three men to go with cards up and down from the front to the back and back up handing them cards out. And they let every person judge the fiddler and give him grades, so much per cent. And after they all played, I told my brother "I won't get nothing." They went to counting, gathered the cards up, telling out the points, how many points each one got, and when they wound up, I had 156 points more than everyone in the bunch. I got first prize.

The following day, the *Tuscaloosa News* described the event:

> The Fiddlers' contest at the Casino last night played to a ca-
> pacity house. More than a thousand people were present and all
> enjoyed the program. Judging was done by secret ballot, every
> adult in the audience participating. They awarded first prize,
> $25 to Charley Stripling of Kennedy, Ala; second prize, $15 to
> Henry Ledlow of Tuscaloosa County; third prize to E. D. Monkey
> Brown, a local insurance man.
>
> A special feature of the program was a number by attorney R. C.
> Price, who had to demolish his fiddle to get it to stop playing.[47]

The Stripling Brothers—Recording Artists. Stripling's success at fiddle conventions made him something of a local hero. His admirers in the community saw to it that Stripling was not passed over by commercial recording companies, as were so many Alabama fiddlers. According to Ira Stripling, their first recording session came about in the following manner:

> Mr. Carey Walker down here in Kennedy noticed they was
> going to take some trial recordings up in Birmingham, and so
> he asked me if we would go. And I told him we would. And so
> he called the man up and talked with him and I was standing
> by him when he was talking. So the first thing he asked, he
> asked if we sung. We just played mostly. He told him he
> wouldn't be interested unless we sung.
>
> Mr. Walker says, "They're good. I'd love for you to hear them."
> He said, "Well I don't think I'd be interested unless they sang."
> Mr. Walker turned to me and asked if I'd be willing to pay
> our expenses up there for him to listen at us play, and I told

him, "Yeah." He says, "They'll pay their expenses. You won't be out nothing just to listen at 'em."

He said, "Well, I'll listen at 'em but I don't think it'll do 'em any good."

On November 15, 1928, the brothers traveled to Birmingham where the Brunswick-Balke-Collender Company had set up a temporary recording studio in the Bankhead Hotel.[48] Ira Stripling recalled the occasion: "When we went up there that night, they had some bands that sounded good to me and he [Manager Jack Kapp] just frown up and ask them if they didn't have anything better than that. Bands just sounded real good to me and he wouldn't take anything they had. I didn't think there was any use for us to even wait for a trial. I told Charlie, 'We'd just as well go.'"

They stayed, however, and finally got their opportunity to audition. In Ira's words, "The first piece Charlie started, he [Kapp] started smiling. Didn't play over what you'd call—what old people called a stanza—you know, played only one stanza and he motioned to him to stop. Says, 'We'll try that. What else do you have?' Charlie told him and started to playing that. And so he didn't play but a little piece and he stopped him again. Then's when he told us he'd try us and if it made good, we'd hear from him in about two weeks. We didn't hear anything from it till Charlie heard it playing in a music store in Fayette."

The first tune recorded by the brothers in that session was "Big-Footed Nigger in Sandy Land," a piece Stripling had heard Henry Ledlow play at a fiddlers' convention. The second was "Lost Child," which Stripling learned from Pleas Carroll, but embellished. It is believed to be the source of the popular fiddle piece "The Black Mountain Rag"[49] and has been re-released on the "Old-Time Fiddle Classics" album produced by County Records (#507) and on the Stripling Brothers album (County 401).

Before returning to Kennedy, the two brothers played on Station WAPI, which had moved from Auburn to Birmingham during the previous year. "After we went up there," recalled Stripling, "then we just got calls far and near, and we got more than we could fill." While playing for dances and contests, they awaited word about the trial recording. Ten months passed before it came, in unexpected form. According to Charlie Stripling:

It went on a couple of weeks and we didn't hear from him and there was people asking me every once in a while, "Didn't y'all make some fiddling records?" I got to where I'd tell 'em we didn't. I thought he'd made a flash out of us and it was no good. . . . But over in August, I was in Fayette, and Mr. William-son, a jewelsman, when I walked in the jewelry shop, he had that record, now, we made up there at Birmingham, playing it. And he says, "Charlie, didn't you all make some fiddling records sometime past?"

I says, "Well, we made one, but I haven't never heard nothing from 'em and I decided it wasn't no count."

Well, he says, "It's *good*." And he asked me how much they paid, and I said, "Didn't pay anything."

And he says, "If I was you, I'd get in touch and find out where they're coming from."

Eventually Stripling contacted the Brunswick Company in Chicago. Jack Kapp, who had supervised the recording in Birmingham, expressed surprise that the Striplings had not been paid. He told them to come to Chicago prepared to record a dozen selections, and promised to pay them when they came. According to Stripling, "I didn't have much confidence in him, because he hadn't paid us for the first one. And I said, 'Well, what about sending us our expenses to pay our way over there?' He said, 'Find out how much it is.' I went out there to the depot and found out, and he wired it to me. The next morning we left and went to Chicago."

In Chicago, on August 19, 1929, the brothers recorded sixteen tunes, all of which were released on the Vocalion label. Some also were released on Australian and Canadian labels. The tunes included traditional breakdowns like "Wolves Howling" and "Dance All Night with a Bottle in Your Hand"; four waltzes; and the only two vocals the brothers ever recorded, "Weeping Willow" and "Railroad Bum."[50]

Before the recording session Kapp informed the brothers that they should not play anything that had already been recorded. "You know, the old-timey pieces like 'Turkey in the Straw' and 'Hen Cackle' and 'Leather Breeches' and all like that had been recorded," said Stripling. Thus he played several tunes of his own composition, among them the "Kennedy Rag," named after his hometown, and "The Coal Mine Blues." The latter was composed when Stripling, a cotton farmer who had never been near coal mines, began playing for dances in the mining camps of Walker County. The tune was very popular among the miners who inspired it. Stripling's "compositions" were committed to memory and to the recording machine, but not to paper, as he had never learned to read or write music.[51]

The records made in Chicago were well received. Charlie Stripling recalled: "The records come out and made a hit and was selling like hotcake. Every where I went they had 'em and was selling 'em. We could have got on, then, with the Victor Company. That agent come through there. He told us, said, 'I could take one of these records down there and play it. My company would give you a job, right now.' "

However, the brothers had a contract with Brunswick-Balke-Collender. Upon its expiration, Dave Kapp, brother of the Brunswick agent, invited them to record for Decca in New York. There, on September 10, 1934, they played fourteen tunes, ten of which were issued.[52] Except for the traditional tune "Chinese Breakdown," most were waltzes, fox-trots, and "ragtime breakdowns," such as "Down on the L & N," that Stripling had composed for round dancing. Kapp was not difficult to please, recalled Stripling: "He'd tell me to play over one, and I'd play over it, and I'd think to myself, 'Well, he won't take that,' but he wouldn't grumble about it. He'd just say, 'Okay,' and then he'd ask me what was the name of it and ask me how come it's the name it is, and make a record of it then."

On the recording trip, the two brothers from Kennedy, population 277,[53] were able to see a small portion of New York City. Later they told local historian Joe Acee, "The excitement of the big city was a curiosity to us, just as we might have been a curiosity to the people there."[54]

Their final recording session was March 12, 1936, in New Orleans, where Decca had set up a temporary studio.[55] The fourteen numbers they recorded were again a mixture of traditional tunes, such as "Mayflower," and original compositions, such as "Coal Valley," named for a mining camp where they performed, "Big Four," named after a local fishing hole, and "California Blues," named after a state they had never visited.[56]

As was the case with most country artists of the day, the Striplings did not get rich from their recording efforts. When given a choice between being paid a flat fee of $50 per record ($25 per tune) or receiving a 1¢ per-record royalty, the brothers chose the former. Stripling explained: "He was going to hold us back, now, if we took a royalty. Hold us back until the last record was released. But you see, he was so long about paying us for that one we made in Birmingham, I was afraid we wouldn't get anything. So that's the reason we made the choice of just a'getting paid. I told my brother, 'I've always heard it said a bird in the cage is worth two in the bush. We might go back and wait for that pay and not never get nothing,' so we took it."

Thus the brothers received $50, divided between them, per record, plus expense-paid trips to Chicago, New York, and New Orleans in exchange for recording forty-six tunes. It was not grand pay, but the fact that they were artists for a major recording company helped them get other jobs that did pay well. For instance, Charlie remembered a job at a theater in Fulton, Mississippi. "In two nights down there, just me and my brother . . . we got more than I got for a bale of cotton. I sold a bale of cotton the next week and we got more out of them two nights playing down there than I got for a bale of cotton. And that man, owned that theater, told me, 'You got us the largest crowd we've ever had here.' "

Despite the supplemental income the Striplings received from their recordings and performances, Ira Stripling eventually found that he could not afford to continue as a musician: "It was in the thirties, during that Panic. Got to where we couldn't get enough out of it to justify all of us a'going. I had some business in town . . . I'd have to hire someone in my place for the business when I left. And I just turned it over to he and the boys [Stripling's sons]. They could realize more out of it than I could and do about as well. The boys got to where they played real good."

Thus, for financial reasons, the 1936 recording session in New Orleans was one of the last performances for the Stripling Brothers, as a duo.

Local Fame. Charlie Stripling, however, continued to perform regularly with his children and other local musicians—at theaters, schoolhouses, dances, and contests—for the next thirty years. He farmed for a living, supplementing his income with his fiddle: "I made enough playing the fiddle from the first start to have done me, I guess, to have lived on the rest of my life, but I had a lot of sickness and hospital bills and doctor bills, and it took a lot of it to pay it. But that was a way to pay it."

Stripling had married Tellie Sullivan, age 14, in 1919. They farmed and ran a country store in Pickens County before moving to Kennedy in 1926. In 1934, Tellie died, leaving Stripling with six children, all under 15. He later married Myrtle Wheeler and three more children were born.[57] Eventually all nine children could play one or more instruments. A tradition developed at family gatherings: During a musical session, the family would play a tune, then each member would pass his instrument to the next musician and play the following tune on a different instrument.[58]

The oldest sons, Robert and Edwin, were accomplished performers

Charlie Stripling with his wife Tellie and first son Robert in Pickens County, 1920. Photo courtesy of Robert Stripling.

by the time they were 10 and 11. With their father, they played for dances held in homes all over the area. Robert Stripling recalled how the host of the dance would send someone with a car to pick them up and bring them over unpaved, sometimes impassable, back roads to the dance. Later Stripling bought a used Graham-Paige for $160 and traveled to dances and contests in it, fabricating broken parts when needed and stuffing tires with rags when they went flat on the way.[59] At many dances, the younger son, Edwin, appeared to fall asleep. Said Ira Stripling, "A lot of people think he *was* asleep. Said he'd go to sleep, but he'd sit there and play that mandolin right on; he'd never miss a lick of time or chord or nothing." Stripling also performed with his sons at schoolhouses during the Depression. He said, "I'd take my boys and we'd go out to these little country schools and just charge 10¢ for admission. But see, we got it all, and we could buy a bag of flour for $3.50 or $4, and I could still make my living thataway."

Dannie Strickland of the tiny Moore's Bridge community, twenty-five miles from Kennedy, remembered such performances: "There was always a big crowd. Everybody enjoyed them. And when they played in Birmingham, we always had our radios on ready to hear them." She said that people in her community liked Charlie Stripling, not only because he was a good fiddler but because he was a religious man who attended church regularly and could speak about the Bible well.[60] It was his custom to include sacred numbers, such as "Jesus, Hold My Hand," at every performance.[61]

Stripling also continued to enter contests with much success. A. K. Callahan has said, "All Charlie Stripling had to do was stick his head in the door at a contest and they'd give him first prize."[62] Besides having a full rich tone, good technical ability, and a driving style, he was a showman who won many prizes with his trick fiddling on such tunes as "The Lost Child" and "Pop Goes the Weasel."

Stripling recalled that he frequently won at Palmetto, in Pickens County: "I was playing at Palmetto one night—Palmetto High School down below Kennedy—I went down there seven years and got the first prize ever time. And I come out that night, and there was a bunch of them standing out in the front yard of the school, and there was high steps, and when I come down them steps I heard somebody say, 'Who got the first prize?' Somebody said, 'Charlie Stripling, the one that always gets it.' And I walked on down there close to them and I said, 'Well, I have been lucky.' The way they give prizes, I didn't know if I won them or not, but if they give them to me, I took them. And there was a fellow standing there that was a stranger to me—I'd never seen him before—and he said, 'My friend, it ain't just luck with you. You fiddle for it. I heard you play.' That made me feel good."

Others, however, thought that he was often given the prize because of his reputation as a contest winner and as a recording artist. Stripling remembered the year in Palmetto when some contestants spoke to the manager before the start of the competition: "They suggested concealing the judges where they couldn't see the one that's playing and said I wouldn't get it. I didn't know they'd done that and I noticed, though, when they went to playing that I didn't see no judges; usually had 'em picked out and set out on a seat separate. And after it got around and all of 'em played, why Mr. Smith, he says, 'Now, it's been suggested we conceal the judges here tonight at this fiddlers' convention where they couldn't see the fiddling. Now they are awarding the prizes. They'll call the numbers that won the prizes and I'll call the name.' And one of the judges back behind the curtain said, 'Number three won first prize.' Says, 'That was Charlie Stripling.' And after it was all over with . . . Mr. Smith come around there and patted me on the shoulder and he told me about what they had done. He says, 'I think they ought to be satisfied now. If they're not, they should be.' "

Though Charlie Stripling won a prize in almost every contest he entered, it was not always the first prize. He admitted to Pinson that there was "a bunch of fiddlers from around Tuscaloosa that I dreaded at fiddlers' conventions, because they was *good*." E. D. "Monkey" Brown and his brother Charlie were good fiddlers as well as crowd-pleasers, and were hard to beat. Another strong contender was Jimmie Porter of Steens, Mississippi, who had a beautiful tone and could play waltzes very well.[63] Robert Stripling recalled that his father also dreaded playing against Pearl Duncan Morgan, the vigorous young fiddler from Caledonia, Mississippi.[64]

Keeping Up With the Times. After World War II, Stripling remained an active fiddler even though the frequency of fiddlers' conventions and home dances decreased. He became the fiddler of choice at large community dances because, over the years, he had developed a repertoire of dance tunes that pleased many tastes:

> When we was playing for dances, I played for so many dances 'til I learned different kinds of time. I first commenced playing old breakdown music for old-timey square dancing, and back then when I first started playing they didn't know anything about round dancing; you never seen nothing like that when you were out in the country where they had the dances. And when I got to going to Columbus, Mississippi; Parrish, Birmingham, places around towns where they round-danced . . . I didn't know much time for that, but I learned it. I seen I had to if I kept my job, if I kept a'getting called. After we got broadcasting stations—radio, I'd listen and get a lot on that.
>
> [When] I first commenced playing for round dances about all I could play was something what they called a Fox-trot. But sometimes somebody would request me to play a two-step. I didn't even know how to play it, but I sure learned it . . . course, I could play a waltz. And I found out there was different times to all that. Some wanted a real slow draggy kind they called a "toddle" and I just sorta begin to get on that when they got that "Twist," a new kind of a dance. That was a different time.

After Stripling's sons married and moved away from Kennedy to raise their families, Stripling was able to find other good musicians to play for dances at all the American Legion huts and National Guard armories in west Alabama. He recalled the first dance he played at Berry with a new band, called, simply, "Charlie Stripling's Band," consisting of fiddle, guitar, mandolin, steel guitar, and tenor banjo: "They had it on a Thanksgiving night . . . and there was a large crowd out there that night; it being a holiday, and them folks liked our music. They got to coming from Birmingham; there was people coming from Tuscaloosa, Meridian . . . Columbus. That was a large building; you know, the National Guard armory is a large building, and they got to where they'd just fill that place up. There's lots of folks just come to listen to the music, told me they did—but they got to where so many come they didn't hardly have room to dance."

The band continued to grow in popularity, and by 1958 Stripling was playing to large dance crowds two or three nights a week—in Mississippi on Fridays, near Tuscaloosa on Saturdays, and frequently at Mayfield on Thursdays. It was at the Mayfield Community House one Thursday night that Charlie Stripling, aged 60, played for the last time. Suffering severe stomach pain, he was taken from the dance to the hospital. After a long stay in the hospital, he fell victim to arthritis. He said that eventually "I got back to where I could play a little, but the boys had all left me and I lost interest and got out of practice." When he was interviewed in 1963, Stripling no longer had a fiddle in the house.

Charlie Stripling died in 1966. In 1971, County Records reissued thirteen of the Stripling Brothers' recordings, enabling the music that once delighted audiences in west Alabama to reach new generations of old-time music lovers across the nation.

Joe Lee
Master Fiddler
(1883–1964)

Joseph Alexander Lee worked in cotton mills throughout his life. He never won a state championship nor made a commercial recording, yet he was one of the nation's most influential old-time fiddlers.

Joe Lee with guitarist Paul Ray in Rome, Georgia, 1939. Photo courtesy of Paul Ray.

Lee was born in Etowah County in 1883 and as a child began working in textile mills around Gadsden, Attalla, and Alabama City. He also began fiddling as a child, playing music with his father and several of his six brothers. He persisted in both his mill work and his fiddling, and in 1916, at the age of 33, moved to Lindale, Georgia, to work at Pepperell Mills. There Lee was heard and admired by several young men who later became recording artists and fiddlers of national repute. Charles Wolfe called Lee "one of the legends of old time Georgia fiddling," explaining that Lee taught Lowe Stokes his style. Clayton McMichen, influenced by both Stokes and Lee, became such a popular recording artist that he was able to pass his style on to "generations of fiddlers."[65]

Stokes, McMichen, and Bill Shores, another fiddler who attributed his style to Joe Lee, were all associated with the Skillet Lickers, a string band that recorded extensively during the twenties and thirties. It is difficult to find a fiddler active during that period who did not learn some of his tunes from Skillet Lickers recordings, played on hand-cranked "Graphifones." Most fiddlers interviewed for this book said that they enjoyed the playing and humor of fiddler Gid Tanner, but it was Clayton McMichen's style that they imitated. McMichen played with a "long bow," meaning that he drew the bow across the strings in long strokes, playing several notes per stroke, while Tanner and many older fiddlers moved their bows rapidly back and forth, producing one note with each pass of the bow. The short bow style could be powerful and rhythmic, but could also sound "jerky" and, after a while, monotonous. However, a good fiddler who drew a long bow could produce a strong rhythm as well as a smooth flow of notes. Young fiddlers of Alabama who tried to learn the "Georgia long bow" style of playing from Skillet Lickers recordings did not know that the artists themselves attributed their style to an Alabama fiddler.

Joe Lee had moved to north Georgia when Lowe Stokes was 16 years old and Clayton McMichen, 14. At some point, the two, along with many other musicians, began going to Lee's home for extended music sessions. Stokes considered Lee "the best old-time fiddler I ever heard." In Stokes's words, "He could just set and play pretty all day and all night . . . play all them ol' hornpipes, and he could really play 'em, too. I learned that 'Katy Hill'—I'd win most of my prizes on that 'Katy Hill'—I learned that from him . . . And a lot of them hornpipes I used to learn to play from him. He [knew] lots of pretty waltzes, too . . . A lot of times he'd make up a tune and just play it by itself, play it good. He wouldn't have no name for it. Boy, me and ol' Mac would get in there and start playing with him. We'd have three fiddles playing."[66]

Stokes told interviewer Joe LaRose that he did not play exactly like Joe Lee, "except on the tune 'Katy Hill.' And he played that 'Katy Hill'—boy, I never heard anybody play it like that. I learned it just like him and put it on a record just like him. And he bought that record. 'Boy,' he says, 'that sounds just *like* me.' "[67]

Bill Shores, who was born and began playing the fiddle in Cherokee County, Alabama, also moved to north Georgia as a young man and became an admirer of Joe Lee: "I learned more about old-time fiddling from Joe Lee than from any other man . . . Joe could sit down with you and play with you all night and never play the same tune twice . . . And he could fiddle better. He had the most nimble fingers for a big man I ever saw."[68]

Lee was close to six feet tall and had large hands. Roger Aycock, a classical violinist, observed, "His hands were so big . . . he'd play in third position without shifting. His little finger was bigger than my middle finger. It was amazing to watch him play . . . He's the only fiddler of that sort I ever saw who played in three positions, in minor keys and flats."[69]

Aycock also considered Lee's ear for pitch remarkable. Paul Ray, a guitarist who frequently accompanied Lee, said that Lee could leave a fiddle in its unpadded wooden case, shake it, listen to the vibration, then tune another fiddle to it.[70] Though Aycock never saw Lee tune in that manner, he agreed that if anyone could do it, Joe Lee could.[71]

In the late 1920s, Lee took part in many of the entertainments and contests that accompanied the nation's revival of interest in old-time fiddling. He performed locally with two younger brothers: Jim Lee accompanied him on the guitar and Mitchell Lee buck-danced to their music wearing a loose-fitting jacket with a long, flapping tail.[72] Joe Lee also traveled with a group of well-known musicians assembled by "Fiddling Bud" Silvey to perform at the fiddlers' conventions Silvey promoted in the late 1920s. For instance, in 1927, The *Sand Mountain Banner* announced that Lee would appear in Albertville with "Fiddling Bud," Arthur Silvey, Bill Helms, Hoke Rice, and Lowe Stokes, as well as a number of fiddlers from Alabama and Tennessee. He appeared with a similar group in Fort Payne.[73] However, Lee seems to have stayed away from large championship contests like those held in Atlanta each year. Lowe Stokes described Lee's discomfort at competitions:

. . . he couldn't win a prize to save his life. He'd play with you in a band and just play awful good. But you put him out on a stage to play for a prize up by hisself—boy, he's so nervous he just couldn't start hardly. And when he gets started, why, he couldn't—he'd get messed up; he gets nervous, you know—then he couldn't hardly stop.[74]

Apparently Lee was content to let his famous protégés win the prestigious contests while he entered competitions in and around Rome. In October 1925, the *Rome News-Tribune* reported that Lee took first place in a fiddlers' contest that drew participants from several counties. The following month, it reported that area musicians Lowe Stokes, Clayton McMichen, and Mrs. J. P. Wheeler had won the top three prizes at the big Atlanta contest, with no mention of participation by Lee.[75]

Lee also left the business of making commercial recordings to his younger friends. According to Bill Shores, "Joe was a hard-working fellow, worked in a cotton mill all his life, a loom fixer and a weaver. He'd go out somewhere and play a square dance till 2 or 3 o'clock in the morning and then go home and get up next morning and go down to the mill and work ten hours a day. He was pretty much a homebody fellow; never did think too much about putting something down for posterity."[76]

Mrs. Lee and Paul Ray remembered that Lee actually wanted to record, and on several occasions made plans to do so. While the studio sessions never came about, Paul Ray made several acetate disc recordings of Lee and himself playing at home in 1940. One of these, which was recently found in Ray's auto-body shop, contains Lee's rendition of "Georgia Wagoner." Beneath a frenzy of static, one hears Lee's rich tone, powerful bowing, and his rapid and precise fingering. With subtle variations upon the tune each time he repeated it, Lee demonstrated his technical skill and creativity, without diminishing the drive and character of the piece.[77]

Lee certainly had the talent and the connections he needed to become a famous fiddler, yet he chose to stay at home. Roger Aycock surmised:

For a big man, he had an awful gentle dispostion. I think that's why he stayed at home instead of traveling. As much as he liked to fiddle, nothing would have suited him better than to go with a group and make a living at it. He couldn't make a living at it here, so he worked at the Lindale Mills and played on the side.[78]

His "side" work consisted mainly of playing for square dances. Said Ray, "If you got $4 or $5 or $10 from playing a square dance, that was a whole lot of money. And if they wanted to dance past midnight, they'd put some money in his pocket. He was honest. He wouldn't beat you out of a dime."[79] Lee's son Charles remembered, "When I was a real small child he used to play for dances and he'd come in and he'd give me a quarter . . . He'd usually wake me up. I'd hear my mama say, "Don't wake him up. Give it to him tomorrow.' But he would."[80]

Lee joined the church some time in the late 1940s and told people that he had quit playing "Turkey in the Straw" and started playing "Amazing Grace."[81] His days as a dance fiddler were over, yet he continued playing his hoedowns and hornpipes at home, alone and for numerous visitors. At home, according to Paul Ray, "he'd get up nearly every morning and play before he went to work, and the first thing he done when he got home and hit the door was play that fiddle. He was just a natural-born fiddler."[82] Charles Lee recalled, "Every few days people would come in from out of town. Sometimes they'd write a letter and say they were coming into town next week. People would spend the weekend . . . he'd help people who weren't too good; he'd give tips . . . He always enjoyed it."[83]

When Lee was not playing a fiddle, he was likely to be prying it open. Roger Aycock recalled:

> He always had a fiddle he wanted to trade. He never kept one long. No matter how good it was, he'd trade it or sell it and get another one. He must have owned 200 or 300 fiddles, at least, in his life . . . And he didn't believe in the adage, "If it ain't broke, don't fix it." Every fiddle he got, he'd take it apart and work on it whether or not it needed it. He'd open it up, thin the top, or put in a new bass bar.[84]

In the course of his life, Lee made a number of violins. Paul Ray remembered some old wooden steps at the cotton mill that Lee used for such purposes. Lee transformed the steps, constructed from curly maple, into fiddle backs.[85]

Joe Lee died in 1964 after a long life filled with hard work and excellent music. He had worked in cotton mills for sixty years, had played the fiddle longer than that, and had influenced more fiddlers than he could ever know. His fiddles made from cotton-mill steps are fitting symbols of his life.

Fiddling Tom Freeman
Alabama's Most Publicized Fiddler
(1883–1952)

Tom Freeman was born in 1883, began fiddling in 1892, and fiddled incessantly for sixty years thereafter. He was so thoroughly identified as a fiddler that all who knew him called him "Fiddling Tom," a name now engraved on his tombstone. Tom Freeman never fiddled professionally; he did not make commercial recordings or "win" statewide fiddle conventions, yet the Jasper *Mountain Eagle* announced his death in 1952 with headlines that read "Fiddling Tom's Fiddle Is Silent Now; Familiar Figure Dies of Heart Ailment," the *Cullman Tribune* published an editorial entitled "Fiddlin' Tom," and the *Birmingham News* wrote, "Famed Fiddling Tom Freeman Dies, Nimble Bow Is Stilled."[86]

Tom Freeman had a knack for capturing headlines throughout his life. A reporter for the *Birmingham Age-Herald* wrote that "next to Nero, he's the most publicized fiddler Birmingham's seen in many a day."[87] Newspaper readers of Walker, Cullman, and Jefferson counties were often treated to folksy accounts of Freeman's latest fiddling exploits, such as the following:

> He [Freeman] was in to see us a few days ago and told how he had just about stampeded the Walker County Fair by beating the Mid-West fiddling champion at the fair in a fiddling contest that caused black snakes 'way over in the woods to stick their heads out of their holes and listen. There were no judges; he won by getting most of the applause. Tom can certainly play that fiddle. When he gets started he saws faster and faster until the roof blows off. We are betting on Tom in future fiddling contests. He won a $10 prize in Cullman recently and didn't half try.[88]

Freeman's fame was not solely the result of his talent. Other fiddlers have described his fiddling as "rough," "jerky," and too erratic to be accompanied by other musicians. Bob Kyle wrote that Freeman "fiddled like a Model-T warming up when it had water on its spark plugs."[89] However, former Congressman Carl Elliott of Jasper, who heard Freeman often during political campaigns in the 1940s, regarded him as a fine and enjoyable country fiddler.[90] It is probable that "Fiddling Tom" was not accomplished in matters of tone and technique, but fully made up for such faults with his zesty delivery

Fiddling Tom Freeman of Bug Tussle. Photo courtesy of Mr. and Mrs. J. C. Freeman.

of breakdown tunes. He could make his listeners clap their hands, stomp their feet, and have a good time.

Freeman's personality and image, rather than his music, were responsible for the amount of publicity he received. To newspaper writers and their readers, "Fiddling Tom" represented backwoods Alabama. A colorful character with a minimal education, he was associated with moonshine, feuds, signs and portents, rural politics, and hoedown music, the ingredients of good "local color" writing. In 1941, Freeman himself became a writer when he produced a manuscript called "The Bug Tussle Murders," which reveals more about his life and philosophy than it does about the moonshine feuds he intended to expose. It shows him to be a simple, kind, and humorous man who came by his colorful ways naturally. He did not have to don overalls and a straw hat and blacken his front teeth when he performed, as the professional country musicians did. Even in his blue serge suit and rakish felt hat, he was a backwoodsman whose words and music entertained his listeners and provided merry copy for journalists.

Freeman was born February 3, 1883, in the southwest corner of Cullman County, an area described by State Senator Thomas A. Walker in 1859 as being "so poor a buzzard would have to carry provisions on his back or starve to death on his passage."[91] Freeman wrote that when he was "a lad of a boy," times were "sure enough hard." His mother would dye hand-woven domestic with oak bark to make his Sunday pants, "so when I got them on I thought I [was] rich when I'd go to meeting."[92] Freeman was equally self-sufficient when he decided to become a fiddler:

> I can remember when I'd go to old-time breakdown dances, when the fiddler would lay his fiddle down, I'd grab it and he'd have to choke me loose from it—I dearly loved a fiddle. So when I [was] only nine years of age I decided to make me a fiddle out of a gourd, and I did so . . . there [was] no spool thread them days, only ball thread, so I doubled and twisted threads together and I put twelve threads more in one string than the other and that should change the sound so it wouldn't all go alike. So then I cut the hair out of a horse tail and bent a hickory stick and tied the hair to each end and that was my bow for my gourd fiddle. The first tune I ever learned to start was "Carry Me Back to Georgia to Eat Corn Bread and 'Lasses." So that started me on my fiddling career . . . Then it wasn't long til I [was] going playing for breakdown dances.

In 1903 Freeman married Ida Pamela Williams, and until the children came along, she traveled to dances with him, hopping out of the wagon to beat the metal rim back onto the wooden wheel whenever it would come off.[93] He "played many times all night long and until the sun would be an hour by next morning," and felt, "I [was] then just warmed up good."

In 1905, Freeman took up whiskey-making, an occupation that had become widespread in north Alabama during the Civil War, after the state legislature made it unlawful to use grain in the manufacture of whiskey. This new law created a demand for liquor, and the "outlayers" in the woods became the natural suppliers. Some actually obtained contracts to make it for the Federal government.[94] During Freeman's twenty-year career as a "wildcatter," he found himself "in some close places—had the limbs and twigs shot from treetops down on me," but managed to elude the law by using a system of red warning flags, hoot-owl imitations, and posted lookouts, as well as by giving free whiskey to law officers. He also supplied "the best standing people such as church members and a lot that I knew was against me. When their family got sick I gave them whiskey for sickness and they wouldn't turn me up."

Freeman's fiddle playing also helped prevent his arrest. One night several detectives arrived at his home. They inquired about his fiddling and he replied, "Yes, I am one of the best old break-down fiddlers you ever heard pull a bow, and also I have a girl that's a knockout in dancing." When one detective asked for a drink of whiskey, Freeman took a chance, went to the edge of his yard, and "pulled out a pint of the best wild cat moonshine that a man ever put down his throat." He poured it into a large "goblet glass" and passed it around the room. By the time it had gone around one time, he knew he had "the whole bunch won over." Then, said Freeman, "I opened up on some of my best breakdown tunes." After an hour and a half of music, the agents left "rejoicing" with a gift quart of whiskey and without a prisoner.

Freeman was able to build a house and barn with the profits from his whiskey-making, but he grew to regret his involvement in the trade: " . . . where there's whiskey there's no peace in [the] family. For a man that fools with whiskey is always looking for the law to knock on his door at any time of night. It's one of the miserablest lives a man ever lived. It gets a man's character."

Freeman maintained that he quit the business in 1924, a year before he was found guilty of manufacturing whiskey. This occurred when a nephew caught operating a still within one-half mile of Freeman's home testified that the still belonged to Tom Freeman. On October 7, 1925, Freeman was tried along with ten other alleged moonshiners and sentenced to Kilby Prison for one and a half to two years.[95] He appealed the decision, but when it was affirmed, Freeman entered Kilby Prison in his usual colorful manner:

> So I decided one day in May 1927 that I'd just go on down. So I went on down fiddling along, went by the capital and talked to Hon. Bibb Graves, who was governor, and then went on up to the prison late one evening. Honorable Sherley from Birmingham was warden at that time. I went up and entered just myself as Fiddling Tom Freeman from Cullman County. I told him with tears in my eyes that I was not guilty but I had made up my mind to just come on rather than leaving the state.

Though Freeman's family remembered that he was miserable in prison, he later wrote that his time at Kilby was made bearable by his fiddling:

> I was treated as good as a daddy could of treated me as long as I stayed there. I just fiddled for capitol folks that come in and called me out of bed at 10 and 11 o'clock in the night for me to fiddle for them. I trusteed all the time I stayed there. They let me go out by myself to play for breakdown dances . . . so I kept from one to two fiddles in there all the time I stayed there and I kept them going.

In his book, Freeman described harsh beatings of prisoners but declared that he was "never taken before the man" because he was a fiddler. Freeman's experiences of being arrested, going through the state legal system, and playing his fiddle for officials while he was in prison led him to discover new uses for his fiddling. After leaving prison, he no longer played for dances, but began "fiddling people out of trouble" and "fiddling for candidates."

Freeman did not hold with those who believed the fiddle was a "devil's box" because it could entrap the soul and lead it from the path of righteousness. He believed, instead, that his playing could reform people who had gotten on the wrong side of the law. He wrote:

> I can fiddle any man on earth out of trouble. If he got 200 year in [the] pen and will honestly say he will live a better life and try to do better if he [is] out of prison and mean it, I can get him out of any prison in the world. But I want a man or woman to

tell me he wants a chance and that he won't let me down . . . I like to help a person that will do right and try to help their selves.

Freeman's most publicized efforts in behalf of lawbreakers came with the Bug Tussle mail fraud case of 1938. Bug Tussle is an unincorporated community near Bremen in Cullman County. Originally named Wilburn, this community supposedly received its more colorful name in 1912 when a resident declared the town should be named Bug Tussle after he had watched two tumblebugs struggling to roll a ball of dirt across a road.[96]

For several years prior to 1938, a number of Bug Tussle residents had been ordering items on credit from mail-order catalogs, making fraudulent claims as to their ability to pay and their financial worth. According to postal inspectors, orders had been submitted in the names of babies and cats. The *Birmingham News* reported that "even a cat at Bug Tussle . . . had a Dun and Bradstreet financial worth of AA and a credit rating of A plus." Although the customers had ordered simple things including chambray shirts, overalls, brogans, mattresses, stoves, and rocking chairs, they failed to pay for them. One company had long since stopped filling orders that came from Bug Tussle.[97]

It was estimated that mail-order houses had been defrauded of $3,500 by the time twenty-six residents of Bug Tussle were arrested and brought to court in the back of a truck.[98] Among them were one of Freeman's daughters and a niece. When Freeman decided to accompany them to the federal court in Birmingham to fiddle for leniency, he intensified an already colorful situation. Though the judge would not allow him to play in the courtroom, pictures of "Fiddling Tom" and articles about his efforts to fiddle his kin out of trouble appeared on the front pages of both of Birmingham's daily newspapers.

In the following years, the *Cullman Banner* frequently mentioned Freeman's trips to Birmingham to fiddle in behalf of friends, such as one who had been arrested for driving while intoxicated: "Freeman says that Judge Abernathy let his friend off for only $25 when Freeman granted his requests for 'Rye Straw,' 'Leather Britches,' and 'Cake Waltz.' "[99] People often sought Freeman's intercession with the law. In his book, he narrated the story of a woman who rushed up to him in the courthouse. Her daughter had been in jail for ten days on a vagrancy charge. She said, "Uncle, I've been praying for a week to see you, for I knew you could get my girl out of jail." After

AY MORNING

THE BIRMI

FUTURE I
REALTO

Present And

Activities I

Cited By

Fiddler Fails In Court

Prepared to defend his daughter and a niece not with his gun but with a fiddle, Fiddling Tom Freeman, of Bremen, was in town Thursday to fiddle Mrs. Meedia Boyd and Mrs. Ruby Freeman out of their difficulties with the federal government.

Fiddling Tom Freeman, of Bremen, is one guy who'll probably try to fiddle his way right into heaven. Next to Nero, he's the most publicized fiddler Birmingham's seen in many a day.

Thursday Tom came to town to fiddle his daughter, Mrs. Meedia Boyd, and a niece, Mrs. Ruby Freeman, out of their entanglements with the federal government. The couple, residents of the Bug Tussle vicinity, pleaded guilty before Judge T. A. Murphree to charges of using the mails to defraud.

Tom's fiddling talent went to waste, however, because Judge Murphree gave the women five years' probation each, after they explained "we didn't mean to do nothing dishonest." The vicinity of Bug Tussle was bathed in the light of publicity recently when about 30 residents of the area were charged with using the mails to defraud by misrepresentations to a well known mail order firm. Mrs. Boyd and Mrs. Freeman faced similar charges. Most of the cases are still to be

play for somebody, though, so after the trial he bustled down to Probation Officer Foster Jordan's office and sawed away on "Shortenin' Bread." He said he hoped to show his appreciation to Judge Murphree by playing "Leather Breeches" for the jurist at a private serenade Friday morning.

The weight of Tom's bow has been felt in many circles, he says. "Last year I fiddled for four candidates in the election in my county and every one of them won," he declared. "I fiddled for Frank Dixon, too, and look what he done."

The United States' chief executive also has had the benefit of Fiddling Tom's music. Tom revealed. "I ain't lost a candidate since 1932

This photograph of Tom Freeman appeared on page 1 of the *Birmingham Age-Herald* on August 19, 1938. Photo courtesy of the *Birmingham Post-Herald*.

extracting promises of future good behavior from the young woman, he was able to get her released.

Freeman felt he was successful in helping people with their legal problems because local officials knew he "really went to war in their behalf in getting them in office." Freeman had started fiddling for candidates in 1932 during Franklin D. Roosevelt's first presidential campaign. Roosevelt was revered by many country musicians, not only for his political philosophy, but because he was fond of fiddling. When he visited Warm Springs, Georgia, for hydrotherapy, Roosevelt was known to invite local fiddlers to play for him.[100] Perhaps that was one of the qualities that made Roosevelt "the only man who could make a Democrat out of Fiddlin' Tom Freeman, who was born and raised a Republican."[101] Freeman fiddled in behalf of Roosevelt during the 1932 campaign and believed himself partially responsible for Roosevelt's victory. Thereafter he wielded his bow in behalf of candidates for office on all levels of state and local government.

Of course, Freeman was not the first to mix fiddles and politics. The two have long been associated in Alabama. In the twenties and thirties, candidates for office inevitably dropped in to say a few words at the numerous fiddle conventions across the state. They also hired fiddlers and string bands to attract crowds to their speeches. For instance, local election committees in Franklin County, both Democratic and Republican, frequently booked Ed Rickard, a popular local fiddler, paying him and providing his transportation to political rallies.[102] Later James E. Folsom made old-time music central to his campaign to become governor of Alabama.

Freeman did not function in the manner of Ed Rickard or Folsom's Strawberry Pickers, however. He chose the candidate that he wanted to win, then proceeded to fiddle for him, either at scheduled rallies or at gatherings that naturally occurred when he would walk into town and start playing. He never met some of the candidates he supported, but informed them by letter of his efforts in their behalf. He proudly displayed the letters of appreciation he received in return.

One politician who "felt the weight of Freeman's bow"[103] was Carl Elliott of Jasper, former representative to Congress from Alabama's seventh district. Elliott began his political career at the age of 26 by running for county judge in Walker County, where he had recently moved and set up a law practice. Elliott recalled meeting Freeman early in the campaign:

> I looked around one day and he [Freeman] was here, and he said that he wanted to fiddle for me in my campaign. I said, "Fine,

you're welcome to join if you want to and I'd be glad to have you do anything you want to do." So he started going around with me and he would fiddle . . . Now, Fiddlin' Tom didn't go everywhere I went that year, but he went to a good many places. I specifically recall, to this day, seeing Fiddlin' Tom at Old Turpentine, also at Sumiton, at Sipsey, and Blooming Grove.[104]

At such political gatherings Freeman would precede Elliott to the stage. "When he got to a place, usually a back-country place, the first thing he'd do was announce that I was winning everywhere, everywhere he'd been. And he'd leave the impression that he'd been about everywhere," Elliott said. Freeman then would play a few tunes to warm up the crowd. According to Elliott,

> And while he said that he had omniscient powers of some kind that told him that I was going to win, I didn't win. But that didn't make any difference; it was close and he enjoyed it . . . he enjoyed fiddling for people, and if he did a lot of fiddling for a fellow, well, so far as he was concerned, that was a successful campaign.[105]

When Elliott ran for Congress in 1948, Freeman offered his services once more: "Again he had an insight which led him to pronounce that there was no question that I would be a winner and he wanted to give me the benefit of his help. And of course, I said yes." Freeman played at every political meeting that he could get to in the nine-county district, and this time Elliott won.[106] In similar manner, Freeman played for Congressmen Luther Patrick and Carter Manasco, Governors Frank Dixon, James E. Folsom, and Gordon Persons, as well as a host of candidates for local office.[107]

Journalists enjoyed reporting on Freeman's political activities. They often quoted his claim that he had never "lost a candidate," called his fiddle the "Candidate Special,"[108] and wrote punning headlines, such as "Fiddling Tom will Call Tune on Inauguration Day."[109] Upon hearing that Freeman had lost his favorite bow, the editor of the *Cullman Banner* requested that everyone look for it. "After all," he wrote, "there is a presidential year coming on, and there is no doubt but that there will be plenty of candidates who will need Freeman's help on his fiddle."[110] Even Freeman's obituary in the *Cullman Tribune* began with a lighthearted reference to the subject: "Candidates will have to get themselves elected this year. They can't depend on Fiddling Tom Freeman to 'swing' them into office with his famous 'Leather Britches' or any other tune."[111]

Those who read of Freeman in newspapers and did not know him personally may have regarded Tom Freeman as a shameless publicity seeker and object of humor. Writers of the tongue-in-cheek articles in the Birmingham dailies certainly did nothing to dispel such opinions. Yet Freeman's associates respected him. Henry Arnold, a staunch Republican and author of the jesting obituary in the *Cullman Tribune*, also included a tribute in the same issue which praised Freeman's personality and enthusiastic attitude toward politics.[112] He was a responsible man who supported his seven children with a well-tended farm and maintained a happy relationship with his wife.[113] He was popular in Walker and Cullman counties, where he was known for his "big friendly greeting,"[114] and was on speaking terms with everyone—farmers, judges, and congressmen, as well as the newsmen who so often quoted him. Although he seldom owned a car, he had only to set out on foot, carrying his fiddle, and he was soon picked up and driven to his numerous and widespread destinations.[115] Carl Elliott considered him a "good, sweet fellow, a joy to be around."[116]

Part of Freeman's appeal came from his "winsome voice"[117] and his store of tales about the old days in Cullman and Walker counties. He could tell about all-night fiddlings, mad-dog scares, and graveyards full of moonshiners. He could tell about passing off groundhog skins as "mountain coons" to a local merchant. He could tell about the old-timers, such as John Harris, whose house became infested with fleas. To get rid of them, Harris had his wife spread pine straw under the floor of the house and set it afire. "That was the cause of them losing everything they had," Freeman would say. "Burnt up everything—house and all—but it done away with all the fleas."[118]

Because of Freeman's lively music and tales, he was frequently invited to perform on the radio in Birmingham and at local civic clubs. A report on a meeting of the Cullman Kiwanians noted that their "entire program was taken up by the highly appreciated and unusual antics of this great fiddler."[119] When the Rotary Club decided to sponsor a fiddlers' contest as part of the first Strawberry Festival in 1939, the headline "Calling Fiddlin Tom" appeared in the *Cullman Banner*.[120] Freeman served as master of ceremonies of the annual event for several years afterward. The fact that civic leaders repeatedly sought Freeman's presence at their programs shows that they considered him a talented and popular entertainer.

In some ways Freeman was like hundreds of other fiddlers across the state: he played because he loved the instrument, and he generously used his talent to entertain and to raise money for community causes. He carried his love for the instrument further than most, though, and his belief in the powers of his fiddle to do more than entertain set him apart from the average fiddler. That, plus his backwoods upbringing and his natural association with subjects like Bug Tussle and moonshine, attracted the attention of journalists looking for interesting local-color stories. As a result, fiddlers who won more contests and made records that sold throughout the world received far less attention in Alabama's press than Fiddling Tom Freeman, a simple country fiddler.

E. D. "Monkey" Brown
The Fiddler Who Became a Literary Character
(1897–1972)

"Next'll be Monkey Brown, champeen of Tuscaloosa County," said Fatback. *"Monkey's brother is his guitar picker. Monkey kin play that fiddle o' his'n in any conceivable position o'the body. We look to see him try. What'll it be, Monkey?"*

Monkey, an angular young man, brought his chair to the platform. His brother, obviously younger, followed.

"Old Cow Died in the Forks of the Branch,"*said Monkey.*[121]

Thus Epp "Monkey" Brown of Tuscaloosa, Alabama, was introduced to the nation at a fiddlers' contest in Carl Carmer's *Stars Fell on Alabama*. The book, published in 1934, described the six-year sojourn in Alabama of an English professor from upstate New York. Carmer wrote of Alabama, "not as a state which is part of a nation, but as a strange country in which I once lived and from which I have now returned." Readers across the nation became fascinated by the colorful, quaint, gracious, and violent land that Carmer pictured.

Carmer taught English at the University of Alabama in Tuscaloosa from 1921 to 1927 and spent some of that time, according to J. Wayne Flynt, "wandering back roads, listening to storytellers, sampling moonshine, and judging fiddle festivals."[122] He kept thorough notes of his experiences and encouraged his students to bring in the names of fiddle tunes, quilting patterns, superstitions, and other aspects of Alabama folklife.[123] Intended for a scholarly article on Southern folklore, his notes became a popular book, instead.

Stars Fell on Alabama is a mixture of fact and fancy. Carmer took, he admitted, "the liberty of telescoping time."[124] Thus, in the book

E. D. "Monkey" Brown with his wife, Adelle, and son Murl, ca. 1918. Photo courtesy of Bertha Brown.

"Monkey" Brown found himself at a fiddlers' convention in Valley-head (De Kalb County), far from his Tuscaloosa home. A west Alabama fiddler, Brown entered contests in Pickens, Fayette, Lamar, and Tuscaloosa counties, and was popular in eastern Mississippi. Only a large convention, offering prizes of $25 to $100, could have drawn him and his brother across the state and into the mountains of northeast Alabama. Aware of this, Carmer described the Valley-head convention as the "biggest this year," with fiddlers coming from all over the state, and he had "Fatback" Shelton award Brown a "box of seegars" for traveling the greatest distance. Yet, as he described the contest, it became an ordinary local event in which the top prize was a $5 gold piece, awarded in sympathy to old man Ventress, who had ten children and "needed it wuss."

While "Monkey" Brown never went to Valleyhead,[125] Carmer, who was a fiddler himself, had obviously seen him perform at conventions around Tuscaloosa. He described Brown's antics well:

> One of the fiddlers flipped his fiddle behind the back of his chair and sawed away. The crowd laughed and the lickered one shouted again. "Play that fiddle all over the lot, Monkey. Show 'em you kin." Monkey raised the fiddle above his head and went on playing. Then he lifted his left leg, put the fiddle under it and still his fingers flitted on the strings, his bow kept moving.[126]

Indeed, Brown could perform those tricks and more in his version of "Pop Goes the Weasel." The tune was one that fiddlers across the South delighted in playing at contests. It was customary to begin with the violin held in a normal position, then, upon reaching the word "Pop" in the song, to pluck a string and shift the instrument to a radically different position, swiftly and smoothly, without losing a beat of the music. The more contorted the position, and the smoother the transition, the louder the applause. Brown mastered the art of "fiddle wrestling" so well that he received his nickname from it. According to one story, J. P. Shelton, the master of ceremonies at many Tuscaloosa conventions, remarked, "That boy can do more with a fiddle than a monkey can with goobers," and the name remained with Brown thereafter.[127]

"Monkey" Brown could play with the fiddle atop his head, said fiddler Tully Boswell, and "put it on each shoulder, put it behind him, put it between his legs. He would sit down, put the bow between his toes, sit there and play that way and you couldn't detect a flaw in it anywhere."[128] He also could play the tune lying on the floor with his back arched and his bowing arm stretched under it to the fiddle he held in his left hand.

But Brown was more than a trick fiddler. He played standard fiddle tunes, such as "Lost Child," "Wolves a'Howling," "Polly Ann," "Rock that Baby, Lucille," "Billy in the Low Ground," and "Sally Gooden," rhythmically yet smoothly. Bob Kyle called him a "fiddling machine," who "fiddled from the top of his head to the bottom of his toes."[129] As he played, he pumped his bowing arm in a way that reminded Tully Boswell of the "monkey motion" valves on a steam locomotive.[130]

Espie D. Brown was born in 1897 in the community of Coker (Tuscaloosa County). Though he was known mostly as "Epp" and later as "Monkey," people also called him Ed because of his initials. One of twelve children, Brown had an older brother, Ben, who had a fiddle.[131] "I commenced to want that fiddle when I was 8 or 9 old," Brown told Bob Kyle, and added:

> My brother wanted $5 for it and I didn't have $5. He wouldn't credit me, wouldn't even let me hold it in my hands. When crops were laid by I hired out to clear a briar patch and thicket at 50¢ a day. In ten days I had $5 and bought the fiddle. She had a pearl star in her back.
>
> I ventured to Echola at the age of 12 and won my first prize of $2.50. That went to my head. Shortly thereafter I read in the paper about a fiddling convention in Carrollton. A cousin of mine who was a good straw beater and I decided to take her in. We boarded a train at Coker. I had on knee britches but I won the first prize of $7.50, just like I deserved it.
>
> We didn't want to spend it for a room to sleep in so we started hoofing it to Reform, spending part of the night at a Baptist preacher's house.[132]

Eventually, said A. K. Callahan, Brown got a better fiddle. He picked enough cotton at "15¢ a hundred" to send $15 to Sears, Roebuck for the fiddle he played the rest of his life.[133]

When his younger brother was 10 years old, Brown began to teach him to fiddle. "If I missed a note," remembered Charlie Brown, "he'd slap my jaws and make me do it right."[134] The child developed into a skillful, flamboyant fiddler and one of "Monkey" Brown's strongest rivals. Audiences loved it when the two traded comic stunts in "Pop Goes the Weasel" or harmonized on a graceful piece called "Beautiful Life."[135]

"Monkey" Brown also became the inspiration of another fiddler from Tuscaloosa County, Tully Boswell. Boswell worked with Brown at Southern Life and Health Insurance during the day and entered fiddlers' contests with him at night. He first heard Brown in 1919 at a small convention in Bethany:

> We went through the contest, three pieces each, but on the last round, Epp stole the entire show . . . He played so much better than all the rest. The crowd just kept cheering on the last round till they just turned him loose and let him fiddle himself out . . . they just turned the whole school building over to him and you talk about the cheering and clapping and hollering.[136]

Boswell recalled a contest the next year in Columbus, Mississippi. Arriving late, Brown was told that the competition was closed. When he went to the back of the building to play with other musicians, however, a woman in charge of the event heard him playing and decided to reopen the contest.

> It looked like their ruling him out had just put fire in his veins. In other words, it stirred up all the talent that he had. That man went out there, got on that stage and played like he had never played, and do you know, he stole that entire show.[137]

Brown received first place in that contest, and in numerous small contests around Tuscaloosa and Pickens County. He could not easily walk away with first prize in the larger contests, however, because of strong competition from other west Alabama fiddlers. Newspaper accounts show that in 1925 he was a finalist, with Charlie Stripling, in the state-wide contest in Birmingham won by Y. Z. Hamilton. It was there that a representative from a record company approached the brothers about recording. Brown turned him down, saying that the two country boys might get killed or lost in New York City.[138] In 1927, Brown was selected to compete with eight other fiddlers at the Casino in Tuscaloosa and placed third, behind Stripling and Henry Ledlow. In 1929, he tied for first place at the Fayette convention with Stripling, Jimmie Porter, and his brother Charlie Brown. In the following years, he does not appear to have entered the Fayette conventions, leaving it to his brother to battle Stripling for those honors.

He continued playing around Tuscaloosa, however. A. K. Callahan, who chaired many of those events, recalled: "Whenever Bob Kyle, Charlie Brown, Monkey Brown, and John L. Dickey played in a contest, it was absolutely nip and tuck. You couldn't tell who was

A gathering of Tuscaloosa County fiddlers in 1971 included, clockwise from lower left, A. K. Callahan, Tully Boswell, E. D. "Monkey" Brown, Charlie Brown, and Bob Kyle. Photo courtesy of Calvin Hannah.

going to win till the last man was out in the ninth inning. But Monkey would win his share."[139]

"Monkey" Brown continued to play as long as there was a place for his music. As fiddle conventions and square dances became extinct in the 1950s, he put up his fiddle. In 1971, however, a photo in the *Tuscaloosa News* showed Brown, 73, playing with Tully Boswell and Charlie Brown. Bob Kyle wrote, "These men cannot play like they used to. But don't count them out. They're practicing again."[140]

"Monkey" Brown did not have an opportunity to regain his former skills; he died of cancer in 1972. Yet he is captured in *Stars Fell on Alabama* as a limber young man whose fingers "flitted" on the strings. The last we see of him, "Monkey was in full swing,"[141] playing for the square dance that followed the Valleyhead fiddlers' convention.

The Johnson Family
Sand Mountain's Famous Music Makers
(ca. 1880–1962)

For nearly a century, the Johnson family was an important part of good times on Sand Mountain. They provided the fiddle and broom-straws for the earliest dances there and developed into a popular string band whose music, via radio and public performances, reached audiences across northeastern Alabama until 1962.

The family first came to the area in 1854 when William Johnson, his wife, and five children urged their mule-drawn wagon up the steep sides of a plateau in northeastern Alabama and prepared to spend the night. They were on their way from Cobb County, Georgia, to settle in the Arkansas Ozarks. The next morning, however, after observing the gentle lay of the land and the sandy loam that covered the massive plateau, they decided to travel no farther. They bought a large section of government land and helped establish the com-munity of Hustleville, so named because those living there had to hustle to survive. Into the new home went a family fiddle which had been damaged when water swept through their wagon as the Johnsons forded Big Wills Creek shortly before ascending Sand Mountain.

During the Civil War the Johnsons remained on Sand Mountain, where divided loyalties turned neighbor against neighbor, and at the close of the war they welcomed the flood of settlers from Tennessee, Georgia, and the Carolinas who came to establish small farms on the fertile land. By this time two of William Johnson's sons had acquired a workable fiddle and were playing at the square dances that followed the log rollings and house raisings taking place every-where on Sand Mountain. There the two, George M. and William S. Johnson, would take turns playing fiddle and beating straws, thus providing all the melody and rhythm the dancers needed.[142]

For the rest of their lives, the two brothers continued to play music and to encourage others to do so. William's grand-nephews remem-ber him as an old man who would walk up and down the dirt road in front of the house playing the fiddle and singing. Though he could play jigs and reels, his favorite tune was "Murillo's Lesson," an anthem from *The Sacred Harp*.

George Johnson delighted in playing the fiddle, beating straws, and buck-dancing. He continued to host great gatherings of musi-cians and to buck-dance until his death at 84 in 1936. With his wife, Elizabeth, he raised nine children, six of whom became the "Famous Johnson Band" that entertained the people of Sand Mountain and

The Johnson Family String Band, ca. 1920: Standing are Ras Johnson and his wife Ella; seated from the left are Adous, Dan, and "H" Johnson. The guitar, mandolin, and two fiddles were made by Adous Johnson. Photo courtesy of Guy and Byron Johnson.

the rest of northeastern Alabama for the next half century.[143] George's first son, W. H., who was born in 1879, became a fiddler, and the next son, John, born in 1883, learned to play the banjo. Thus by 1900 a small Johnson family band was established and expanded as the other sons matured. Adous joined the band with the first string bass in north Alabama, which he played with a bow. Soon afterward came Ras on the guitar and Leo and Dan on fiddle. In 1916 when Ras married Ella Greene, who played mandolin and piano and sang with the Greene family band, the Johnson band was expanded to include her. However, it was diminished by the death of John in the flu epidemic of 1918. The band remained without a banjo player until the 1950s when the members invited Burt Stewart to play with them on the radio.

Entertaining Sand Mountain. Sand Mountain in the 1920s was dotted with small farms, and other than a few storekeepers, teachers, bankers, and mechanics, people worked at home. They received their mail and voted in communities with names such as Friendship, Red Apple, Harmony, Flat Rock, Solitude, Jay Bird, and Double Bridges. And they sent news of illness, death, rainfall, marriages, visits, and other happenings to a weekly newspaper, the *Sand Mountain Banner*. A look at the *Banner* during that period shows that though the people on Sand Mountain were isolated from those in the valleys and from one another during the week as they worked on their farms, on weekends they gathered at all-day "singings" and church meetings, oratorical contests, benefits for the needy, spelling bees from the "Blue-Back Speller," "Virginia reels" sponsored by the Business and Professional Women, fiddle conventions, high-school football games and student plays, box suppers, and picnics at Pierce Lake (which had a special sheltered walk from the ladies' dressing room to the water so that men could not "ogle").

The Johnson family band was likely to be at many of these gatherings. Almost every issue of the *Banner* mentioned their appearance at a church entertainment, picnic, land auction, dance, or fiddlers' convention. They performed at similar events off Sand Mountain, such as the picnic on Lookout Mountain sponsored by the Modern Woodmen of America, who advertised "Fried Chicken, cold drink stands, watermelons and the best of all, one of the best bands in this section will furnish music . . . that's the Johnson band of Albertville. If you have never heard this band, you don't know what you've missed."[144]

The Johnson band was popular because it had something to offer everyone. First, it was an old-time string band with a guitar, bass, mandolin, and three fiddlers who could play the old breakdowns they had learned from their father and uncle and the other old-timers of Sand Mountain. W. A. Bryan of Boaz, who often listened to the Johnsons and to the much-recorded Skillet Lickers band of Georgia, said that the Johnsons ran "a very close second" to the Skillet Lickers in their renditions of old-time tunes, and that no band could beat them at "Sally Gooden" and "Leather Britches."[145]

They were a gospel quartet, as well, when four of the members stepped forward to sing and play hymns beloved by older people in the audience. And Ella, joined by Leo's wife Elma, could croon the latest tunes that the young moderns of Sand Mountain listened to on their phonographs. The varied program, tied together by Ras Johnson's homey and humorous patter, left audiences feeling thoroughly entertained.

The Johnsons traveled to the fiddlers' conventions that were held at every crossroads community around Sand Mountain—Nixon's Chapel, Sardis, High Point, Hartselle, Crossville, Geraldine, Boaz, Grant (at the D.A.R. School), and many others. Byron and Guy Johnson, sons of Ras and Adous, recall that the Johnson band quite often carried away the $10 first prize for "best band" while Leo Johnson would bring home a prize of $7 or a gold watch for being judged "best fiddler." At times the band performed at the contests but did not compete in them. For instance, at a fiddler's convention held in 1924 at the City School Building in Albertville, it was announced that "The Famous JOHNSON BAND will have charge of the opening exercises, followed by single fiddling, banjo, bands, etc., etc."[146]

The band's most consistent and best-paying jobs came from auction companies: the J. W. Oliver Auction Company of Collinsville, the J. P. King Auction Company of Albertville, and the Clark-Wheeler Auction Company from McMinnville, Tennessee. From the original settlers of the area, these companies bought large tracts of land, subdivided them into lots, and auctioned them off to home builders. Every week, full-page advertisements appeared in area newspapers inviting everyone, "especially the ladies," to auctions which offered free barbecue, prizes, twin auctioneers, fiddle contests, and band concerts, most often by the "FAMOUS JOHNSON STRING BAND," though occasionally the Clark-Wheeler Company would hire Uncle Dave Macon and Sam McGee, popular Tennessee musicians. After one auction, the *Gadsden Evening Star* wrote, "The famous Johnson string band of Albertville furnished music and it attracted much attention for it is rated as a really first class musical organization."[147]

In 1926 the Johnsons began to travel the hilly, unpaved roads and unbridged rivers of north Alabama in their new Ford, the bass in the back seat with its neck sticking out the front right window and the band members and their additional instruments arranged uncomfortably around it. In this manner they journeyed to Auburn to play on the radio and to Atlanta to record for Okeh.

The Johnsons on the Air. When Alabama's first full-power radio station began broadcasting from Auburn in 1925, its management urged all Alabama communities to send performers to represent them on the air. It is not surprising that merchants of Marshall County selected the Johnsons. The *Sand Mountain Banner* announced that businessmen of Guntersville, Albertville, and Boaz had each contributed from 25¢ to $2 to pay the expenses on the Johnsons' trip to Auburn, and noted that only one out of the fifty-nine citizens approached had refused to contribute.[148]

Thus the Johnsons drove two hundred miles to perform on WAPI. Few on Sand Mountain owned radio sets, and Guy and Byron Johnson recalled being driven five and one-half miles through a heavy storm to the home of Lon Brown. They joined a roomful of neighbors who had come to hear the broadcast. Apparently Mr. Brown had the type of "radi-ow" described in a Freed-Eisemann advertisment in the *Banner*: "Squeals like a cat, fights like the neighbors in Hogan's Alley, and demands a burglar's kit and 'overtime' to keep it in order."[149] After tinkering with the large horn speaker, he gave up and plugged in earphones, which meant that all present had to take turns listening. Lucky was the person wearing the headset when the first string band to play on the only radio station in Alabama struck up "Dixie."

Almost Recording Artists. In 1928 the Johnsons had an opportunity to expand their fame. After auditioning in Gadsden, they were asked to make records for Okeh. They signed a three-year contract under the direction of Polk Brockman,[150] an important figure in the recording of country music. It was he, an Atlanta record dealer, who had caused Ralph Peer of Okeh records to first record Fiddlin' John Carson in 1923. The success of that experiment had led to the recording of the Skillet Lickers and many other fiddle bands of the twenties and thirties.[151]

In Atlanta, on August 1, 1928, the Johnsons recorded at least five tunes and possibly more. According to information on file at the Country Music Foundation, instead of recording the old-time breakdowns they played so well, they performed hymns and popular tunes:

THE COLLINSVILLE COURIER, COLLINSVILLE, ALA.

AUCTION
WEDNESDAY
JANUARY 13, 10 A.M.

417 ACRES
FARM of J. P. COX

Three miles southwest of Collinsville on Big Valley Highway, 1-2 mile of Vernon Church and School, one of the best farms in Big Wills Valley

Fine Red Cotton Land, Five Good Houses and other good Outbuildings. In one of the best communities in DeKalb county, fine location just three miles from Collinsville High School. Mr. Cox has moved from Collinsville to Florida and is selling this farm and investing in other property there, and giving his friends an opportunity that they have never had, to buy this farm in small tracts.

Be sure to take advantage of this sale and buy a home or for an investment **on easy terms, 1-3 cash, balance 1 - 2 - 3 years with int.**

FREE!
One Big Gold Cash Prize
Many other prizes all through the sale.
FREE Refreshments For Everybody FREE

MUSIC by FAMOUS JOHNSON STRING BAND
They are the "World's Best"

J. W. OLIVER AUCTION
J. W. OLIVER, Auctioneer   COMPANY   COLLINSVILLE, ALABAMA

Full-page advertisements, such as this one in the *Collinsville Courier* of January 7, 1926, kept the Johnson name before the public.

"Murillo's Lesson," with "What a Friend We Have in Jesus" as an introduction; "Holy Manna," "Daisies Won't Tell," "Silver Moon," and "Everbody Works but Father."[152] The last tune was a comical number which had been used on the minstrel stage and had been published as sheet music in 1904 and 1905.[153] In it Ras, joined by Leo on the chorus, complained that "Everybody works 'round our house, but our old man," to the accompaniment of three fiddles (two doing rhythmic bowing behind one lead fiddle), a guitar, and Adous's bowed bass (playing a rhythmic counter-melody).[154]

The Johnsons left Atlanta with assurances that "Everybody Works but Father" would be released and that arrangements would be made for the band to play on WSM in Nashville, the "Grand Ole Opry" station. But for some reason that the Johnsons never understood, none of the records were released. According to Byron and Guy Johnson, the family was not interested in pursuing the matter. On the way home from Atlanta, while the band members discussed future engagements, Dan had stated firmly that he "wasn't fixing to go nowhere." Forty-seven years later, Adous explained the decision: "I guess what kept us from becoming famous except on Sand Mountain was the fact that we stayed in the Albertville area. Daddy didn't want us to leave home and we really didn't want to leave either. Our family has always been very close and keeping our family ties was more important than money or fame."[155]

Good Times at Home. E. C. Littlejohn explained that the Johnsons were "close-knit." Their home in Hustleville was in a "sockfoot": "You go down in there and you'd go down to the end and turn around to get out. All that lived down in there were the Johnsons. They didn't have to mix with other people to have fun; they just enjoyed their family."[156] Byron and Guy Johnson recalled that one brother seldom went anywhere without the other four. When they went to the bank each spring to borrow money for seed, all five would sign the loan in handwriting so similar that it seemed that one had signed for all.

And though they could have entertained themselves happily, they welcomed company. Ras's daughter-in-law, Ruth Johnson, remembered that the yard "was covered every Saturday and Sunday—just gangs of people from town." In addition to being musicians, the Johnsons were much interested in games. They enjoyed Rook, croquet, checkers, marbles, and horseshoes, and they worked to develop their skills in them. According to Byron Johnson, "The only thing they were serious about was killing time." To the Johnsons, raising a crop was secondary.

Music was at the center of activities at the Johnson gatherings. George Johnson was in the habit of inviting any good country musicians he met to stay and live with the Johnsons, and many took him up on his offer. During the twenties and thirties, Clayton McMichen, Gid Tanner, Fate Norris, and Lowe Stokes, all members of the famed Skillet Lickers, were frequent guests of the Johnsons. Earl Johnson (no kin), the well-known Georgia fiddler, and later, Arthur Smith, the highly influential Tennessee fiddler, came to stay in Hustleville and play under the big trees beside the Johnson family home. Sometimes the professional musicians would stay the whole week between performances, and during these visits, little farm work was done. Instead, there was almost continuous music with breaks for games and food, vast quantities of it. One visitor to their home, Earle Drake, a Birmingham guitarist, marveled at the huge amounts of food set out for the family and their Sunday visitors.[157] Vistors may have found one fault with the hospitality: the Johnsons were teetotalers, who did not allow their guests to drink on the premises; yet fiddlers came, drawn by the good humor, food, and music at the Johnson home.

Saturday Nights with the Johnsons. The Johnson band continued to perform until 1962. During the 1950s, the dark days of old-time music when television and rock 'n' roll had taken their toll on the fiddler's popularity, the folks on Sand Mountain still enjoyed the Johnsons' show on radio station WABU-FM, followed by a dance at the National Guard armory.

The "Sand Mountain Jamboree" would open with a rendering of "Turkey in the Straw" by the Johnson brothers joined by Burt Stewart playing banjo, clawhammer-style. The next number would perhaps be a more modern tune like "Drifting and Dreaming," sung by Ella, Elma, and Elma's daughter, Imogene. Announcer Jesse Culp would then deliver some earnest words of shopping advice from sponsors such as J. B. Roberts and Sons Clothing Store in Albertville, a supplier of Star Brand Shoes, Hunter's Community Store, or the Sand Mountain Truck and Tractor Company, while the band softly played an appropriate tune, perhaps "Anytime You're Feeling Lonely" or "Chicken Reel." Each program was a race with the clock, the band trying to honor all requests mailed in during the week, before rushing off to play for a hall full of dancers at the armory. There would be hoedown tunes like "Flop-Eared Mule, "Eighth of January," "Paddy on the Turnpike," "Black Mountain Rag," "Sally Gooden," "Flatwoods," and "John's Got a Wooden Leg," to which the guests in the studio added whoops, hand-clapping, and foot-stomping. There would be sacred tunes such as "Shall We Gather at the River," "Hide Me, Rock of Ages," and "Where the Soul Never Dies," and there were swing tunes like "Coconut Grove" and "In the Mood."

Occasionally a number would be cut short with a laugh because W. H., 80 years old and hard of hearing, was playing out of tune. In 1950 a more serious interruption occurred. Near the end of the broadcast, Dan, having just finished playing Uncle William's favorite tune, "Murillo's Lesson," suffered a stroke. As he was rushed to the hospital, Ras explained the problem to the listeners. By the time Dan was delivered to the hospital, the parking lot there was filled with anxious friends and fans of the Johnsons. Dan never recovered and died two years later. At this, the band attempted to retire, but were dissuaded by large numbers of requests that they continue the radio program.

Adous and Ras Johnson, Fiddle Makers. Even after the Johnsons grew too old to keep up their active performance schedule, some of them continued their involvement in another form of music-making. Adous had begun making fiddles in 1925. He first repaired the old family fiddle that had been damaged in the Johnsons' move to Alabama in 1854. Before gluing it together, he studied the instrument's internal construction with the idea of making another. Wood from a maple tree behind the Johnson home became his first handmade fiddle, shaped by a pocketknife and thinned with a curved pane of window glass. Uncle William put strings on it before the first coat of varnish was applied, and it is almost certain that he played "Murillo's Lesson" on it. Over the years, Adous acquired more precise measuring and cutting tools and began to order fine German woods after he had depleted the maple tree population on the Johnson land. Later he took one of his fiddles to Professor T. M. Thomason, a violin instructor in Birmingham, who provided him with a blueprint of a Stradivarius violin and some trade secrets about the internal workings of violins. He got other pointers from fiddlers such as Clayton McMichen, who was asked to try out a fiddle that Adous was completing. After playing it for a moment, McMichen opened his pocketknife and, to the astonishment of those present, began carving on the neck. He stopped only when the fiddle suited him, then told the maker, "You need to cut it out more here," advice that Adous followed in making instruments thereafter.

As Adous received requests for more fiddles than he could make, he pressed his brother Ras into service, and the two men continued to make the instruments until Adous was 90 years old and had completed two hundred fiddles. Some of them had been given to well-known fiddlers, like Earl Johnson; others were purchased by lovers of old-time fiddling who never learned to play them. Adous, who kept careful records of the outcome of his checker games, kept no record of the purchasers of his instruments.

In 1979, the Alabama state legislature honored the two brothers with House Resolution 21, which commended them for offering "the best of Alabama's native craftsmanship in designing and manufacturing fine-quality violins." On the occasion, Ras told a reporter, "We had the dream, that maybe by making these fiddles that our name would live after we were dead and gone and people would remember the Johnson fiddle."[158]

Though the Johnson band is now silent, it is still remembered for its music and for the fiddles produced by Adous and Ras Johnson.

Famed Georgia fiddler Earl Johnson holds a fiddle made by Adous Johnson, who stands beside him. Behind are Ras, "H," and Leo Johnson. Photo ca. 1950, courtesy of Guy and Byron Johnson.

Its long tenure as Sand Mountain's leading band is due in large part to the kind of people who live there. A recent article in the *Birmingham Post-Herald* noted the "unshakable sense of place," the "healthy respect for tradition," and the "powerful community identity" among the residents of Sand Mountain.[159] The Johnson family, who had provided music for social gatherings since the settlement of Sand Mountain, was vital in developing that sense of community.

CHAPTER

4

FIDDLING THE BUTTONS
OFF THEIR SLEEVES

Celebrations, Square Dances,
and Fiddlers' Conventions

Fiddles have long been a part of festivities in Alabama. In St. Stephens, the capital of the Alabama territory, a young couple was honored with a "shivaree" on their wedding night in 1813. Friends silently gathered outside the couple's room, then burst into a variety of noises, some produced by drums and tin pans, some by violins.[1] The instrument has been brought out at the end of house raisings, logrollings, and corn shuckings,[2] not only in pioneer days but well into the twentieth century. Fred Watson of Dale County wrote of peanut shellings in the 1920s that ended in square dances;[3] Ed Rickard of Russellville played in the 1930s at homes where "they'd give a cotton picking or a log rolling or a big quilting . . . and a big dance that night. Danced until daybreak." He also took part in "serenades" at Christmastime. He and friends, some with faces blackened, men in women's clothes and vice versa, would gather outside a house. "I'd shoot a firecracker and start to fiddling. A lot of them would hit on tin buckets. Sometimes they'd sing. I'd play two or three tunes; then they'd bring out a big cake and give us some, and so on."[4]

Fiddlers often received special invitations to social gatherings. In 1907 the Oliver Hall Company in Collinsville held a Smith reunion for everyone in the county with that name. Hall invited "a number of fiddlers, the old-fashioned kind, fiddlers who will play real music that will appeal to every citizen of De Kalb." Afterward it was reported that fifteen hundred people turned out for the event, and fiddlers "enlivened the proceedings with impromptu concerts during the day."[5] More common were the Fourth of July celebrations across

This string band was active in the mining community of Johns, near Bessemer, in the late 1890s. The standing guitarist has not been identified; to his right are Porter Miller, Lucian Rainey, J. T. Cargile, and Silas Avery. Photo courtesy of Bessemer Hall of History.

the state at which political speakers and fiddlers were the chief sources of entertainment. In 1925, W. F. Harrison of Grove Hill placed a "Notice to Fiddlers" in the *Clarke County Democrat*: "You are cordially invited to come to the barbecue at Grove Hill, July 4th, and bring your fiddle." The appeal was successful: "Immediately after dinner, a number of old-time Fiddlers were gotten together and for some time they entertained the crowd with many of the old airs."[6] And of course, some considered fiddlers essential at wedding celebrations. When she married in 1889, Mrs. Martha Ballard of Lamar County remembered that "the fiddlers were ready by dark for the big square dance on my wedding night,"[7] and in 1898 Francis Bartow Lloyd observed, "It takes some fiddle music to round off a weddin match down in the Panther creek settlement."[8]

Musicians like these, believed to be from Fayette County, were popular additions to community outings. Photos courtesy of the Brackner Collection, Birmingham Public Library Archives.

In Bibb County, fiddlers were needed to provide the music for buck-dance contests. "That was our *favorite*—a good buck-dancer," said Harmon Hicks:

Now, this wouldn't be at a regular square dance . . . There'd be a couple of string bands—cost you a dime to go in—a whole dime. And they would put three men up there for judges. They'd put up $5 for the best buck-dancer and naturally he had the opportunity to pick out the tune he wanted to buck-dance to— a lot of them have better time than other tunes. And then there'd be maybe a dozen of them men . . . there wasn't no women. But it was some of the best buck-dancing, just like somebody beating a drum. The noise that they were making was absolutely on the tune. My daddy told me about a man who was old when I knew him, but they'd set a cup of water on top of his head, and that guy could dance all over the floor and that cup of water would never fall off.[9]

A fiddler could turn an ordinary event into a party, as well. In Limestone County, recalled Bill Harrison, musicians would gather for jam sessions and impromptu fiddle contests on Saturdays and rainy days:

> My father was the proprietor of a "general merchandise" store in the Salem Community, about fifteen miles northwest of Athens. Some of my earliest and fondest memories center around the sounds of the old-time fiddle and fiddle bands heard in profusion in and around his store on Saturday . . . since Saturday was "trade day," large crowds were almost always present.[10]

A popular fiddler playing at home after supper could draw a crowd. James Cole of Athens remembered neighbors gathering to listen to his father, D. A. Cole (photo on frontispiece): "I remember as a little boy—when I was maybe 4 or 5 years old—how I used to sit on the floor and listen to him play. And he would play to entertain. People in the community would come to our house just to listen to him."[11]

Charlie Stripling's daughter, Elsie Mordecai, recalled evenings when her father was fiddling at home: "People would come from all over and hang in the windows. They'd come on flatbed trucks and fill up the house. So many people would sit on the bed that the slats would break, and under the bed was Mama's canning jars."[12]

Fiddling for Dances

In other homes, the bed was purposely dismantled. "They'd knock the bed down and carry it out and go to dancing," said Jimmie Porter.[13] Until the 1930s, dances in the home were common, Tom Hill remembered: "Square dances—they used to have a lot of them. At that time that's about the only entertainment there was. There'd be a dance at somebody's house celebrating someone's birthday, or didn't even have to be a celebration; if they wanted to have a dance they just had it. About every two weeks on an average, round somewheres there was a square dance."[14]

In the mining camps of Jefferson and Walker counties, according to Gaines Arnold, "if they had someone to play, they might have four or five or six dances a week."[15] They were family affairs; anyone tall enough to dance was invited to do so. James Cole remembered being swung off his feet as a child by big "corn-fed girls,"[16] and Jimmie Porter recalled that "old folks really danced. People as old as my daddy . . . Some of 'em would be crippled up where you thought they couldn't dance, but they'd get 'em out."[17]

For two weeks prior to Christmas, dances were held almost nightly. Moreover, before a new home was occupied by its owners, its empty rooms and smooth new floors invited dancers. In his history of Marion (Perry County), Captain W. L. Fagan described a "housewarming" in 1827 celebrating the opening of the most elegant house in the area:

> The ball opened with a "stag dance," when Thos. H. Nelms, with his famous violin, "Pine Bark," gave the boys "Miss McLeod" in his inimitable style. Ben Franklin Hornbuckle played for the next set "Billy in the Low Ground." There was "lofty dancing,"—not much regard for steps—every man for himself. A "stag dance" was necessary on the opening of every dance, for the young men possessed such an excess of agility, that a "breakdown" was needed to render them sufficiently graceful to be partners for the ladies.
>
> The sedate, pious guests were in an adjoining room keeping time to the music with spoons and quills, beating and mixing five gallons of eggnog.[18]

A housewarming in Centreville in 1898 appears to have been more genteel. The *Centreville Press* reported that "Mr. and Mrs. Lavender gave a dance at their new home last week, that was enjoyed by the young people. They intend moving this week."[19] Such housewarmings were common through the 1930s. In Moore's Bridge (Tuscaloosa County), when the new general merchandise store was built in 1933, the community was invited to dance to the music of Bud Robertson's boys before the shelves were stocked.[20]

Dances in Bibb County in the 1920s, as described by Harmon Hicks, were much like those held throughout the state:

> Dances was all in homes . . . Back in them days they'd build houses with a lot bigger rooms than they got now. They would just move all the furniture out into another room. Maybe they'd have two rooms where you could sit in the doorway and both rooms would be full of dancers, but you could be playing music for both of them.

It was over long about 12 o'clock. They wouldn't hardly ever dance later than 12 on Saturday night. By then they'd want to know where it was goin' to be next Saturday night. So somebody would say, "I'll have it at my house" . . . and they'd say, "Hey, can you play next Saturday night?" and if I could, I would.[21]

Matthew Hill played with his family band for dances around Pinson: "They'd clean out a room . . . Sometimes in warm weather they'd have the windows up and people 'd be standing outside, looking in the window. We'd back up in the corner and they'd give us an old cane-bottom or split-bottom chair. People would use the rest of the room for dancing. They'd sprinkle meal on the floor. Sometimes their feet would slip out from under them."[22]

Theirs were not the fashionable galops, polkas, and waltzes imported from the Continent by dance masters in the 1850s, but simple dances brought to the American colonies by British settlers in the 1700s. English folklorists Cecil J. Sharp and Maud Karpeles first observed these dances, which they called "running sets," in Kentucky in 1918, and were astounded: "We realized at once that we had stumbled upon a most interesting form of the English Country-dance which, so far as we knew, had not been hitherto recorded, and a dance, moreover, of great aesthetic value." Sharp believed the dances to be descended from pre-Christian religious ceremonies. In a figure called "Cage the Bird," for example, three dancers circled around a central dancer. Sharp proposed that this figure originally may have been a sacrificial rite, the central dancer being the victim. He believed that such dances had disappeared from southern England prior to the publication of Playford's *English Dancing Master* (1650), but were still being done in northern England and the Scottish Lowlands during the colonization of America.[23] "When these people moved to this country," wrote Lloyd Shaw in *Cowboy Dances*, "they still held their ancient forms unchanged and crystallized, fossils, if you will, for all time."[24]

Of course, long before the dances came to America they had lost all significance other than social. They were unsurpassed in sociableness, however. In Alabama they were usually done in a circle, the friendliest of geometrical forms. Any number of couples could form a set, the maximum determined by the amount of room available. With hands joined, the dancers moved right and left with a smooth, gliding step and did a few preliminary swings before embarking upon the heart of the dance, a series of "visits." One couple moved about the circle, doing a figure such as the "Ocean Wave" or "Cage the Bird" with every other couple, and ending each visit with a do-si-do that provided the two men an opportunity to swing each other's partners. When the first couple had finished its round of visits, the second couple began.

Though done rapidly, the dances were not exhausting. Couples not involved in one of the visits could clap, buck-dance, or chat until it was their turn to dance. Nor were the dances mentally fatiguing. Unlike modern square dancing, there was no demand that the caller provide an original, varied, and challenging program. Out of perhaps fifty figures done in Alabama, each community had only six or eight that they did regularly. Dancers drew pleasure from doing familiar figures in smooth, unflustered style, their feet sliding across the rough floors in unbroken rhythm.

The fiddler was the only person likely to be weary at the end of a dance. Said Jimmie Porter, "I played for those things until I was

Dancing at a community school in Coffee County, Alabama, under the direction of a WPA recreation supervisor, April 1939. Farm Security Administration photo by Marion Post Wolcott, courtesy of the Library of Congress.

just worn out . . . It's too long. When you play until all of them get around, you're going to be just about holding out a stub!" Tom Hill said that he played the buttons off his sleeves, and Ed Rickard claimed that he wore out thirty-six bows fiddling for such dances in Franklin County.[25] Yet they continued to play because they were vital. With small groups of dancers meeting in homes throughout each county, fiddlers, be they champions, children, or "scratchaways," were encouraged and recognized. In Fayette County in the 1890s, according to Ida Miles Tarwater, there was a fiddler who was considered "socially unacceptable" by many of the young ladies of the area. They humored him, however, because they wanted him to keep fiddling at their parties.[26] Others were more direct in obtaining the fiddler's good will and paid him, often from a hat that had been passed among the dancers. In the twenties and thirties, Claude Cassidy's band of four played around Sand Mountain for "a dime on a corner." Halfway through a set, they would stop and take up a dime from each man. "A lot of them wouldn't have a dime but they'd dance all the same . . . We'd play hard sometime for two or two and a half dollars—but that was a lot of money then."[27]

During the Depression, fiddlers in Jackson County were encouraged by the Federal government. In 1936 the Federal Emergency Relief Adminstration built Skyline Farms, one of twenty-six rural community projects in the nation, whose purpose was to provide work, home education, and agricultural training for displaced tenant farmers and their families.[28] To create a sense of community among participants, the Resettlement Administration encouraged folk dancing and music. Professional musicians went to the communities, encouraged by director Charles Seeger to be "barefoot musicians" who would "search out the grassroots culture within the homestead populations."[29] Chester Allen obtained a place on the Skyline Farms construction crew because of his ability to play the fiddle and guitar. He and fellow workers played for Friday night dances in an outdoor pavilion built especially for such purposes. They also accompanied the dancers on a trip to Washington, D.C., in 1938, to perform at the White House for Eleanor Roosevelt. There, reported the *Birmingham Age-Herald*, "eight couples danced the figures kept alive in the South despite the modern round dances. They 'opened and shut the garden gate,' 'Ocean Waved,' and 'Broad Sashawayed.' "[30] Allen and the Skyline Farms band were also recorded by the Library of Congress at that time.

While old dances were being done at Skyline Farms and elsewhere across the state, the "modern round dances" mentioned by the *Age-*

Dancers at Skyline Farms near Scottsboro who later performed before Franklin and
Eleanor Roosevelt at the White House. Farm Security Administration photos by
Ben Shahn (1937), courtesy of the Library of Congress.

Herald were making inroads into their popularity. Round dances were those in which one danced exclusively with one's own partner, whether waltzes, fox-trots, or two-steps. The old community dances were called square dances, though they were done in large circles. In the 1930s, dancers began requesting popular tunes for round dances between square-dance numbers.

Dances were now moving from private homes into public halls. On Friday and Saturday nights across the state, locally popular dance callers and fiddlers like Monte Crowder in Huntsville, the Johnsons of Albertville, and Charlie Stripling in west Alabama were starting to attract large crowds to school gymnasiums, National Guard armories, and American Legion halls. Commercial dance halls were being built. Some were nicknamed "snuffdipper's balls"; some that condoned alcoholic beverages were called "bloody buckets."

At public halls, where as many as a hundred dancers would participate in a square dance, the progression was streamlined. A solitary couple no longer danced its way around the set. Now couples were designated as "lead" or "home" couples (or "one's" and "two's"), and all lead couples moved simultaneously to the right to dance with home couples. No one stood awaiting his moment to dance. When the lead couples had progressed completely around the circle, the caller would lead all the dancers into a "Grapevine Twist," or wind them up into "A Little Ball of Yarn," or direct the men to swing every woman in the room, one by one. Thus, the dances were still lengthy. Earle Drake, a professional musician who played at the Ben Hur Dance Hall in Birmingham in the 1930s, recalled:

> They had saxophone and drums, and they played "Stardust" and contemporary music and then they played the square-dance music also . . . We'd play what they call "two and one." In other words, two round dances and one square dance. But one square dance would last an hour and a half. There'd be so many on the floor, 'til the time you got 'em round and called all the square dancing—good night—half the night was gone. Then you'd play two dances and it's time to play another square dance. I'll tell you, it's hard work. And get through and they hand you a half a dollar or a dollar.[31]

Through the years the ratio of square dances to round dances decreased, thus decreasing the demand for good breakdown fiddlers. At the Crystal Ballroom in Bessemer in the late 1940s, it was customary to do two square dances; the rest of the evening was devoted to round dancing.[32] When Tom Sutton played for dances at Clements

High School (Limestone County), it grew harder to find people who knew how to square dance. He played contemporary music for round dancing, with an occasional breakdown when someone managed to gather enough people for a set.[33]

By the mid-1950s, few people in Alabama were doing the old-fashioned dances, either in homes or at public dance halls. Western square dancing, a descendant of those dances, was becoming a national craze, however. Brought to the attention of the nation by Lloyd Shaw of Colorado in the 1930s, Western square dancing had grown in popularity during World War II and by the 1950s had become America's main alternative to rock 'n' roll. Yet that phenomenon did nothing to restore the fiddler to his place of honor. Instead, because the Western dance figures were more complicated than their ancient predecessors, dancers formed clubs which met weekly for instruction and practice and turned to the phonograph rather than the fiddler for music. That was not Shaw's intention. In his influential dance manual, *Cowboy Dances*, he wrote that when a group was learning to dance, piano music would suffice, but "if the group begins to get good, they will want authentic music, which means that a good old-time fiddler must be found, and it is surprising how a little inquiry will usually discover one in any community."[34]

Instead, beginning groups turned to phonograph records and found them addictive. Gene Dunlap of Birmingham, a caller as well as an old-time fiddler, explained:

> The caller was more comfortable with the records, because that's what he'd practiced to at the house . . . He was used to that; the dancers were used to it, and it was just smoother and better. That record's just as steady as it can be. It looks good to have a band, but the records would really be better.[35]

On special occasions in the 1950s, recalled Dunlap, the square-dance clubs of Birmingham would join together to hire a fiddle band, but that practice soon ended. Callers who had worked out dances to fit popular songs, country-western hits, and Broadway tunes as well as traditional music, felt limited by the bands' repertoires and missed the predictability of the commercial recordings.[36] Bands that did attempt to keep abreast of the caller's current favorites, such as "Mack the Knife" and "Mona Lisa," had to rehearse often, then found the square-dance groups were unable to compensate them adequately for their efforts.[37] While callers, dancers, and musicians agreed that live music was better than recordings, the convenience and affordability of the commercial recordings won out over the authentic old-time community fiddler that Lloyd Shaw had favored.

Displaced from the dance floor, fiddlers lost their most important audience. Their need to have a stock of good breakdowns to play at dances had preserved traditional tunes through the centuries. Their desire to propel the dancers through sets on the strength of their bowing arms had kept the tunes vigorous. Now the reels and horn-pipes that delighted dancers tended to seem repetitive and indistinguishable to the seated audience. There was less reason to play them.

With the folk revival of the 1960s, old-fashioned square dancing to live music became part of gatherings at community centers across the state. Later, country-dance groups using live music were established in Birmingham and Huntsville; yet on the whole, the fiddler never regained his prominence as a dance musician. Fortunately, fiddlers had another source of recognition—the enthusiastic audiences of statewide fiddlers' conventions. That story has a happier ending.

"Crossing Bows for the Championship": Old Fiddlers' Conventions

"Last Friday evening, the date set for the Fiddler's Contest, brought together the largest audience perhaps ever assembled in Westmoreland Hall," wrote Dr. W. H. Johnson in 1924, describing the first of the "old fiddlers' conventions" that he organized in Athens, Alabama. "The crowd began arriving by dark and by 7 o'clock there was not standing room in this immense auditorium." People had traveled for miles to witness the event. "At 8 o'clock," continued Dr. Johnson, "the curtain went up and seated on the stage were many citizens of the county and adjoining counties with fiddle and well-rosined bow, ready for the contest, each eager for the start, and the audience was in a receptive mood."[38]

The scene described by Dr. Johnson had occurred many times before in schoolhouses and county courthouses across the state of Alabama and was to be repeated on hundreds of occasions in the following decades. It is likely that the practice of holding fiddlers' conventions came to Alabama with the pioneers. In Virginia, one of the states that furnished settlers to Alabama, such contests had been taking place since at least 1736, when the *Virginia Gazette* of Williamsburg announced a fiddlers' convention with the grand prize of "a fine Cremona fiddle."[39] Though contests were certainly held prior to 1900 in Alabama, they did not begin appearing in newspapers until after that date. Newspaper announcements such as the following serve as our main source of information about early fiddlers' conventions:

> The Old Fiddlers Convention will be held in Jackson, August 14, 1903. The Baptist Ladies here have arranged to have a grand concert at the College. The old fiddlers of the county have kindly consented to play for them. Such performers as the Barnes of Suggsville, Daffin, Woodard, and Pete Stringer of Grove Hill and the jovial Kos Moyer of Mobile. Others from Salitpa and Thomasville, with our home talent, headed by our genial big-hearted Capt. S. T. Woodard gave assurance of one of the finest concerts ever held in Jackson. This will not only be an evening of soul stirring, side-splitting pleasure but an opportunity to help in a splendid cause. Let everybody get ready for the biggest thing of the season.[40]

A report afterward noted that the fiddlers' convention "was quite a success and largely attended, as was the Grand Concert at night."[41]

These articles indicate the origin of the term "old fiddlers' convention." In 1903, only "the old fiddlers of the county" were invited to participate. The fact that they were old is verified by John Simpson Graham's history of Clarke County, written in 1923. Graham compiled a list of men born in the first half of the nineteenth century and living in the county when he arrived in 1875. All the fiddlers named above, except Kos Moyer, appear on Graham's list of "The Old Men of Clarke County."[42] The reports also show that such an event was more than a contest. It appears that the fiddlers gathered earlier in the day, then gave a concert that night. There may have been a competition, but as the articles do not mention prizes, it is possible that the affair was truly a gathering or "convention" in the original sense of the word. Over the years the "old fiddlers' conventions" became competitions between musicians of all ages, playing a variety of instruments, yet in many areas they were called by the traditional name. In other areas they began to be called "old-time fiddlers' conventions," a title suggesting that the practice of having contests was old, not the fiddlers themselves.

In the early 1920s, news of fiddlers' conventions began to appear regularly in county newspapers across the state. Scholars often attribute the new popularity of conventions to Henry Ford's attempts to revive old-time music and dance in the midst of the Jazz Age. In Alabama, however, the frequency of fiddlers' contests began to increase prior to 1926 when Ford sponsored his highly publicized conventions. It is clear, though, that the surge in contests in Alabama came from the same impulse that inspired Ford's efforts. Contest announcements often disparaged modern music. At a 1922 fiddlers' convention at the Soldier's Home in Chilton County, it was said that " 'Alabama Gals,' 'Leather Breeches,' and 'The Old Hen Cackle,' would vie with the latest jazz nerve wreckers,"[43] while the announcement of a contest in Guntersville in 1923 elaborated on that sentiment:

> All lovers of old time music in Marshall and adjoining counties are urged to attend this great musical event, and make it a Red Letter Day in the campaign to restore the Fiddle and Bow to the Sacred place they once occupied in the hearts of our forefathers of the ante-bellum period. It is the opinion of the promoters that the Jazz Period of music in the South is rapidly passing and that the early future will witness once again the triumph of the music made immortal in prose and poetry by such men as Joel Chandler Harris and Bob Taylor.[44]

The contests of the twenties may have begun as serious efforts to "keep alive the music of our yesteryears,"[45] but they flourished because they were entertaining. They continued in rural areas across the state throughout the 1940s, but were held most frequently during the gloomy days of the Depression. "Depression has no effect on music," wrote the organizers of the annual Elkmont convention in 1932, "and this year is expected, of all years, the very best music."[46] Admission prices and prize money were reduced during the Depression, but the size of the audience and the numbers of contestants grew.

In 1934 the *Limestone Democrat* remarked upon the popularity of the events: "That old fiddlers' contests are popular amusements in Limestone has been repeatedly proven lately. These annual events at Athens and Elkmont were largely attended recently and the one at Clements High last night played to 'standing room only.' It was estimated that fully 700 persons were in the building to enjoy the program."[47] In southwest Alabama, contests were so numerous in the thirties that a reporter observed, "As the football season dies, the fiddler's conventions open full blast."[48]

While the majority of fiddle contests took place in schools and courthouses, they could be held anywhere and for any reason. Sam

Woods of Millry, writing of his boyhood in Washington County at the turn of the century, recalled that fiddle contests furnished the main entertainment at summer barbecues.[49] Many communities across the state celebrated the Fourth of July with picnics, baseball, political speeches, and fiddlers' conventions followed by street dances.

Contests were occasionally sponsored by private entrepreneurs. When an auction company sold parcels of land on Sand Mountain, it could call forth a crowd by announcing "Free Music and Fiddlers' Contest. Cash prizes to the best old-time fiddler."[50] The Ben-Hur, a dance hall in downtown Birmingham, would lure weeknight crowds with announcements of an "Old-Time Convention."[51] In rural areas, the proprietor of a medicine show could draw upon the talents of local musicians by putting on a fiddlers' convention. Arlin Moon of Holly Pond recalled a man who stopped nearby, set up signboards advertising his product, announced a fiddlers' contest, then treated the crowd to an enthralling sales pitch between fiddle tunes. According to Moon, the salesman sold "what they called a snake oil, a wormwood oil . . . he put it on a piece of soft pine wood. Of course, any kind of oil would go right through it. He'd turn it over and show the people how it went through that piece of wood. He'd say, 'Now, it'll go through your flesh like that.' " Though Moon was skeptical of the sales pitch, he was happy to accept the $2.50 he won as best fiddler.[52]

Privately sponsored fiddle contests made up a small percentage of those reported in Alabama's newspapers, however. Old-time fiddlers' conventions were more likely to be held under the auspices of such groups as the Woodmen of the World, the United Daughters of the Confederacy, the American Legion, the Baptist Young People, and the Ladies' Missionary Society. By far the largest number of contests was sponsored by local parent-teacher organizations, with the proceeds earmarked for the improvement of public education.

The Schoolhouse Conventions. Schools in Alabama's rural counties have always led a hand-to-mouth existence. The Superintendent of Public Education in 1888 reported to the Governor: "At no time in the past has the school fund of the State been what it should have been. Ever since the system was inaugurated it has been crippled for want of an adequate means to build and furnish schoolhouses and to give free tuition to the children of the State for longer than three or four months a year."[53]

For many decades thereafter, the citizens of rural communities struggled to provide safe, pleasant schools for their children and to keep the doors of those schools open for eight or nine months per year. E. F. DuBose, principal of Joe Bradley School in Merrimack (Madison County) from 1923 until 1946, recalled that there was usually only enough state money to keep his school open for three months. Inevitably a letter would arrive from the State Board of Education announcing that no more public money would be forthcoming. Fortunately, he could rely on funds from the Merrimack Mills, which had built the school for the children of its employees, supplemented by the proceeds of frequent fiddlers' conventions.[54] In other communities the teachers and parents bore the burden of keeping the schools in session. Alice Harper Strickland, who began teaching on Brindlee Mountain in Marshall County in 1939, recalled one year when a lack of funds made it necessary to close the school a month early. All the teachers decided to teach one month without pay so that the children might complete the full eight-month term. "When the people in the community heard this they got busy with auctions and box suppers, donations of pigs and cows to be sold, and raised the money to pay each one of us for that last month of school."[55] At the time, Mrs. Strickland was making $60 a month. In nearby Cullman, teachers in 1938 had a twelve-month base pay of $63 a month. Only three towns in Alabama paid less, noted the *Cullman Democrat*, but Cullman was one of the few communities that paid salaries promptly.[56]

Even when there were enough public funds to keep the schools open, local citizens needed to provide money to keep the facilities in working condition. In 1945 the Alabama Education Survey Commission found the value of Alabama's school plant facilities to be the lowest in the nation.[57] Heating and sanitation facilities at many rural schools consisted of potbellied stoves and outdoor toilets. Money for "luxury" items such as library books, sewing machines for domestic-science classes, athletic uniforms, and stage curtains had to be provided by the community. The fiddlers' convention was a highly popular means of raising the needed funds. Those who reported the results of their contests to the newspaper often mentioned profits of $80 to $100, a sum that could pay a teacher's salary for a month, with money left over for school improvements.

The town of Coffeeville on the Tombigbee River in Clarke County is typical of the small communities across the state that held frequent schoolhouse fiddlers' conventions. Coffeeville had a one-teacher school until 1910, when the faculty doubled. In 1926 the first high school was built. Thereafter the PTA raised school funds

with annual contests. In 1937 the school burned down after a fiddlers' convention. Attributed to a faulty flue rather than to sparks
flying from the bows of fiddlers, the fire did not end the conventions,
which continued into the 1940s. Electric power lines did not reach
Coffeeville until 1935, nor a paved road until 1948. Prior to the early
1950s, only one telephone line reached the community, providing
service for just six homes. Until a bridge was built in 1960, a ferry
provided access to the west.[58] Despite the difficulties of traveling
to Coffeeville, people turned out in large numbers for the contests:
The auditorium "could scarcely hold all of the people who came to
the fiddlers' convention Friday night [December 1935] . . . Contestants came from many places to afford the audience, many of
whom came long distances, much pleasure and entertainment during the evening."[59] The fiddlers' conventions in Coffeeville and
small communities across the state were popular because they gave
rural people a merry reason to break the daily isolation caused by
unpaved roads, unbridged rivers, and lack of telephones. They provided music, laughter, and the opportunity to support the local
school system.

While communities shared similar goals in putting on fiddlers'
conventions and generally followed the same steps in organizing the
events, there was great variety in the way contests were run. For
instance, in setting the date, the planning committee might hold a
one-time event to meet a specific financial need; it might propose
an annual convention to be held at a fixed time each year; or it
might be flexible in setting the time, as were the organizers in Verbena:

> I know that you too have been wondering when Verbena
> would have its annual Fiddlin' Bee, for I have been wondering
> the same thing for some time past. You see, the weather and
> other things have kind of worked on us, and we have been wait-
> ing for it to clear up a mite before we announced the date. The
> groundhog has now made his prediction that the weather will
> be good from now on, and we intend to start something.[60]

Once the date had been set, organizers could send personal invitations to area fiddlers or rely on a notice in the local newspaper.
The announcement might be a simple statement of the time and
place of the contest, or it might be a detailed report of the activities
planned and the well-known fiddlers who had already committed.
It might contain promises: "If you love good old-fashioned music
played in the good old-fashioned way by good old-fashioned fiddlers,

come and you will get the treat of your life."[61] Or it might open with a rhyme:

Come young folks, come old folks; Come, everybody, come!
Come to hear the fiddlers and make yourself at home.
Be sure to check your chewing gum and razors at the door,
And you'll hear more music than you ever heard before.[62]

Quite often the committees did not bother to send such notices. Announcements made at other fiddlers' conventions and reminders to schoolchildren by their teachers made up the bulk of the advertising. Alice Harper Strickland recalled that fiddlers and other musicians would sometimes give a small matinee at school "hoping that the parents would turn out that night in full force."[63]

The types of prizes to be given varied from contest to contest. Cash prizes were simple to arrange, as the money could be taken directly from the admission receipts and awarded to the winning musicians. Thus, at some contests, the winners of each category went away with money in their pockets, the three top fiddlers perhaps taking home $10, $7, and $5 at most, while the best guitarists, banjoists, and others received an average of $2 apiece. At the Old-Time Fiddlers' Convention in Summit (Blount County) held in 1930, the first prize was a $5 gold piece, the second was $3 in silver, and the third was "a $2 bill with the corner already torn off."[64] At Simcoe (Cullman County) the winners were awarded percentages of the proceeds: band, 15%; fiddler, 7 1/4%; guitar, 5%; banjo and mandolin, 2% each.[65]

Since distributing the gate receipts among the contestants diminished the amount of money that could be raised for the school, some contest organizers preferred to give prizes of merchandise donated by local merchants. At Union Grove (Chilton County) in 1927, the fiddlers who did not win the $5 first prize or the second prize of $2.50 could look forward to one of the following prizes: a twenty-four-pound sack of flour, $1, a half-gallon bucket of lard, three gallons of gasoline, 50¢, a 35¢ package of coffee, a 25¢ pair of socks, or two 10¢ handkerchiefs.[66] One of the prizes given at a convention in Clanton in 1926 was a $2 sack of Full o' Pep Egg Mash.[67] In Verbena in 1921, John Burkhalter took home a pig when he came in second to Watermelon Johnson, who won $7.50.[68] Charlie Stripling of Kennedy once was awarded a can of corn at a fiddle contest in Sulligent.[69]

Stripling may have been part of a group of fiddlers who expressed displeasure with such prizes. On the afternoon of April 4, 1928, a meeting was held at Kennedy High School prior to a fiddlers' contest that night. Its purpose was to organize the "Fiddlers Association of North West Alabama" which would include the counties of Fayette, Lamar, Pickens, and Tuscaloosa. The *Sulligent News* reported:

> It seems that the fiddlers of the district are not satisfied with the amount they receive in prizes from some of the organizations where the fiddling is the main attraction.
>
> It is the desire of the fiddlers to bring this business up to a standard and have some uniformity of awarding prizes. It developed at this meeting that in some instances they furnished all the attraction and prizes awarded were some cheap article without any material value. They emphasized the fact that they had always been given a square deal at Fayette and Kennedy.[70]

It is unlikely that the group ever brought any kind of uniformity to the organization of fiddle contests in the widespread communities of northwestern Alabama. Further discussion on the topic was postponed until a meeting scheduled for the following July 4, but if such a meeting was held, it was not reported in the county newspapers. Prizes of merchandise continued to be given in the small schoolhouse conventions, usually in combination with cash prizes. Thus a fiddler who did not win one of the top prizes might be consoled, thanked, and encouraged to try again with the award of a sofa pillow, a homemade cake, or a package of Red Moon Chewing Tobacco. He also might be treated to refreshments, a bowl of chicken stew, or a full dinner at the close of the contest.

The choice of the master of ceremonies was an important one, and most planners invited a prominent citizen such as a mayor, county judge, state legislator, or school principal. In Tuscaloosa, J. P Shelton and A. K. "Temo" Callahan, both state legislators, often filled this role, while in Clarke County, Coma Garrett, Jr., the Judge of Probate, was a popular master of ceremonies. Judge Frank Turner of Washington County also "proved himself an expert in this capacity," wrote one reporter. "While, naturally, he did not enter any of the events, he gave his moral support by 'beating straws' for the fiddlers, giving samples of hog calling, Jew's harp playing and in many other ways entering into the program in a way which kept the fun at high pitch throughout the long and varied program."[71] Masters of ceremony were required to have strong voices. Jimmie Porter, who played in many of the contests of northwestern Alabama, remembered that, lacking public-address systems, "they just got up and hollered."[72]

The announcer might begin by informing the contestants and the audience of the contest rules. These varied from location to location. One invariable rule, however, was that violinists were ineligible. Fiddle contests were not for classically trained musicians who could read notes from a page. "No violin playing will be expected or desired," wrote the promoters of a Clarke County contest. They would permit only "plain old-time fiddling."[73] In Madison County, according to "Jack" Jackson, a fiddler could be held suspect if he "trembled his fingers," meaning that he played with a vibrato.[74]

Another rule frequently mentioned in newspaper announcements was that the fiddlers must play only authentic old-time fiddle tunes. The writer of the article would usually name a few tunes as examples. W. E. G. Sutton, describing the contest to take place in Verbena, promised that

> out of the past will be brought those famous old melodies of the days when dads and gran'dads and their sweethearts tripped lightly to the strains of "Johnny, Will Your Dog Bite?," "Tom Sawyer," "Devil's Hornpipe," "Highland Fling," "Sally, Put the Kettle On," and many other olden time pieces which are entirely foreign to knowledge of the younger generation.[75]

There seems to have been no restriction on the categories of old-time tunes that could be played, however. While a contestant today is usually required to play a waltz and a breakdown, entrants of earlier contests were free to choose the types of tunes they played best. A fiddler with a beautiful tone and smooth bow might play a waltz or a parlor tune, such as "When You and I Were Young, Maggie," in competition against a fiddler known for powerful breakdowns. Only the musical tastes of the judges would determine his success.

Convention rules might also cover the use of accompanists. In some contests the fiddler was required to play alone, while others allowed him to have a guitar or other backup instrument. At one Clarke County convention, there were separate contests for accompanied and unaccompanied fiddlers.[76]

When the preliminary announcements had been made, the fiddling began. Frequently the contestants would be seated on the stage, and upon a signal from the master of ceremonies, they would strike up a familiar tune en masse. S. M. Taylor, a graduate student at the University of Alabama, described the "grand overture" in her master's thesis in 1925:

. . . and although this invariably brings the audience to its feet with yells, I must confess that it is the greatest conglomeration of tones, and the furthest from ensemble music that ever came to my ears. For this fiddler is no sodden conformist; he has his own individual conception of how "Turkey in the Straw," "Arkansas Traveler," and "Dixie" should be played and—he plays it that way—and although each interpretation is pleasing because of its rhythm and queer harmony, when played individually, no word in the English language can describe the sound when they play together.[77]

A different reaction to the massive ensemble appeared in the description of a 1929 convention in Grove Hill: "While the judges were out, all the contestants came out and played and this was declared by many to have been the best feature of the entertainment."[78]

When it was time to start the competition, the master of ceremonies would announce the number of tunes that each musician would be allowed to play. This was determined by the number of contestants and other activities, such as political speeches, banjo contests, recitations, or hog-calling contests, that were planned for the night. No matter how tight the schedule, there seemed to be time for antics. Fiddlers cackled like hens, brayed like mules, and trilled like mockingbirds as they played. Like "Monkey" Brown, they were fond of playing "Pop Goes the Weasel" in all conceivable positions. Bob Kyle noted that Brown's younger brother, Charlie, was also a showman at contests:

Charlie Brown and I were at each other's throats. When we'd go to a fiddle convention, he was playing against me and I was playing against him. And he played a tune called "The Cackling Hen, " and that night at Alberta . . . I went over and asked him, "Would it be all right if I tune my fiddle up same as yours, 'cause I'm just going to be playing against you anyhow, and same way with you." And he said, "All right." And so we went to war, but somebody had made Charlie a rooster suit. It had a long red tail that stuck out about six feet—red. And when he'd play that "Cackling Hen," he'd cackle. You couldn't tell it from a rooster. And when he'd get down, he was sort of hump-shouldered-like anyhow, and he'd bend over, with the tail going up and down . . . well, I had to follow that, and that was the hardest thing that I ever had to play in all my life. And I played harder than I ever had before. I tried to kill him. I tried with all my might to kill him, playing the fiddle . . . You wouldn't be-

Tenbroeck School in DeKalb County was the site of a long series of fiddlers' conventions. It also hosted ca. 1918 a summer music school, at which an itinerant teacher provided instruction in vocal and instrumental music. Photo courtesy of B. L. Kelly and Bob Scarboro.

Above and on the following page, Charlie Atkins, who grew up in Lamar County, demonstrates two of the positions in which fiddlers rendered "Pop Goes the Weasel" at local fiddlers' conventions. Photos by Kim McRae Appel.

lieve how natural he looked as a rooster. The crowd just went crazy.[79]

Despite Brown's costume and Kyle's efforts, neither took first place. "A little old boy named Dickey that lived two or three blocks away from the school won the money," Kyle concluded. Unless a fiddler knew the judges well, as the fiddlers often did, it was hard to predict the winners. Judges could be politicians, musicians, or fans picked from the audience. Certainly there were no uniform standards of judging. While one judge enjoyed trick fiddling, another might prefer graceful waltzes, while another could be moved to award first place to a small child as encouragement.

Sympathy sometimes determined the winner. Gaines Arnold of Quintown won second place in a Walker County convention at which the judges were three music teachers and a car salesman. The day after the contest, one of the judges confided that Arnold had actually outplayed the winner, but first place had been given to a man who had been badly injured in a mine accident.[80]

If a contest was judged by audience applause, virtuosity could easily be overcome by sympathy and local favoritism. Often serious fiddlers refused to play at contests that were to be judged by the audience. Bob Kyle once drove from Tuscaloosa to Sumiton, only to find that the contest was to be judged by applause. When he tried to convince the master of ceremonies that judges should be used instead, he was told, "You either play or don't play." Kyle remembered his reponse:

> "I'm going to play, and I'm going to play by your rules and I'm going to learn you something." I went on out and sat on the stage, took my fiddle and tuned slowly and sort of listened at it, just acting the fool. Then I laid it up there and hit it a time or two, and about four or five hairs flew out of the bow. I looked like I couldn't understand what it was all about. Still hadn't played a lick, and by that time the crowd was already applauding, and just as they got applauding good, I cut loose on the tune and they never did stop while I was playing.
>
> And I went around and told this fellow, "I didn't play better than anybody else, but I think I learned you something about letting the crowd judge."[81]

Because of the vagaries of judging, fiddlers seldom claimed to be champions on the basis of schoolhouse contests. Everis Campbell's standard remark upon winning a contest was, "Well, they got sorry for me and give me first prize."[82] When someone noted that Charlie Stripling won most of the contests he entered, Stripling replied, "Well, I have been lucky. The way they give prizes, I didn't know if I won them or not, but if they give them to me, I took them."[83]

One aspect of conventions that varied from area to area was the type of activities that accompanied the fiddlers' competition. In early contests, such as the 1903 contest in Jackson, audiences mainly heard fiddling, with an occasional interlude of dance exhibitions or recitations. During the twenties and thirties, however, other instruments began to appear on the program. The organizer of a 1921 contest in Verbena seemed uncomfortable with this trend when he wrote, "This affair will be for the fiddlers, and banjoists, but mostly for the fiddlers. There will be a prize for the best string orchestra, too, but don't get your mind off the fact that fiddlin' will be the main show."[84] In Clarke County, where other musical and comical contests were threatening to overwhelm the fiddle competition, the officials of a 1929 convention requested that contestants "confine their efforts to fiddling," for "this is what the people have come out to hear."[85] However, in Limestone County during the same year, organizers of the annual Elkmont convention applauded the trend that was in evidence there and in other communities:

> Each year, as these contests are held, they get better, with a more varied program, better fiddling, and there have begun to appear all kinds of instruments now at these contests. The group music is also given a prominent place in our program this year, and we expect many good bands or groups.[86]

Harmonica and banjo players, guitarists, and singers began to compete. Some conventions had a competition for string bands, which usually included a fiddle, guitar, and banjo, though they might also have a mandolin, cello, or string bass. Others had a "group" category that allowed various combinations of instruments and singers. The number of bands or groups entering fiddlers' conventions across the state grew steadily throughout the thirties and forties.

Most fiddlers' conventions included a few nonmusical competitions, as well, giving hog callers, husband callers, and pretty girls their moments of glory on the stage. In Clarke County, where the 1903 contest was described as "side splitting," the organizers maintained the tradition by enthusiastically offering a variety of comical contests. The *Clarke County Democrat* observed in 1937: "While these events are styled 'Fiddlers' Conventions,' they have come to include mirth-provoking stunts of every conceivable character and are extremely popular with those who like an evening of fun."[87] Inhibitions were overcome by the promise of merchandise prizes, such as seventy-six items collected for the Coffeeville contest of 1937.[88] People were encouraged to enter the liars' contest: "Those thinking of entering should not worry about the competition, because Ian Robinson will be placed at a 50 percent handicap, Charlie Cotton, 60 percent and Rev. G. E. Daughtry at 75 percent."[89] Newspaper announcements warned readers to keep their hogs closely confined on contest nights. At a 1934 convention in Suggsville, "chief interest centered around the hog calling contest, in which there were seven entrants, and when W. C. Tarleton, winner of first place, had completed his demonstration, so many hogs had risen from their beds and congregated about the community house that they had to be run away before the program could continue."[90]

Thus fiddlers in Clarke County shared the evening with yodelers, buck-dancers, acrobats, rooster crowers, whistlers, comedians, and liars. Mingled with music were contests for the prettiest girl, the ugliest man, the most popular baby, and the truck bringing the largest crowd. Yet, in Clarke County, as at all other contests, the best fiddler was the champion of the night. He took home the largest prize of the evening, usually $5 in cash.

Although fiddlers faced the possibilities of erratic judging, trivial rewards, and being overwhelmed by a variety of hilarious contests, they continued to participate. Bob Kyle, for instance, went to as many as four conventions a week in Tuscaloosa, Bibb, Pickens, Fayette, and Jefferson counties, often traveling with A. K. Callahan. Callahan remembered driving sixty miles without lights and brakes to reach a contest, and Kyle recalled continually watching for the sheriff because their car tags had expired. They carried kindling with them, so that when the car broke down they could keep warm while fixing it.[91] Such dedication was not born of the desire for yet another prize necktie, but of the desire to mingle with other fiddlers, learn new tunes, and contribute to worthwhile causes.

Moreover, the contest fulfilled a fiddler's most important requirement: an attentive, enthusiastic audience. The promoter of the annual fiddlers' contest at Crossville (De Kalb County) was aware of that need when he wrote, "A large audience of around 400 people always greet these players and bands, and give them somebody to do their best before."[92] Such audiences encouraged the fiddler to keep in practice, to hone his skills on the instrument, and to develop a repertoire of well-played, crowd-pleasing tunes.

Limestone County Conventions. Limestone County, in particular, provided the kind of audiences that stimulated musicians. Alton Delmore attributed the success of the Delmore Brothers, nationally popular radio and recording artists of the thirties and forties, to the audiences of the Limestone fiddlers' conventions where they first performed. In his autobiography, *Truth is Stranger than Publicity*, Delmore described their first public appearance at a fiddlers' convention at Clements High School in western Limestone County: "There was a good crowd there and those people know fine music when they hear it. Many song writers and singers come from down in that part of the county. That night, one of the judges was a singer, music teacher and song writer." Having worried that their soft voices would not be heard above the noise of the crowd, the two young brothers were pleased when they won the audience's rapt attention and second place in the contest. Delmore concluded, "If the crowd had not quieted, there probably would never have been an act called The Delmore Brothers . . . I am grateful for all the good music lovers who lived down there in that community."[93]

Before becoming stars of the "Grand Ole Opry," the brothers continued to enter local fiddlers' conventions. Limestone County provided them many opportunities to perform and gain local celebrity; contests were held in the schoolhouses of Elkmont, Cairo, Athens, Rockaway, Goodsprings, Rogersville, Cartwright, Cross Key, West Limestone, and East Limestone, among others.[94] Delmore wrote that the turning point in their career came at the annual contest of the Athens Agricultural High School, which he considered to be "by far the biggest and most important contest of the entire country."[95]

The Athens convention had begun in 1924 under the leadership of Dr. W. H. Johnson, principal of the Agricultural High School, with the support of Harris Rogers, a fiddler who lived near the school. Dr. Johnson publicized the contests well, conducted them in an elegant manner, and afterward wrote detailed descriptions for the county newspapers. His reports re-created the excitement and grandeur of the Athens convention.

For the first contest in 1924, Dr. Johnson had arranged "a delightful program, one that would keep the audience interested from the very first note of the orchestra until the close of the program at ten of the clock." Though "this was a fiddler's contest and violins were shunted to one side and no violin player was allowed to participate in the program," the Fuller Orchestra entertained with classical selections until the curtain rose at 8 o'clock, revealing a stage full of contestants. Dr. Johnson stated that each contestant would be allowed to play one piece, and if encored could play a second.[96]

John Chambers, of the western part of the county, was the first to play. Dr. Johnson's report noted that Chambers "is recognized as one of the most expert handlers of the fiddle bow in the country and to make his playing more interesting, he used a beautiful fiddle that he made with a pocketknife. He was given a rousing encore and played for his second number 'The 8th of January.' " Among other contestants were Harris Rogers, "our own brag fiddler," to whom the audience showed its appreciation by not wanting him to stop, and the Reverend Spot Starkey, who "gave a fine rendition of old-time tunes which he used to play for dances before he went into a different field of endeavor." Mrs. Delia Mullins of Madison County earned rounds of applause, and the playing of Robert Reynolds, her brother, "was like that of his sister, without flaw, and met with instant approval by the audience." In response to a demand by that audience, the two played a duet.

In the 1924 contest, only fiddlers competed. Other entertainment included recitations, one string-band number, and various types of dancing. After "one of the most enjoyable evenings ever known in Athens," the winners were announced: John Chambers, first prize; Harris Rogers, second; Spot Starkey, third; and Mrs. Mullins, fourth.[97]

A year later, the second contest was held. "The immense hall was packed from front to rear and more than one hundred people were turned away for lack of room." The program consisted of the fiddling competition, won by John Watkins, a number of variety acts, and a new competition for bands.[98] At the third contest, in 1926, Mrs. Mullins claimed the first prize that some thought she should have received in 1924.[99]

In 1927, "Athens and Limestone County witnessed the greatest old fiddlers program ever given in this county. The Agricultural school was host to the old fiddlers and when the stage curtain raised, there were exactly twenty-five people on the platform to entertain more than eight hundred people crowded into the auditorium," said another report. The program had proved successful enough to become an annual event; the last Friday night in February was pronounced the official date. In addition to the fiddle competition, which was won by J. B. Carver, there were now prizes for the best band, "single other instrument," and buck-and-wing dancer.[100]

In 1928, crowds assembled long before the doors opened. "This year we had fourteen old fiddlers,[101] six banjo pickers, five guitar pickers, four harpists, five buck-and-wing dancers and thirteen groups or string bands on the stage," forming "the greatest array of old-time musicians ever assembled on one platform in this section of the country." This contest honored the memory of the late "Uncle Harris Rogers, the greatest old fiddler of all. It was he, who more than anyone else, lent inspiration to the beginning of the old fiddler's contest at this place." Mrs. Emma Crabtree was judged best fiddler of the contest and was awarded $10 in gold.[102]

In 1929, Dr. Johnson still marveled at the success of his creation:

> This program was begun back in 1924 as an experiment. At that time it was thought that the new would soon wear off and as a consequence the programs would only last a year or two and something else would be necessary to take their place. But not so, for the interest is increasing from year to year. The auditorium was packed to capacity, over 800 people managing in some way to find standing room. There were 120 people who entered the various contests. There were 83 different numbers on the program, necessitating a run of nearly four hours to take care of the contestants.

John Chambers, who had won the 1924 contest, was named best fiddler in 1929.[103]

Announcements for the contest to be held on February 28, 1930, promised "the gathering of these old-time musicians with new strings and well-rosined bows to make the audience forget the cares and vexations of this life for a few hours." Dr. Johnson wrote that "these are rare occasions. They bring people together who know nothing of what is termed 'classical music' but who do understand and appreciate what the fiddler interprets from the greatest instrument that has ever been made."[104] In that year and the following, however, the results of the contest did not appear in the paper.

In 1932 the *Alabama Courier* reported that "Superintendent W. H. Johnson acted as the publicity manager, sending out letters to all the fiddlers in Limestone and the adjoining cities. A special effort was made to get every ambitious musician to participate in the contest and demonstrate his ability with the bow." As a result, ten fiddlers, ten guitarists, four banjoists, a ukulele player, and eight harmonica players entered.[105] Twenty bands, among them the Delmore Brothers, competed for the group prize, which turned out to be a box of cigars. Delmore captured the excitement of the event in his autobiography: "There was a big crowd there and everything was decorated and all fixed up like the president of the United States would be there . . . There were some bands there that would have given Bob Wills some strong competition if Bob had been there." The Delmores tied for first place in the band competition with "three pretty girls." In the runoff, the girls got a tremendous hand from the audience, but when the brothers finished singing "The Columbus Stockade Blues," "men threw their hats into the top of the house and everbody screamed." The audience "really went wild" when the Delmore Brothers sang the "Browns' Ferry Blues," a song they had composed especially for the Athens contest about hard times in one of Limestone County's small communities.[106] Alton Delmore also won first place for guitar playing, and D. A. Cole was awarded $7 as the winning fiddler.[107]

Over 150 contestants participated in the tenth annual "get-together of those who would keep alive the music of our yesterdays" in 1933, when Osburn Echols won the fiddle competition.[108] Contests were held in 1934 and 1935, though no reports appeared in the papers; then the contest quietly ended. During the 1935–36 school year, Athens Agricultural School became Athens High School, and Dr. Johnson was replaced by a principal who did not continue the contests.

Limestonians were not left in silence, however. Clements and Elkmont high schools continued to have their large contests each March, and when West Limestone High School was opened in September of 1935, it held its first annual fiddlers' convention the following April.

World War II broke the momentum of the Limestone County conventions. Though they were held sporadically thereafter, the days of the annual schoolhouse fiddle conventions were over. Yet, wrote Bill Harrison, "old-time music held on tenuously, mainly in the extreme north Limestone County hills, in the form of little-known gatherings in the homes of musicians and enthusiasts."[109] In 1966, Harrison and a fiddler named Sam McCracken were inspired to revive the contest tradition when they read an article in a Nashville newspaper that "lamented the apparent death of old-time fiddling." According to Harrison, "A survey by a few devotees of old-time music here in Limestone County revealed the opposite. Old-time music, it was found, had experienced a vigorous survival." This was proved when their first convention, held in an old schoolhouse, was successful and led to a second one at West Limestone High School, which attracted 2,000 people.[110] When the organizers formed the Tennessee Valley Old-Time Fiddlers' Association in 1967 and moved the contest site to Athens College, they met the same enthusiastic response from lovers of old-time music that had overwhelmed Dr. W. H. Johnson at his first contest in 1924 and the Delmore Brothers at the outset of their career.

The Courthouse Conventions

In some counties it was customary to hold fiddlers' conventions in the county courthouse on the first Monday night of a circuit-court term. The surprising link between fiddling and jurisprudence developed in Alabama's pioneer days. Circuit court convened twice a year in each county, and, according to Wellington Vandiveer of Talladega County, "The week of court was a time for gossip, recreation, social amenities, and horse swapping. Preparations were made for it many days in advance. It was the one real large event in the history of the town and county and the pioneer made of it a frolic and relaxation."[111]

On the opening day of court, crowds converged upon the county seat—plaintiffs, defendants, attorneys, jurors, witnesses, relatives, folks who came to admire the oratory of the lawyers, and people who wanted to sell mules, chairs, medicine, and assorted merchandise to the assemblage. In the public wagon yard at night, wrote Frank Lawrence Owsley,

> . . . they gathered in groups around the fires built near their wagons, swapped stories, and traded horses and mules—no tricks being barred. Some of the wagoners were fiddlers and banjo players, and once business was disposed of, they kept their instruments singing day and night, both from the urgings of their companions and from their own unalloyed enjoyment of playing. Then, too there was always rivalry between players as well as the natural desire of each musician to learn some new song or musical "trick" from the other.[112]

It is not difficult to imagine that as the hours passed and the liquor jug made its rounds, the wagon-yard rivalries grew into serious competitions, attracting large crowds and provoking arguments and bets. It is possible that some of the contests may have become so intense that they were settled in court the next day. It is more likely that the custom of courthouse fiddlers' conventions was born when someone realized there was money to be made by moving the music indoors and charging admission. At any rate, conventions coinciding with the opening day of circuit court were held long after wagon yards had disappeared.

Sponsored by a civic organization or a committee of prominent citizens, the courthouse conventions were usually well-organized events which attracted fiddlers from a large area. Fayette and De Kalb counties, in particular, supported long series of these conventions. Their organizers, like Dr. Johnson of the Athens Agricultural School, were committed to the preservation of old-time fiddling. Educated and articulate, they provided their local newspapers with detailed, sometimes highly embellished and nostalgic accounts of the fiddlers' conventions they sponsored.

Fayette County Conventions. As the poem "Fiddler's Jubilee" indicates, Fayette County was rich in fiddlers. That poem, published in 1907, humorously described a fiddlers' convention in Fayette at which only four of the fifteen expected fiddlers actually played. The courthouse conventions, held when circuit court convened early in September and the middle of March, attracted many more fiddlers. In 1919 the Fayette chapter of the United Daughters of the Confederacy began sponsoring the contests,[113] though they had doubtlessly been held prior to that year under other sponsorship. Twice a year, between 1919 and 1947, the U.D.C. directed contests which attracted large crowds and the best fiddlers of west Alabama.

Led by Mrs. W. W. Monroe, Mrs. Dean Walters, and Mrs. Felix Robertson, the organization publicized the conventions elegantly. Announcements spoke of "the followers of Stradivari" and "fiddle 'n' bow artists," and often quoted Longfellow:

> And the night shall be filled with music
> And the cares, that infest the day,
> Shall fold their tents, like the Arabs,
> And as silently steal away.[114]

Despite these genteel touches, the women demonstrated a true understanding of their subject. An announcement of the contest to be held September 8, 1930, contained a complete and accurate description of old-time fiddling:

> These Conventions have always been a source of amusement to the large number of people who attend, the music being different from the ordinary music of the day as most of it has been transmitted from one generation to the other without being in

the form of written music, and learned and played entirely by ear, and as "variety is the spice of life," everybody seems to enjoy the peculiar wiggling of the bow passing across the fiddle.

The usual number of prizes will be awarded to the best fiddlers playing the old-time pieces such as "Turkey in the Straw", "Billie in the Low Grounds", "Lazy Kate" or any of the other gals. As fiddlers have about 100 pieces to select from, any tune they may choose to play will be acceptable.[115]

Mrs. Belle Robertson (1862–1945) is generally recognized as the guiding spirit behind the contests. An editorial in the *Fayette Banner* about the conventions noted that "Mrs. Robertson is a lover of the violin, and for years she has helped to make these entertainments worthwhile."[116] Though she was one of Fayette's wealthiest citizens, she is remembered as being "down-to-earth" and having a deep appreciation of pioneer customs and traditional music.[117] To encourage wide participation in the contest, she led the U.D.C. to offer sizable cash prizes to winners and $1 consolation prizes to all other fiddlers. Charlie Stripling recalled, "A lot of them would play even if they couldn't play much, just to get in and get them that dollar."[118]

It was important to have a good number of entrants, as the U.D.C. conventions appear to have been for fiddlers only. Reports of the events mention no other instruments, comical contests, or variety acts. An account of the September 1930 convention noted that twenty-one fiddlers entered and provided "a three hour program of the best music of this kind."[119] "Monkey" and Charlie Brown of Tuscaloosa, Jimmie Porter of Steens, Mississippi, and Charlie Stripling of Kennedy were consistent winners. Stripling won so often that eventually Mrs. Robertson paid him not to enter, as it discouraged the other fiddlers.[120]

Audiences filled the courtroom, drawn by the opportunity to hear the area's top fiddlers. After the spring 1930 convention, headlines in the *Fayette Banner* read, "Fiddler's Convention Draws Thousand People Monday Night,"[121] as was the case at many of the conventions. They were lively audiences. Jimmie Porter remembered that "if you played a good piece that they liked, they'd nearly tear the floor down."[122]

With the proceeds from the contests, which the group referred to as "a movement of mountain music," the U.D.C. funded various projects. Most important was the Holland M. Bell Club House, built in 1935. Constructed of logs "in pioneer fashion," it was used as a meeting place and a "shrine for relics."[123] All the furniture was handmade. When the clubhouse was featured in the *Birmingham News–Age Herald*, the headline read "Mountain Music Hovers Over Fayette."[124]

The clubhouse no longer exists, but another project, a marble drinking fountain erected in 1929, still stands on the lawn of the Fayette Courthouse. It was built for the comfort of those attending the contests. On its base are engraved the words "Made Possible by the Fiddlers Convention." It is probably the only tangible sign in the state of the contributions made by fiddlers to their communities.

The Fayette County fiddlers' conventions were seldom mentioned in newspapers after the 1930s, yet U.D.C. ledgers indicate that they were held twice a year through at least 1947, with an average profit of $40 per convention. It is interesting to note that in 1945, both the lowest and highest profits were made. After the March contest, the U.D.C. deposited $2.15; the September event brought in $67.55. That contest, held one week after the official ending of World War II, attracted a large and celebratory crowd to the Fayette County Courthouse.

De Kalb County Fiddlers' Conventions. On the other side of the state, another series of contests took place under the sponsorship of William Van Jacoway, Sr. In 1933, on the occasion of the 26th Annual De Kalb County Fiddlers' Convention, Jacoway wrote:

> Conventions of this kind are being held and have been held periodically over the country, but none other for twenty-six years without a break in time and place. Therefore, if this record serves as a measure of interest in the perpetuation of the old-time tunes . . . the Blue Ribbon goes to those who reside among the mountains and valleys of this section of the country.[125]

Jacoway, who organized the long series of De Kalb County conventions, was born in 1873 and spent most of his eighty-two years in the valley between Sand and Lookout Mountains in northeast Alabama. He was a civic, political, and religious leader in Fort Payne, where he owned the county's largest department store. Fascinated by the history and folkways of the area, he wrote a county history which was published in 1925,[126] and he shaped his fiddlers' conventions into monuments to the past.

The primary purpose of the fiddlers' conventions, according to Jacoway, was

ALABAMA, Wednesday, August 10, 1933.

——25TH ANNUAL——

DEKALB COUNTY Fiddlers' Convention

AT COURT HOUSE

MONDAY NIGHT

August 15th, Fort Payne

The power and charm of music is not confined to the human heart only, but its power and influence touches the savage breast of the forest. Therefore, in these perilous times when the hearts of men and women are being tossed upon the sea of despair and uncertainty, forget it by attending our 25th Annual Fiddlers' Convention August 15th.

The Biggest, the Funniest and the most Soul-Inspiring Event in the history of the fiddle and the bow. The old time tunes will rekindle the smoldering fires of youth, retouch the golden heart-strings of a broken chord, rejuvenate and transplant the soul to the green fields of memory's ecstatic joys and pleasures of the LONG AGO.

Come and be thus transformed into a boy or girl just for the night.

HOG CALLING CONTEST FIRST PRIZE $2.00

Judge Alf Hawkins, who, on similar occasions, delights in telling of the Virginia Reel and the old Square Dance among the hills and mountains of North Alabama, will be Master of Ceremonies.

ALL PRIZES PAID IN CASH.

Doors Open 8 P. M.   :   Admission 25 and 35 cents.

JUDGE ALF HAWKINS.
MAYOR C. M. T. SAWYER.
JUDGE L. L. CRAWFORD.
IRA HOUSTON.
W. V. JACOWAY.

Publicity Committee.

Advertisement for the De Kalb County Fiddlers' Convention, which appeared in the *Fort Payne Journal* on Wednesday, August 10, 1932. Photo courtesy of the *Fort Payne Journal*.

... to perpetuate the memory and the music of the old-time fiddler, to revere the Past, to show the present generation of young men and women that there was sweeter and more inspiring music emanating from the fiddle and the bow than will ever be found in the present day jazz, with its Fox-trot, Camel Walk, "Bear-Hug," and all other kindred round dances, and to further prove to our boys and girls that father and mother played just as important [a] part in the realm of innocent amusements as those of this day and generation.[127]

Though each year he involved leading citizens in planning the conventions, Jacoway's personality and philosophy were visible in every announcement and report. He wrote that fiddlers' conventions provided the opportunity not only to hear good music but also to "drink again at the Fountain of Youth, albeit just for tonight."[128] He promised that the touch of the old-time fiddler would lift "the veil of the past ... permitting a vision of the pictures on Memory's walls."[129] It would "rekindle the smoldering fires of youth, retouch the golden heart-strings of a broken chord, rejuvenate and transplant the soul to the green fields of memory's ecstatic joys and pleasures of the LONG AGO."[130]

On the first Monday night of the August circuit-court term, people poured into the De Kalb County Courthouse from nearby communities and counties as well as from Tennessee and Georgia, arriving long before the doors opened at 7 o'clock. Immediately they would fill every seat, while "a few yearling boys" would try to gain admittance to the balcony by climbing the fire escape,[131] and "a great plethora of Fiddle and bow artists" would be tuning in the anterooms.[132]

Banjos, guitars, and other stringed instruments were also being tuned, for the contest had included them from the beginning. In 1930 it was reported that "43 fiddlers, 21 string bands, 11 banjo pickers and 10 guitar pickers were present. Thus it is not difficult to understand that the big audience was treated to three hours of the old-time music, laughter and recreation."[133] Laughter was provoked by contests involving cracker and melon eaters, ugly fiddlers, and husband callers. Nostalgia was evoked by the oldest-fiddler award, which, given Jacoway's love of the past, had more than usual significance at the De Kalb conventions. For instance, in 1929 Jacoway wrote:

During the past year the convention lost its oldest fiddler in the death of Uncle Bill Lyons. Taking the honor this year ... was

Uncle J. M. Blalock . . . of Lookout Mountain, who first attended the convention twenty years ago when he was 55, and Monday night at the ripe old age of 75 as he deftly drew his bow over the fiddle in "Rye Straw" and "Sally Good-un." Although Uncle Jim's fingers, under the weight of 75 winters, have begun to lose some of their nimbleness and elasticity, he was able to catch the swing and rhythm of those old-time tunes that inspired the steps of the old-fashioned quadrille.[134]

Judge Alfred E. Hawkins, who delighted in "telling of the Virginia Reel and the old Square Dance among the hills and mountains of North Alabama,"[135] was master of ceremonies during the twenties and thirties. In 1941, Dick Hunt served in that role. He was the grandson of Colonel R. C. Hunt, a "pioneer of old-time fiddling"[136] who had been master of ceremonies at fiddlers' conventions as early as 1907. All had the task of moving the long and varied program smoothly toward its conclusion and entertaining the audience while the judges, appointed just before the program started, were making their decisions. Reports often mentioned long deliberations by the judges, frequently fiddlers themselves.

When at last the selections had been made, musicians stepped forward for their applause and prizes. At early conventions only two prize winners received cash; the rest won merchandise. However, by 1928 only cash prizes were offered, "the management having decided this the only and best way to make future conventions a success."[137] Perhaps past awards like the $5 safety razor awarded to the youngest fiddler and the pair of shoes given to the best band had influenced the change. Conventions that followed offered more than $100 in cash prizes. On three occasions the top prize was won by Jesse Young of Tennessee, a recording artist and professional fiddler. Once a 14-year-old fiddler named J. B. "Buddy" Durham, "who played his violin from between his legs, behind his back, on top his head and in every conceivable manner one could imagine, brought down the entire house by his antics . . . thereby stealing the show."[138] Durham, whose father was raised on Sand Mountain, was already a professional fiddler, having performed across the country as part of a family band since he was 8 years old.[139] Often the contest was won by area residents such as Frank Davis of Rainsville, Frank Moore of Henagar, and W. H. Johnson of Albertville.

At the close of the evening, before the crowd left "with their souls bubbling over with the melody of old-time fiddle tunes,"[140] there was always a final item on the agenda. Each year Jacoway called for a vote on continuing the event for another year, each year "the vast audience voting almost unanimously in the affirmative."[141]

To Jacoway, whose primary purpose in sponsoring the conventions was to perpetuate old-time fiddling, the receipts at the door seem to have been a troublesome by-product. Proceeds from the 1907 convention were contributed toward a proposed schoolhouse, but subsequent news stories failed to mention the use of profits until 1928, when the *Fort Payne Journal* announced that over $1500 had been contributed to various public enterprises from the proceeds of the events. It reported that the management was now considering a project that would directly benefit fiddlers. An insurance fund, overseen by a responsible trustee, would be established. Upon the death of a fiddler who was in good standing with the De Kalb County Fiddlers' Convention, his family would receive a percentage of the fund. "Had this plan been adopted at first," commented the reporter, "this free insurance would now be worth something to the fiddle and bow artists."[142] In 1932, the insurance fund was still being considered, now as part of a grander vision. The management was trying to interest Henry Ford in erecting a fiddlers' auditorium "because of the unparalleled record of a quarter of a century of Fiddlers' Conventions held at Fort Payne without a break in time or place."[143] It was hoped that Ford would contribute to the insurance fund at the same time.[144]

While envisioning tributes to the fiddler far beyond those attempted elsewhere, the organizers continued to use the funds, probably less than $200 per year, on more mundane projects, such as the reclamation of an unsightly ditch at the rear of the Methodist Church and the creation of a park beside it.[145] The fiddlers' auditorium and insurance fund never materialized, and by 1942 Jacoway was announcing, "All prizes commensurate with proceeds, as no profit is wanted."[146]

World War II brought an end to the De Kalb County Fiddlers' Conventions, as it did to many of the annual courthouse and schoolhouse conventions. Most ended quietly with no public notice of their departure. The *Fort Payne Journal*, however, carried a headline that read, "Abandon Fiddlers' Convention." It announced, "After a period of thirty-five years without a break in the chain of annual Fiddlers' conventions at this place, it is thought wise to skip this year and not have the convention as usual on account of war conditions over the nation."[147] Stating that many of the fiddlers were in the armed forces and that gas and tire rationing restricted travel, the article reported that the conventions would resume after the war; however, such was not the case.

The thirty-five-year record of the De Kalb County contests has now been surpassed by the Walnut Grove Fiddlers' Convention of Etowah County, which celebrated its fiftieth anniversary in 1986, yet it would be difficult for an individual to surpass the record set by William Van Jacoway for devotion to old-time fiddling. Although nostalgic about "the good old days at the barn dance, with the shy ones playing hide and seek in the maizes [sic] of the grand old quadrille,"[148] he was pleased with "the high-powered car" that sped fiddlers to conventions and electric loudspeakers that carried music to the rear of the auditorium.[149] He sought to bring the simple pleasures of the old days into the modern world. During his lifetime he was remarkably successful in his goal of perpetuating "the memory and music of the old-time fiddler."[150]

Fiddling in the Fourteenth Judicial Circuit. The Kiwanis Club of Jasper capitalized on the connection between circuit court and fiddlers' conventions in a novel contest it sponsored in 1929. The contest, which was described as the main feature of a variety show at the Colonial Theater, was to determine the best fiddler of the Fourteenth Judicial Circuit. The probate judge of each of the five counties in the district—Fayette, Lamar, Marion, Winston, and Walker—was asked to select the two top fiddlers in his county for the competition. Prior to the event, the *Mountain Eagle* announced that each of the judges had selected his champions and was bringing a large delegation to support the "fiddling team." J. M. Tingle of Double Springs and T. A. Roberts of Haleyville were to represent Winston County, both having won most of the contests they had ever entered. J. O. Wisenhunt and a fiddler from Sumiton were selected to represent Walker County. Though the names of candidates from Lamar, Marion, and Fayette were never revealed, the judges of those counties all promised that they had the best pair of fiddlers in the state and expected to win.[151]

After the contest, readers of the *Mountain Eagle* learned that the show was the "hit of the season," and the *Fayette Banner*, whose readers were accustomed to excellent fiddling, reported that the audience heard some of the best music ever presented in Jasper. J. M. Tingle of Double Springs was awarded the first prize of $25; while C. W. Morris of Fayette and J. O. Wisenhunt of Walker received $15 and $10 as the second and third best fiddlers of the area.[152]

Fiddling Championships

The contest in Jasper differed from schoolhouse and courthouse conventions in that it bestowed a title along with the prize money. At
its close, J. M. Tingle was entitled to declare himself the best fiddler
of the Fourteenth Judicial Circuit, should he so desire. Occasionally
other organizations across the state sponsored conventions claiming
to be contests to determine the champion fiddler of Alabama, of
several states, or of the entire South. Because there was no official
national fiddlers' body to sanction certain contests, any organization
could sponsor a championship fiddlers' convention. Thus several
fiddlers could—and did—make simultaneous claim to being the
champion fiddler of Alabama.

While the championship contests were usually sponsored by a
local organization such as the American Legion, the Kiwanis Club,
the Band Boosters, or the Ku Klux Klan, they were quite often run
by a paid promoter from outside of the community. One promoter
during the late 1920s was "Uncle Bud" or "Fiddling Bud" Silvey of
Thomaston, Georgia, who directed contests in Albertville, Huntsville, Ft. Payne, and other cities of north Alabama and Georgia. Silvey would place large advertisments in local newspapers announcing
a contest in which "the Georgia, Alabama, and Tennessee Fiddlers
will cross bows for the championship of three states,"[153] and listing
well-known fiddlers who were planning to attend. The "big name"
musicians did not always appear; for instance, the Skillet Lickers,
who had been expected at the 1928 convention in Huntsville, were
not mentioned in later reports of the contest. Yet Silvey's contests
appear to have been reputable, entertaining affairs which awarded
the winners well. In Huntsville, Mrs. Emma Crabtree won a violin,
and the best band, a $25 guitar. Silvey, a fiddler himself, seemed
genuinely interested in perpetuating old-time fiddling. After the
Huntsville contest, he expressed surprise at the number of fiddlers
in the area, finding Huntsville to be "literally alive" with them and
promising to offer larger cash prizes the following year in order to
encourage more of the musicians in Huntsville's mill villages to
participate.[154]

Birmingham's Conventions. In 1925 the Old Fiddlers' Association
of Alabama held a contest to determine the championship of Alabama. Nothing is known of the Old Fiddlers' Association other than
the fact that Y. Z. Hamilton was a member, and that it occasionally
furnished music for square dances sponsored by the Wahouma Klav-

THE CONEY ISLAND
of DIXIE

EAST LAKE PARK

WHERE
THE HEART
OF HILARITY BEATS

KNIGHTS OF THE FIDDLE AND BOW
THURS. FRI. AND SAT. NIGHTS

THIRTY OLD FIDDLERS IN ANNUAL CONVENTION
OF ALABAMA FIDDLERS' ASSOCIATION.

BLACK FACE COMEDIANS—MALE QUARTET—MAN-
DOLINS — HANDSAWS—BUCK DANCING — PRIZE
FIDDLERS' CONTEST—FEATURING

LITTLE WILLIE OF BLOUNT COUNTY

(CURTAIN RISES AT 8 EACH NIGHT)

Turn to left at 80th street for free parking space across the lake.

Advertisement for the Annual Convention of the Alabama Fiddlers' Association, which appeared in the *Birmingham Age-Herald* on May 19, 1925. Photo courtesy of the *Birmingham Post-Herald*.

ern of the Ku Klux Klan.[155] The convention was described as an annual affair, and the press noted that "the occasion of the meeting of the old-time fiddlers in Birmingham has always been one that drew appreciative audiences." Held at East Lake Park, the contest seemed as much a promotion of the resort as it was of old-time fiddling. The 1925 event promised to attract more people than ever because the "phiddlin' phools" had diversified their program, including handsaw numbers, blackface comedians, a male quartet, and buck-and-wing dancing, as well as "thirty-odd fiddlers from all over the state." "Little Willie" of Blount County was the featured fiddler. Opening night brought a record midweek crowd to the park, and the fiddling contest reportedly "brought down the house." On Friday night, attendance doubled. The contest ended Saturday night, however, with no report to the newspaper naming the champion fiddler of Alabama.[156]

A much more impressive fiddlers' convention had been held in Birmingham earlier in the year under the auspices of the Nathan Bedford Forrest Klan. Though it did not claim to be a championship contest, it attracted some of Alabama's and Georgia's finest fiddlers. Announcements promised a "unique affair," organized by an unidentified "expert in affairs of these kinds." The fiddling contests were to be divided into several classes, such as old-time jigs and breakdowns, old Southern melodies, folk music, and patriotic airs. A month prior to the event, a large announcement of the contest appeared in the Birmingham papers, offering $500 in cash prizes and providing a registration form.

Three days before the convention, the sponsors announced that over one hundred applications had been received but only fiddlers with a reputation had been accepted, among them Robert M. Stanley, who had recently played on Radio Station WSB in Atlanta; Kit Tanner [probably Gid Tanner] of Dacula, Georgia; Homer Davenport of Cannon Creek, Tennessee; and Joseph C. Glasscock of Steppville, Alabama.[157]

According to the *Birmingham Age-Herald*, 3,500 people attended the Wednesday-night convention. Y. Z. Hamilton was awarded the first prize of $100 in gold; A. A. Gray, a champion fiddler of Georgia, received $75, and Earl Johnson, a well-known trick fiddler and recording artist from Georgia won the third prize of $50. Five others, all top fiddlers in their home counties, received $25 each. They were W. A. Meek of Birmingham, Cliff Click of Bessemer, D. S. McKee of Notasulga, Charlie Stripling of Kennedy, and E. D. Brown of Tuscaloosa.[158]

Large fiddlers' conventions continued to be held each spring at the Birmingham Municipal Auditorium. They received no mention in the Birmingham newspapers, but were remembered by fiddlers who participated in them. Jack Jackson of Huntsville and Olen Mayes of Short Creek recalled the convention of 1926 at which they received prizes. In 1927 the *Tuscaloosa News* printed an article with a Birmingham dateline about the "Southern Championship" to be held April 21–23, at which A. A. Gray, champion of Georgia; E. E.

Announcement for a fiddlers' convention, which appeared in the *Birmingham Age-Herald* on January 25, 1925. Photo courtesy of the *Birmingham Post-Herald*.

Akins of Birmingham; and the Gibbs Brothers of Huntsville, champion string band of the South, would compete.[159] The 1928 contest was attended by Jimmie Porter, who recalled placing second to Clayton McMichen. W. A. Bryan remembered driving from Boaz to Birmingham in 1929 to see Bud Silvey win the Southeastern Championship.[160] It is not known if these contests were sponsored by the Klan, the Old Fiddlers' Association of Alabama, or by individual promoters. However, the fact that conventions attracting the best-known fiddlers of the South continued, without notice in the state's largest newspapers, speaks of a strong network of fiddlers, linked by mail and possibly by a state fiddlers' association.

Championships at the State Capital. Montgomery was the site of two highly publicized Georgia-Alabama championships in December 1926 and April 1927. The first of these featured some of the most popular country recording artists of the day: Fiddlin' John Carson, Riley Puckett, and Clayton McMichen. Sponsored by the American Legion, the competitions were promoted by "Tanks" Grantham, who had more experience in promoting boxing matches than in fiddle conventions. In one press release he confused Clayton McMichen with Riley Puckett and wrote of a famous blind fiddler, Clayton McKibben, who had won great ovations in all parts of the South.[161] Grantham promised to furnish "a real high class musical bill interspersed with features which are sure to please."[162] These included singing by the featured performers, violin "wrestling" by Charles Loche of Columbus, who played the instrument in all conceivable positions, music by S. L. Norris, who played six instruments at the same time, and an old-fashioned square dance to end the convention.

Grantham's December contest followed a similar Georgia-Alabama competition held in Columbus two weeks earlier. R. L. Stephens of Camp Hill, who won fourth place, was the only Alabama fiddler known to have entered, and Georgia fiddler Clayton Mc-Michen won the title.[163] In Montgomery, McMichen won again, with second place going to J. P. Powell of Tallassee and third place to Charles Loche of Columbus. The following April, Grantham made much of the Georgia-Alabama competition, noting that Georgia fiddlers were coming "to show Alabama Bow Wielders a trick or two." He wrote, "Georgia fiddlers declare that they will take the championship badge back to that state, while Alabamians assume a 'show me' attitude." Among the Georgia musicians said to have entered were Gid Tanner, Riley Puckett, Lowe Stokes, and Fate Norris, none of whom are mentioned in press reports that followed. The convention attracted popular fiddlers from central and southeast Alabama, and they took home the prizes. J. R. Powell became champion fiddler of Georgia and Alabama; D. S. McKee of Notasulga took second place, and A. E. James of Newville, third.[164]

The "National" Championship. Highly promoted conventions like those held at East Lake and in Montgomery in the 1920s were predecessors of commercial fiddlers' contests held across the United States in the late 1930s under the sponsorship of Larry Sunbrock, a promoter of country-music extravaganzas. While Sunbrock used many techniques over the years to draw large crowds, his most successful promotion was the series of national-championship fiddlers' conventions he created.

Sunbrock chose Lester Vernon Storer, a three-quarters Shawnee Indian from Adams County, Ohio, to be his champion fiddler.[165] Called "Natchee the Indian" and "Natchee the Apache,"[166] Storer was a handsome young man who performed in Indian regalia: braids, headband, and fringed jacket. Whether he was a great fiddler is subject to debate. Some, such as the promoter "Happy" Hal Burns, considered him the best, while others thought he was overrated. Dick

Vance wrote that while Natchee played, he would give a blood-curdling screech which covered his lack of ability and helped him win the contest.[167] Curly Fox remembered that Natchee had a pleasing style but knew only about ten tunes.[168]

Sunbrock's "Radio Stars Jamboree," which included "Grand Ole Opry" performers such as Uncle Dave Macon, the Delmore Brothers, De Ford Bailey, and Sarie and Sally, would feature a fiddlers' competition between Natchee and the best-known fiddler of the region. In Ohio this was Clayton McMichen,[169] in Texas it was Bob Wills or Cliff Bruner, and in Alabama it was Curly Fox.[170] Born in Rhea County, Tennessee, Fox had frequently visited relatives in Birmingham as a young man and regularly played for local radio stations. With the help of Clayton McMichen, Fox won a contract with Sunbrock to do a series of tours in which he would challenge Natchee. The contract specified that because he was on a salary, he would be ineligible for prize money.[171]

The first competition in Birmingham took place at the Temple Theater on April 24, 1938. It was billed as the official 1938 Alabama championship event sponsored by the National Fiddlers' Association. Advertisements promised a fiddlers' contest including Natchee, the national champion; Curly Fox, the Southern champion; and twenty-four other fiddlers.[172] Including local fiddlers on the program meant selling more tickets, for each tended to bring his own rooting section to help budge the applause meter in his direction.[173]

When the first championship contest filled the 3,000-seat theater during matinee and evening performances, Sunbrock scheduled a similar event, to be held a month later at the larger municipal auditorium. This time it was announced that hundreds of Alabama fiddlers were expected to compete for the Southern championship.[174]

Both events were similar in format. During the matinee, local fiddlers were given approximately a minute apiece to show their skills, and as time ran out, the remaining fiddlers played in groups. Invariably the applause meter would indicate that Fox was the fiddler chosen to take on Natchee the Indian. The two then would throw themselves into intricate versions of "Listen to the Mockingbird," "Black Mountain Rag," and other crowd-pleasing tunes. Despite Fox's popularity, Natchee would be declared winner of the match. Unable to take defeat graciously, Fox would vow to win the evening's contest. Once, in his outrage over the decision, Fox smashed his prized $3 "Stradivarius," which Sunbrock had purchased for the occasion. That evening a packed house would witness

Fox's victory over the national champion. Any other outcome would have been impossible, given Fox's immense popularity with the Birmingham audience.[175]

Sunbrock's staged competitions were glorious entertainment. For a charge of 25¢ to 40¢, the audiences heard good fiddling in the exciting context of a fiddlers' convention. Local fiddlers had the opportunity to perform on the stage with national stars, and members of the audience were allowed to express their opinions on the outcome. The fact that it had been decided beforehand did not diminish their enjoyment. The 1938 Natchee the Indian–Curly Fox matches are still remembered with pleasure by fiddlers across north and central Alabama who traveled to Birmingham to take part in them.

Fiddlers' Conventions Reborn. Sunbrock's national-championship contests were cashing in on the enormous popularity of fiddlers' conventions during the 1930s. As interest in old-time fiddling diminished in the years following World War II, however, the popularity of conventions naturally declined. Not only were there fewer fiddlers to participate in them, but also there were fewer places and reasons to have them. The small community schools that had sponsored the bulk of fiddlers' conventions had largely vanished, their students now riding school buses to large county schools that did not so badly need nor inspire fund-raising efforts. By the time the folk revival of the late 1960s reawakened interest in the old music, few fiddle conventions were being held in the state. Yet they had not been forgotten.

With the successful revival of the contest at Athens in 1969, fans of traditional music began to remember old contests in their communities and to establish new ones. Decatur, Troy, Grant, Brilliant, Fairhope, Jasper, and hundreds of other communities across Alabama began to hold fiddlers' conventions once again. John Callahan, whose brother A. K. chaired small schoolhouse conventions in the 1920s around Tuscaloosa, began organizing conventions in 1971 and continued to do so until his death in 1981 at the age of 86. Held in shopping malls, which had replaced schoolhouses and courthouses as community gathering places, Callahan's contests gave young shoppers in such cities as Selma, Huntsville, Tuscaloosa, and Birmingham their first taste of traditional fiddle music.[176] The new conventions inspired fiddlers who had been champions in the earlier round of contests to bring out fiddles they had not played in a decade, flex stiffened fingers, and compete once more. They inspired young men and women who liked what they heard to take up the instrument.

Lacking the small schoolhouse conventions that once took place all over the state, today's fiddler cannot compete four nights a week as Bob Kyle did in the thirties; yet there are enough contests held in Alabama and surrounding states that a fiddler who is willing to drive long distances can attend one almost every weekend during the spring, summer, and early fall. Thus, modern fiddle contests are no longer local entertainments whose contestants know each other and their audiences well. They are no longer antic-filled, "side-splitting" affairs in which the fiddler's personality and circumstances are as important as his playing. Instead, most organizers attempt to run straightforward competitions, barring trick fiddling and supplying judges with written critera by which to evaluate the fiddlers. This, of course, affects the music—and performance. Fiddlers concentrating on pleasing a panel of judges with pencils poised above score sheets play differently than they would, were they before a crowd of foot-stomping neighbors.

Today, at the larger contests which attract participants from across the nation, one often hears a "contest" style of fiddling, in which the fiddler plays more slowly and distinctly, developing interesting and technically challenging variations to the basic melody. He strives for smoothness, creativity, and a good tone. This is a change from the older days in which most fiddlers had served apprenticeships at weekly square dances. There, to win approval, they had to develop a driving and vigorous bowing style. Fiddlers who now play only for seated audiences strive for virtuosity, and in the process often slight the vitality, the "toe-tappingness" of the music. One rarely sees old men spring from their chairs to buck-dance to their favorite hoedown as was common at the old-style conventions where fiddlers applied elbow grease in profusion.

Many of the older fiddlers interviewed for this book believe contest fiddling is much better than that which they heard as children. Others complain that modern contest fiddlers take too many liberties with the old tunes and play them too slowly. Yet both the admirers and detractors of modern fiddling attend the competitions, to play in gatherings far from the stage, if not to enter them. W. V. Jacoway wrote in 1924: "It matters not how hot or how cold, how wet or how dry, a fiddler is bound to fiddle and of all the things these old fiddlers like best, it is to get mixed up in a fiddlers' convention."[177] Today's large contests are vastly different from those conducted by Jacoway, yet they continue to be the best places for fiddlers to meet their colleagues, and to trade instruments, tunes, and memories. Fiddlers' conventions still play a crucial role in the perpetuation of old-time music.

5

FIDDLING AND ASSOCIATED SINS

The Fiddler's Image

Brown's Valley in the 1830s was a land, wrote John Gorman Barr, where "white people of a restless and roving class . . . took up their abode," making it "a school for fraud, violence, and theft."[1]

A leading spirit, at the time we chronicle, in the valley, was Major Dempsey Crafts, against whom the tongue of malice could maintain no other charges than that he was most sinfully and perseveringly inclined to fiddling, drinking, and practical joking—accomplishments which rendered him extremely popular throughout the *reserve*, and made his presence absolutely indispensable at the frolic, the hunt, the horse-race, and the house-raising.[2]

The situation in Randolph County was about the same: "Up to 1860 Roanoke was the fighting place of bullies on Saturdays," wrote General B. F. Weathers for the *Roanoke Leader*. "Rus Duke was the Captain of the Jackson Allen Company. Ike Broughton was Captain of the High Pine Co. The two companies would meet in Roanoke on Saturday, drink, fiddle and dance until about 3 p.m.," and then break into fighting.[3]

In the more genteel society of St. Clair County at the turn of the century, the potential for disorder remained. Mattie Lou Teague Crow wrote that the young people of Ashville met at St. Clair Springs to dance and flirt, accompanied by "old folks [who] carried food, shotguns, fiddles, and moonshine."[4]

In the three quotations above, in old folk expressions and tales, as well as in contemporary music and literature, the fiddle has commonly been associated with mischief, moonshine, and shotguns. It has been called the "devil's box," and the expression "as thick as fiddlers in hell"[5] has been used to describe an abundance of something undesirable, such as mosquitoes. In folklore, Satan himself is a fiddler, who will meet aspiring musicians at any crossroads and teach them to play. His students become virtuosos at the cost of their souls. While this belief is usually attributed to Southern blacks, it has roots in European and British folklore, and variations of it have been found among people of various races, economic classes, and geographical regions. Folklorist Herbert Halpert wrote of a white, classically trained musician from Illinois whose uncle had told him "the Devil was in the fiddle." In New Jersey, Halpert heard the legend that "The Devil's Dream," a popular fiddle tune, had been composed by Satan himself. Halpert observed in McKinney and Anderson's *Music in History* (1940) that the violinist Niccolò Paganini (1782–1840) "was thought by even sane-minded people to have been taught to play by the Devil."[6]

In Alabama, humorist Francis Bartow Lloyd of Butler County played upon the concept of the Devil as fiddler in one of his *Sketches of Country Life* (1898):

DANCED OUT OF THE PULPIT

I reckon maybe you have all heard tell of the brethren and sisters and sometimes the deacons and elders, dancing themselves out of the church. But the Rev. Zeb Newton was the first and onliest preacher that I ever heard of dancing himself out of the pulpit. Now, in his young days Zeb had been a fiddler, and as old Mart Mayo says in regard to Daniel Webster, "he drug a right nasty bow, too."

Well, one day whilst out ridin his circuit Zeb met a man in the road and the man turned out to be a fiddler; and when Zeb started in to talk religion with him the stranger pulled his fiddle and tuned up and went to fiddlin. Zeb held forth at old Snake Hill church the next Sunday, and indurin of his sermont he tried to tell the dyin congregation about the fiddler and his fiddle, and still he didn't want to come right out and talk too plain about it. So he went on at it sorter this away:

"I was ridin along the other day—er, and I met up with a wicked man—er, and he was totin a little, long, black box—er, under his arm—er, and it looks like a coffin—er, but it want no coffin—er, and he took somethin out of that little, long, black box—er, about the color of a red rooster cock—er, and he twisted

her years—er, and she says cling, clang, clung, clung—er, and
he drug a long stick acrost her bosom—er, and she says, says
she—er:

> Some loves a gal that pritty in the face,
> But I love a gal that little in the waist,
> Put it in the bandbox, save it, save it,
> Put it in the bandbox, save it till I come."

And the next thing anybody knew Zeb was knockin the back-
step and cuttin the pigeon wing to beat bobtail right there in
the pulpit. It seems like the recollections of that good fiddle
music must of took him back to old times, and he forgot all
about what he was doin and where he was at. He danced around
at such a lively lick till presently he fell backwards out the pulpit
and kicked up a terrible rumpus and confusionment.

The brethren then took and put their heads together and called
a church meetin for that evenin and turned the preacher out to
run with the goats and dry cattle. Zeb he went on down from
bad to worse after that, and it want so very long before we got
the news that he was runnin for office over in Tucker's Mill
beat.

But whilst preachers are but only human flesh and blood and
bones like the rest of us, still they are the salt of the earth, and
the yaller-leg chickens will always roost low when they come
and put up at my house.[7]

The "man in the road" was surely Satan, who was able to silence
Zeb's religious talk by pulling his fiddle out of a coffin-like case,
seductively drawing the bow over "her bosom," and having her sing
a suggestive song. Zeb was unchurched for dancing at the pulpit,
but it was the "devil's box," not the dance, that initiated his down-
fall.

Lloyd also described the plight of Newt Callins, another fiddler:

Newt was about the sorriest white man that ever made a track
or flung a card in the settlement. The boys use to say he was a
fiddler from Fiddler's Green,* and he did drag a right nasty bow.
He could play the fiddle and sing funny songs and swap horses
and tell smutty yarns, but that was about all. He didn't take to
work a single bit, sayin how he was a born genius and didn't
have to work. He was also a natural born loafer. He want worth

his weight in sap saw dust, and the general wonderment was that he could have the big lazies continually all the time and still keep out of the poor house.[8]

Eventually Newt's wife turned him out and, like Zeb Newton, he "went on from bad to worse":

> From playin the fiddle and playin cards, he got to drinkin very hard and lyin and stealin, and playin the devil in generally. The last time I heard from him he had jined the chain gang for ridin off on a horse that belongs to some other man, and if he has ever unjined himself, its more than I know.[9]

In 1977 the novel *Whiskey Man*, by Howell Raines, depicted a fiddler who was no better than Callins. General Drummond drifted about the hills of north Alabama, playing for dances of the moonshine and fighting sort, and courted the spinster of Milo community though he was already married to two women in other counties.[10]

The Fiddler and the Church

Though few people actually believe "the devil rides a fiddle bow" and most have known fiddlers who were as sober and upstanding as the day is long, the stereotype of the fiddler as rowdy and hell-prone still exists. The sermons of fire-and-brimstone preachers have helped to keep it alive.

At the heart of the teachings of most Southern churches is the belief that one must reject the things of this world in order to find salvation. While there are intellectual sins to worry about, such as pride in one's possessions and attainments, ministers have often concentrated on such activities as drinking, card-playing, gambling, dancing, and music-making. In the frontier days, wrote Dickson D. Bruce, Jr., in *And They All Sang Hallelujah*, preachers condemned those popular recreations for symbolic as well as practical reasons. By abstaining from them, believers were able to demonstrate to others "the force of their beliefs in their daily lives."[11] Fiddlers who had been converted were expected to give up their instruments or at least to stop playing secular music; those who did not were subject to the disapproval of other Christians in the community.

Fiddle tunes could be put to higher uses, however. George Pullen Jackson wrote, "Fiddles and all that went with them were generally taboo with religious folk. But the fiddle tunes were too good to

Duke and Tom Kimbrough of Franklin County, ca. 1910. The brothers played for dances until Tom, the fiddler, became a Methodist minister and stopped playing anything except sacred music. Photo courtesy of Chuck Carpenter.

remain the exclusive employ of the devil, and all it took to bring such tunes into books of 'sacred' song was a set of religious words." For instance, "Fisher's Hornpipe," a favorite at fiddlers' conventions, became "The Old-Fashioned Bible" in the *Sacred Harp* hymnal.[12] In turn, fiddlers transformed *Sacred Harp* hymns into fiddle tunes, the anthem "Murillo's Lesson" being a favorite of fiddlers across Alabama.

Some believers saw nothing wrong with fiddling, but were concerned with its associated sins—gambling, drinking, fighting, dancing, and desecrating the Sabbath. For where there was fiddling, the other activities were likely to be as well, tempting the fiddler to go "from bad to worse." He might start with the sin of fiddling on the Sabbath. Churches taught that Sunday should be set aside for rest, meditation, and the study of God's word. Preachers warned against excessive cooking, dining, visiting, and buggy riding on Sunday.[13] The *Alabama Baptist* in 1887 even condemned the Sunday operation of trains, bakeries, and drugstores.[14] Yet musical gatherings on front porches and in backyards on Sunday afternoons were common. Sunday was considered the best day for fiddling, and those who refrained for religious reasons were rare.

A much more serious concern, however, was the proximity of fiddlers to liquor. Captain W. L. Fagan illustrated this proximity strikingly in an anecdote in his "History of Marion, 1818–'35." Leaders of Marion (Perry County) had borrowed a cannon from the town of Cahaba in order to properly celebrate the Fourth of July. After the official ceremony, revellers assembled at the grocery store. "The fiddler, perched on one end of the counter, discoursed sweet strains of music, while the 'boys' made the log cabin quiver with their 'pigeon wings' and 'double shuffles.' " Outside the cannon thundered, fed by a drunken cannoneer. Morning sun revealed that a discharge had destroyed part of the store's gable and roof. "The revellers never discovered the catastrophe, neither did the fiddler miss a single note of his tune, nor the dancers lose one step in their wild quadrilles."[15]

Whether they partook or not, fiddlers were invited to play at parties and dances where whiskey flowed freely. Some gatherings were sponsored by moonshiners to promote their goods, others by people who simply enjoyed drinking as they danced. In the 1930s, Tom Sutton of Athens was paid $1 an hour to play at dances of the latter kind before his conscience began to bother him:

> You know, whiskey and music and women go together. So these people had the dances at one of their homes. Whenever

I'd get there, I'd tell them I'm not going to drink. They'd say, "We know you don't drink, but if you take a notion, here it is" . . . They was always nice. They didn't get drunk. Just drank a little . . . But I really believe that the Bible teaches against drink. I had quit it but still I was going and associating with the people that was drinking. So the Bible says to shun all appearance of evil. And I was sitting there playing. Doesn't that seem evil to you? My conscience wouldn't let me; that's the reason I had to quit it.[16]

Others imbibed freely at dances and fiddlers' conventions. Monk Daniels of Sand Mountain recalled winning an important convention with the help of half a pint of confiscated whiskey that a sheriff brought from his office:

I drank half of it . . . and just before I went to play—there was just one ahead of me—I drank the other half. I went on and played and didn't see nobody, but when it was over I was surprised that they gave me first prize . . . White lightning give me a lift, and I had a nerve. That's what it done—give me a nerve.[17]

Fiddlers who played for dances and other entertainments at which drinking was allowed were also likely to be associated with brawling. Vearl Cicero remembered a "free-for-all" at a dance hall. Someone was hit on the head with a banjo and "it went down around his neck like a tie."[18] The *Cullman Democrat* in 1925 reported on a dance, in a community known as "Rough Edge" among local officers, where one man killed another in a quarrel over a girl. In 1936, a headline in the *Sand Mountain Banner* read, "Youth Meets Death at Dance," and many county newspapers contained similar reports over the years.[19] Such incidents were rare at the home dances for which most fiddlers played, however. Said Gaines Arnold:

Just every once in a while, some fellow would come in a'drinking something. Around these families, we didn't have that. The man of the house would get up and tell them that they was welcome to have a good time, only they wouldn't have no drinking or fighting, and if they came in drinking, they'd just have to put them out. And they would—several of the men would get them and take them off.[20]

Even if a fiddler played only at respectable family dances, he was bound to displease some members of the community. Dancing was a controversial subject, the topic of countless sermons, newspaper editorials, and debates between neighbors. In the 1840s, Betsy Hamilton (Idora McClelland Moore) of Talladega presented the argument in dialect:

> Ole Mis' Freshours is plum agin' dancin'. She crossed her knees, give a big spit o' snuff over in the fire, and said in a religious tone:
> "Ah, Laws! All them ken dance that thinks thar hain't no fire an' brimstone hereafter. Ah, Laws! I thank my stairs dancin' is one sin I won't have to account fer."
> Mis' Green had jes' filled her pipe, an' lit it with a coal o'fire. She said:
> "I wish I had as many dollars as I have danced till atter midnight. An' I'd a sight druther my gals would dance as to play them kissin' games; but I don't see no harm in nairy one."[21]

Mrs. Green and Mrs. Freshours were discussing a square dance that was in progress next door: "The fiddler had come, an' dancin' was gwine on in t'other house. We could hear Iky Roberson's big mouth callin' the dance: 'Balance all! Swing corners! All promenade!' "[22]

Had the dance been a "round dance," with the gentlemen's arm encircling his partner's waist, even Mrs. Green would have been opposed. Until the 1930s, most country people considered these dances immodest and scandalous. Sam Jones, the "mountain evangelist," described them as "hugging set to music."[23] In 1900, those with any doubts about the issue could send 25¢ in stamps to *The Petitioner* of Fruitdale, Alabama, and receive *From the Ball-Room to Hell*, a book explaining "the natural and necessary effects of modern waltzing and why thousands of girls are ruined every year through its influence."[24]

Some believed that round dancing was respectable as long as certain limits were observed. The Hayneville Dancing Club in 1913 condemned the "Turkey Trot" and voted to forbid all dances except the waltz and the two-step, though two members stated there was no harm in the tango "as long as it is not carried to extremes."[25]

Compared with turkey trots and tangos, the old-fashioned square dances seemed innocent amusements, yet to some they were the first step on the road to damnation. The Reverend Fred D. Hale wrote in the *Alabama Baptist* (1887): "A member of the church who dances becomes an ally of the world, and joins in its most cherished amusement . . . I do not mean only the round dances, for the square dances in your parlors, participated in by both classes, lead many in [to] the public halls."[26]

Hale explained that the peril of any sort of dance was its accompaniment. "The stirring music, the intense excitement, the frivolous crowd, the nervous exhilaration, the display of form and dress, the physical contact, etc., make the dance a foe to Christianity, and in many cases even to morality." Such incitements were present at home dances as well as at public dance halls, and "a very large per cent of fallen women do not hesitate to attribute their career to the influence first of all, of the social dance in their own or their neighbor's parlor."[27]

Thus many parents forbade their children to participate in any type of dancing. However, an occasional game set to music was acceptable. In some communities, the Virginia reel was allowed. Though actually an English country dance, it was lively, simple, and old, and had attained the status of a folk game. "Twistification" was also permitted. Mitchell B. Garrett remembered doing it as a child in Hatchet Creek (Clay County):

> A good game with which to end the party, around ten or eleven o'clock, was "Twistification," which bore some resemblance to dancing; but of course it could not be called dancing, because in our community the Terpsichorean art was severely frowned upon and denounced as a cardinal sin. All that "Twistification" amounted to was a spirited romp around the room, with boy swinging girl, and vice versa, first on one arm and then on the other.[28]

Eddie Rozelle, also of Hatchet Creek, stated that the games were often accompanied by fiddle and banjo music, but if they began to seem too much like dances, "they would be called to a halt by the parents."[29] Byron Johnson remembered a "game" that ended abruptly on Sand Moutain:

> The Methodist preacher had a sorghum mill to make syrup. And he decided one summer to have an old-time Virginia reel at his house. So they [the Johnson Family Band] went to play the music and the dancers lined up on both sides of the room and they started the old-time Virginia reel. And they had a candy pulling—they cooked the candy on the syrup pans and pulled the candy.
> A Virginia reel was fine; it was more like playing a game, but one thing led to another and first thing you know, it turned into a regular square dance. So the preacher stopped the music right

in the middle and said they was going to have to quit. It'd turned into a dance.

And one of the leading doctors in Albertville . . . walked out into the floor and said if he didn't want the peas to boil, he shouldn't have put them in the pot.[30]

While the preacher had pure intentions in sponsoring his Virginia reel, Francis Bartow Lloyd hinted that not everyone did. In "Takin Christmas With the Boys," Aunt Nancy Newton allowed a dance in her front yard with the following words:

> If you boys want to git up a dance here it is perfectly all right with me . . . You don't have to work up no weddin match in orderment to dance here, and you needn't to put it out that we are goin to have a candy pullin, and then run it into a dance. No sailin under false colors around Nancy Newton's, if you please. Get your fiddlers and sweep the floor and choose your partners and pitch in and dance.[31]

Nancy Newton's nephews were more discreet than she, however. Lloyd continued:

> . . . in the hopes of keepin Aunt Nancy out of a church rucus, we took good pains to make that dance a strictly family affair. Everybody there that night was kin folks to Aunt Nancy, and we had a plenty for two full sets and some to spare.[32]

A "church rucus," such as the Newton kin sought to avoid, was a serious affair. One seen dancing or violating any other church strictures, would, according to Mitchell Garrett, be asked "to come before the brethren and sisters in conference assembled and make a full confession of his guilt and a solemn promise to mend his ways." If he persisted in sin, he would thereafter be "turned out of the church."[33] Church records of the nineteenth century abound in references to members who were reprimanded by their congregations for dancing. In Bibb County, three women who confessed to the Pleasant Hill Cumberland Presbyterian Church that they had participated in a dance were placed on probation,[34] and a man was suspended from the Geneva Church in south Alabama "for falling into the sin of dancing on an Episcopalian steamboat excursion."[35] Two young women of Cook Springs, site of a fashionable turn-of-the-century watering hole, were called before the Mount Pleasant Church because they had been observed at the dance pavilion. They had gone to watch in astonishment the first waltzing done in their community.[36] It is difficult to find cases in which people have been "unchurched" for fiddling, probably because confirmed fiddlers did not join congregations that forbade their favorite activity, yet it is certain that those who played for dances were condemned as severely as those who danced at them.

In the twentieth century, cases of church discipline of any sort grew rarer, but ministers did not relent in their attack on dancing. Sermons with titles such as "The Dance of Death"[37] were popular at summer tent revivals. Young people who had heard such sermons all their lives attended dances anyway, filled with thrill and dread. According to Eddie Rozelle of Hatchet Creek, "Occasionally someone who did not feel dancing was sinful would dare hold a dance. Should any of the girls attend, they would have to slip out risking reprisal from their parents. Some of the boys, including myself, often slipped away to the back sections of the community and danced with girls out of our circle who were allowed to attend. This was risky business, for boys in that section often resented outsiders coming in and trouble ensued."[38]

W. P. Wilkes of Pike County, knowing that "every youth was expected to 'sow his wild oats' before being accounted a man," found square dances more fertile grounds than other forbidden activities. He hated the taste of whiskey, he was a poor gambler, smoking made him ill, and he feared catching a disease from carousing among houses of ill repute:

> That left only one field for my orgy of wild oat sowing. I began going to the "breakdowns," politely known as dances. With lumbering feet I would prance around the circle stumbling in and out the weaving lines, vigorously swinging this partner and that with toil hardened hands attached to long awkward arms. Practice failed to bring me anywhere near perfection. I was never complimented for being light on my feet or other than heavy on those of a hapless partner who fearfully accepted my bid for a set. But the feral seed were scattered without serious injury to myself or any one else.[39]

Wilkes survived his brief encounter with square dancing and eventually became a respected Baptist minister and scholar.

Not all denominations proscribed dancing. In Marengo County, Episcopalians were known to dance at church entertainments.[40] Others forbade dancing, but found fiddling fully acceptable. Some congregations had enough confidence in their ability to withstand temptation that they actually sponsored fiddlers' conventions. At the turn of the century, the Baptist Ladies of Jackson were putting on annual conventions, and other Clarke County churches, such as the Whatley Baptist and the Centerline Baptist Church of Nettleboro, carried the tradition into the 1930s. The Baptist Young People of Holt in Tuscaloosa County were known to sponsor conventions in the 1920s, as was the Methodist Church of Clanton.[41]

In general, it seems that both secular music and dancing were acceptable in the early days of the Alabama territory prior to the organization of churches; they were condemned in the latter part of the nineteenth century, and they became acceptable once more in the twentieth century. Yet, at any given time in Alabama history, there have been proponents of fiddling but not dancing, square dancing but not round dancing, fiddling of sacred music but not secular, and on and on. In modern society, the evils of dancing and fiddle playing are the least of our worries, yet some fundamental religious sects are holding the line. It has not been too many years since a minister in Russellville told Ed Rickard, "If you belonged to my church, you'd have to put that fiddle under the bed and leave it there."[42]

Alabama Fiddle Lore

Besides being part of the humorous "local color" writings of Betsy Hamilton, John Gorman Barr, and Francis Bartow Lloyd, and the stern anti-dance sermons of evangelists, fiddlers have found themselves the subjects of ghost tales and frightening stories.

Since 1858, people in Coffee County have spoken of the "Dancing Ghost." In *Pea River Reflections*, Judge Marion Brunson explains that William "Grand-sir" Harrison was so fond of dancing that he built a fine dance hall to which he invited hundreds of guests. When he grew old, he ordered that his grave be placed near the dance hall, so that after he died he might still hear dance music. "Without his magnificent presence," wrote Brunson, the hall fell into disuse—to the disappointment of Harrison's ghost, which still haunts the site. Those traveling near it on Saturday night have reported hearing "fiddling tunes and the sound of dancing clogs."[43]

Ghostly fiddling has also been heard in the Chancellor community of Geneva County. There a home dance abruptly ended with the killing of a rowdy intruder. Everyone who attempted to live in the home, thereafter, was driven away by the sound of fiddling which would begin in ordinary fashion but suddenly cease, as though to remind inhabitants of the violent death which had occurred there. Eventually the abandoned house was moved to a new location and turned into a barn. One day as a group of women sat in the barn, picking off peanuts to be used for seed, they suddenly heard fiddle music drifting from under the peanuts. According to Brunson, two of the women ran away, but the rest continued "listening to the fiddling tunes until the eerie notes stopped just as suddenly and mysteriously as they had started."[44]

Fiddlers were likely subjects for scary stories because they often traveled alone late at night after playing for dances. In *"A Night with the Hants" And Other Alabama Folk Experiences*, collected and edited by Ray B. Browne, Cora Lee Pennington of Fernbank (Lamar County) told of a fiddler whose instrument protected him from harm as he traveled home after a dance:

> . . . he had quite a distance to come by himself, and there were wolves in that country. When he got about half way home, he heard a pack of wolves coming on his track. Well, it scared him so bad he didn't know what to do. But he saw an old house off to the side of the road, and he went up to that. And most of the boards were off the side of it, so he just climbed up on the frame of the house. And the wolves was just right behind him. So he just climbed up there and sat down. And he said: "Well, I know that I've not got but a little while to live, and I'm going to play my violin one more time." And the wolves was just all around him trying to get up. So he started playing his violin, and all the wolves just ran away. The violin excited them, and they ran off. And he got down and went on home.[45]

Essie Agee of Clarke County related a favorite family story about her father, a square dance fiddler:

> My father had been fiddling for a dance one night. Along about midnight he was coming home, when it started getting real cloudy, and pretty soon it started to rain. Well, about this time he was close to an old hanted house, so he decided to go in and wait until the rain was over. He knew that there wasn't such things as hants anyway, and so he wasn't afraid. Well, he got in the house and sat down to wait until the rain was over. He hadn't much more than got set down when in came a couple of the boys that had been at the dance. Soon as they got in one of them said: "Now if you hear the old devil playing in here we'll get out, and get out fast." When the fiddler heard this, he decided

to have some fun out of the boys, so he slowly and quietly took
his fiddle out of the case and cut loose on a lively tune. Well,
those boys were right. They did get out and get out fast. They
got out so fast, that the fiddler never did know exactly how they
done it.[46]

Thus, in Clarke County in the twentieth century there were at
least two young men who firmly believed that the devil was a fiddler.
Perhaps they had slipped away to attend a forbidden dance and on
the way home were worrying about the consequences of their deed.
With the flames of hell already on their minds, it took only a few
notes from a roguish fiddler to show them the error of their ways.
How many other fiddlers have played ghostly music near the Harrison cemetery on Saturday nights or fiddled abruptly ending tunes
in the Chancellor community to keep the old tales alive?

Because of the way he has been presented in folklore, popular
literature, and religious teachings, "the typical fiddler" is likely to
be thought of as a mischievous, whiskey-drinking ne'er-do-well,
more attentive to his fiddling than to his wife and children. Some
of Alabama's fiddlers did their best to live up to that stereotype.
Others, like D. Dix Hollis, were pillars of the community and
church, who could dismiss criticism with the words: "It was music
that moved the Evil spirit from King Saul."[47] As we have seen
throughout this book, there is no typical fiddler. Probably the only
characteristic that fiddlers of the past held in common was their
willingness to take chances with the Hereafter, if necessary, in order
to continue playing the fiddle.

While most communities in Alabama had those who demonstrated the strength of their religion by shunning dances and other
frivolous entertainments, there were few in which the fiddler was
totally stifled. If old newspapers, local history writings, and memories serve correctly, there have always been enough people of other
persuasions to keep fiddlers busy playing for weddings, dances, benefits, barbecues, reunions, ice-cream suppers, medicine shows, land
auctions, political rallies, fiddlers' conventions, and other social
events that were part of community life in Alabama prior to World
War II.

OLD-TIME TUNES
PLAYED IN ALABAMA

In the mid-1920s the commercial recording of old-time fiddlers enabled tunes to be introduced into areas where they had never been played before, bringing a degree of standardization to repertoires across the country. This list attempts to document tunes that may have been common in Alabama prior to the growth of the recording industry.

The following were mentioned in newspaper articles and books in which the writers were recalling tunes of earlier days or giving examples of old-time tunes.

Northwest Alabama

Tunes listed in the *Northwest Alabamian* (Fayette), 29 August, 1929, as those likely to be played at a convention where "the veil of the past will be lifted, permitting those present a vision of the pictures on memory's wall, as they unfold to the touch of the old-time fiddler":

Leather Breeches	Sallie Goodin
Billy in the Low Ground	Lost John
Polly Ann	Big Footed Sorrel
Pop Goes the Weasel	Give the Fiddler a Dram
Old Hen Cackle	Dixie
Fisher's Hornpipe	Four Cent Cotton
Sugar in the Gourd	Possum up a Gum Stump

Tunes listed as examples of acceptable old-time numbers for a fiddlers' convention in Fayette (*Northwest Alabamian*, 4 September 1930):

Turkey in the Straw	Billie in the Low Grounds
Lazy Kate	

Tunes listed in "Fiddler's Jubilee," Fayette County (*Fayette Banner*, 2 January 1908):

Lexington on a Bum
Great Big Taters on Sandy Land
Come out girls and dance by the light of the moon (a line from "Alabama Gals")

Tunes considered "the good old tunes of long ago" by D. Dix Hollis of Lamar County, as listed in the *Opelika Daily News* (17 April 1926):

Billie in the Lowground	Turkey in the Straw
Leather Breeches	Gray Eagle
Dixie	Bonnie Blue Flag
Hoplight Ladies	None Greater than Lincoln
Lone Indian	Sallie in the Wildwood
Mocking Bird	

Tunes listed in the *Tuscaloosa News* (28 March 1971) as specialties of "Monkey" Brown of Tuscaloosa, who was active at contests in the 1920s and '30s:

Pop Goes the Weasel	Drunkard's Hiccups
Leather Britches	Wolves A'Howling

Tunes listed in "A Preliminary Survey of Folk-Lore in Alabama," a master's thesis by S. M. Taylor, University of Alabama, 1925:

Lost Child	I'll Never Drink Any More
Hen Cackle	Clucking Hen
Devil's Hiccough	Arkansas Traveler
Ole Time Sorghum Mill	Turkey in the Straw
Wolves A'Howling	

Tunes mentioned in newspaper articles about Tom Freeman of Cullman County and in his autobiography:

Carry Me Back to Georgia to Eat Cornbread and 'Lassis	Hen Cackle
	Cake Waltz
Leather Breeches	Rye Straw

HYMNS

Promised Land	Amazing Grace
Murillo's Lesson	

Northeast Alabama

Standard tunes in the square dance fiddler's repertoire as listed by
A. B. Moore in *History of Alabama* (Tuscaloosa: University Book
Store, 1934), 147:

Fiddler's Dram	Hell's Broke Loose in
Rosem the Bow	Georgia
Sail Away Ladies	Sally Goodin
Leather Britches	Hen Cackle
Sourwood Mountain	Rabbit in the Pea Patch
Sugar Valley	Root Hog or Die
Snowbird in the Ashbank	Wild Goose

Tunes mentioned in reports (1926–31) of the De Kalb County Annual Convention:

Rye Straw	Sally Goodin
Black-eyed Susan	Cotton-eyed Joe
Hell Among the Yearlings	Katy-Did
Arkansas Traveler	Leather Breeches
Hop Light Ladies	Jenny Lind Polka
Bile the Cabbage Down	Katy Hill
Billy in the Low Ground	

Tunes played by George Cole of Etowah County at the turn of the
century, as listed by Mattie Cole Stanfield in *Sourwood Tonic and
Sassafras Tea* (New York: Exposition Press, 1963), 85:

Cindy Lou	Cotton-eyed Joe
Sally Gooden	Boil Them Cabbages
Bonaparte	Down
Shortenin' Bread	

Southwest Alabama

Tunes listed as definitive old-time pieces for a contest in Jackson
(Clarke County), in the *Clarke County Democrat*, 6 May 1926:

Leather Breeches
Rabbit in the Pea Patch

Tunes described as "popular old-time tunes" that assuredly would "be rendered in most approved fashion" at a contest in Grove Hill (*Clarke County Democrat*, 9 May 1929):

Black-eyed Susan	The Waggoner
Needle in the Case	Golden Slippers
The Hen Cackle	Sugar in the Gourd
Irish Washerwoman	Turkey in the Straw
Arkansas Traveler	

Tunes played at a housewarming in Perry County in 1827 (from the *Marion Standard*, 30 April 1909):

Miss McLeod
Billy in the Low Ground

Tunes played by slave fiddler Jim Pritchett (Marengo County), as recalled by Alfred Benners in *Slavery and Its Results* (Macon, Ga.: J. W. Burke, 1923):

Forked Deer	Arkansas Traveler
The Dying Coon	
(an improvised number)	

Southeast Alabama

Tunes played by Ben Smith, a Georgian in an Alabama regiment during the Civil War, as listed by Robert Emory Park in *Sketch of the Twelfth Alabama Infantry* (Richmond: William Ellis Jones, 1906), 101:

Hell Broke Loose in Georgia	Billy in the Low Grounds
Arkansas Traveler	Dixie
Money Musk	The Goose Hangs High
When I Saw Sweet Nellie Home	My Old Kentucky Home
When This Cruel War is Over	The Girl I Left Behind Me

Tunes played at a fiddlers' convention at the Pike County Fairgrounds, listed in the *Troy Herald*, 6 July 1926:

Arkansas Traveler	Tom and Jerry
Gray Eagle	Possom Trot
Shear My Sheep, Stephen	Double Bridges
Soldier's Joy	Hasten to the Wedding

Tunes played by R. L. Stephens of Camp Hill at a contest in Columbus, Georgia (*Columbus Enquirer*, 10 and 12 December 1926):

Sailor's Hornpipe
Arkansas Traveler
Rickett's Hornpipe

Central Alabama

Tunes predicted to "vie with the latest jazz nerve wreckers for first place" at a Chilton County convention (*Chilton County News*, 1 June 1922):

Alabama Gal
Leather Breeches
The Old Hen Cackle

From a list of "forgotten" tunes compiled by W. E. G. of Verbena (Chilton County) in the *Union Banner*, 29 September 1921:

Johnny Will Your Dog Bite?   Tom Sawyer
Devil's Hornpipe   Highland Fling
Sally, Put the Kettle On

Tunes played at a contest in Verbena in 1921, described in the *Union Banner*, 27 October 1921:

Sailor's Hornpipe   Arkansas Traveler
Run Nigger Run   Turkey in the Straw

WINNERS OF FIDDLERS' CONVENTIONS AS REPORTED IN ALABAMA NEWSPAPERS

The following list of winners, organized by county, represents those found during five years of research. It is incomplete for three reasons: (1) The results of a great majority of fiddlers' conventions in Alabama were never given in newspapers. In Clarke County, for instance, of thirty-six contests announced between 1926 and 1941, only five were followed by news reports announcing the winners. (2) The newspapers of several counties known to have had rich fiddle traditions, such as Madison, Pike, and Tuscaloosa, seldom announced or reported on such activities. (3) Time did not allow a thorough search of all newspapers in the state.

The names of winners that were found are listed here as they were printed in the newspapers, though some appear to be erroneous. Only the winners of the fiddle and string-band competitions are included. Readers interested in the names of winning banjoists, guitarists, hog callers, and the like will find most of the newspapers referred to in this appendix in the State of Alabama Department of History and Archives in Montgomery.

Blount County

Oneonta Courthouse: 26 March 1923. Thirty musicians were present; four bands were awarded prizes. Winning fiddlers: 1. Herman Tidwell; 2. C. C. Cornelius (*Southern Democrat*, 29 March 1923).

Chilton County

Verbena School Auditorium: 21 October 1921. Had overflow crowd, said to be the largest assembly in Verbena School; made $100 for the P.T.A. Winners: 1. Watermelon Johnson, Haynes ($7.50);

2. John Burkhalter, Haynes (a prize pig) (*Union Banner*, 27 October 1921).

Soldier's Home at Mt. Creek: 6 June 1922. "Violin experts from all over the country will be on hand" (*Union Banner*, 1 June 1922). Another contest was held at the Soldier's Home in September; winners of that contest: Lee Hays, of West Blockton, "and also an inmate of the home" (*Chilton County News*, 14 September 1922).

Verbena School Auditorium: 16 October 1925. Cleared $150 for the benefit of a new school auditorium. Winner: Robert Johnson ($5); other fiddlers: Mr. and Mrs. Jim Robinson, "Watermelon" Johnson, Mr. and Mrs. Tom Coker, Mrs. Robert Johnson, Vernon Clark (*Union Banner*, 29 October 1925).

Thorsby: 7 February 1926. Drew a record crowd. Manager, Professor Bean. Proceeds to benefit the Domestic Science Department of Thorsby Public Schools. Winners: A tie between Watermelon Johnson, F. Smith, and Harley Ray resulted in F. Smith winning $5, and Johnson $3. Other entrants: Jim Courtney, Jim Robinson, Ward, Charley Eiland, Price F. Smith, J. C. Price, Fate Courtney, and Bill Courtney (*Union Banner*, 11 February 1926).

Clanton Court House: 11 March 1926. Methodist Ladies of Clanton, Circle #2, took in $161.86 for tickets and nearly $100 for a cake contest; many were turned away after all seats and standing room were taken; fiddlers were in attendance from Tallassee, Centreville, Calera, Prattville, and all parts of Chilton County; fiddlers were treated to supper after the program was over. Winners (in order): J. C. Price, Powell, F. Smith, C. N. Eiland, Henry Cleckler, Tom Coker, J. C. Terrell, Tom Courtney, B. W. Hopper, Harley Ray, Jack Courtney, A. P. Williams, Jim Bullard, W. A. Wright, W. D. Clark, Norrell Weaver, W. T. Hand, L. L. Courtney, Mrs. J. M. Robinson, Mrs. Coker (*Union Banner*, 18 March 1926).

County Picnic: 22 July 1932. A fiddlers' contest was part of the entertainment. Manager, Mr. Stapp (*Union Banner*, 7 July 1932). Winners: 1. Fonza Smith, Maplesville ($2.50); 2. Lexie Mims, Clanton ($1.75); winners of $1 were Alvin Smith, Archie Cleckler, Dewey Blalock, Archie Deloach, Joe Deloney, E. N. Watkins, Percy Pitts, Jr., Henry Cleckler, and J. S. Jones (*Union Banner*, 28 July 1932).

Clanton, County Courthouse: 4 December 1932. Sponsored by the Pilot Club. A men's chorus also sang sacred songs; event was termed a "huge success." Proceeds of $40 went to the Red Cross and to help pay for a piano in the courthouse. Winner: an unnamed fiddler from Elmore County (*Union Banner*, 8 December 1932).

Clarke County

Grove Hill: 10 May 1929. A county-wide contest. Professor Jernigan, manager. Contests for best fiddler, no accompaniment, $5 award; best fiddler, with accompaniment, $2; best string band, $5; best harmonica player, $2; best banjo player, $2; best buck-dancing, $2; best novelty music, $2 (*Clarke County Democrat*, 9 May 1929). Winners, fiddler without accompaniment: E. J. Megginson of Thomasville; 2. Barney Pugh, Dickinson; 3. R. M. McIntyre, Coffeeville. Other participants: W. L. Porter, Allen; W. N. Harrison, Grove Hill; William Pugh, Dickinson; and Cleve Walker, Winn. Only two entrants in fiddler with accompaniment; winner: Barney Pugh (*Clarke County Democrat*, 16 May 1929).

Suggsville: 19 October 1934. Sponsored by the Suggsville Study Club. Fiddlers' convention was the main event; other contests for Jew's harp, hog calling, buck dancing, and spinning, as well as "epicurean delights." Mrs. W. M. Barnes, organizer (*Clarke County Democrat*, 27 September 1934). Winners: 1. Roland Stringer; 2. W. J. Fowler (*Clarke County Democrat*, 25 October 1934).

Coffeeville: 15 November 1934. Proceeds to benefit school. Contests for fiddlers, string bands, guitar players, harmonica players, piano players, hog callers, and buck-dancers (*Clarke County Democrat*, 15 November 1934). Judge Coma Garrett, Jr., was master of ceremonies. Extremely large audience was unusually attentive, appreciative, and orderly. Winner: R. M. McIntyre of Coffeeville ($5); Tollie Brunson of Grove Hill, 7 years old, pleased the crowd; Fred Hicks of Coffeeville also played well (*Clarke County Democrat*, 22 November 1934).

Coffeeville High School: 13 December 1935. Judge Coma Garrett, Jr. was master of ceremonies. The auditorium could scarely hold the large audience. Contests held: baby popularity, pretty girl, ugly man, group players, fiddlers, guitar players, harp players, buck-dancers, and hog callers. Winner: F. E. Hicks; others: Woodrow Mauldin, George Clanton, Razz McIntyre (*Clarke County Democrat*, 19 December 1935).

New Prospect: 3 April 1936. Realized $84.50. Winners: 1. Tollie

Brunson; 2. Henry Lee Hudson; 3. Herman Reid (*Clarke County Democrat*, 9 April 1936).

Cullman County

Cullman Strawberry Festival: 16 May 1940. Tom Freeman, "Cullman County's famous Bugtussloneon," conducted the contest. Winner: Billy Cantrell ($5); band: Radio Wranglers ($5) (*Cullman Banner*, 24 May 1940).

De Kalb County

De Kalb County Courthouse, Fort Payne: 18 May 1907. Proceeds toward a contemplated school building. Prizes: $5 and $2.50 in gold; fiddlers and banjoists invited; "all out-of-town fiddlers will be entertained free and special arrangements have been made to take care of out-of-town people who attend the convention" (*Fort Payne Journal*, 1 and 8 May 1907). Cleared $75 for the school building. Entrants: S. L. Jones, Collinsville; Albert Cox, Alabama City; J. N. Hunter, Round Mountain; Dr. J. C. Carroll, Henagar; J. M. Cunningham, Blanch; John Honea, Skirum; W. R. Johnson, Crossville; George W. Bell, T. J. Cook, and W. A. Watts, Fort Payne; J. T. Moody, Sylvania; William Robbins, Porterville; Joe J. Tolbert, Henagar. Winners: S. L. Jones, $5 in gold; W. A. Watts, $2.50 in gold; J. T. Moody, a "fine hat" (*Fort Payne Journal*, 22 May 1907).

Powell Junior High School: 23 November 1929. Prizes for best string band, vocal quartet, fiddler, guitar player, banjo player, buckdancer, and Charleston (*Fort Payne Tribune*, 7 November 1929). Results: large turnout "despite rough weather"; $83.30 taken as admission; proceeds to the school. Winners: 1. Frank Davis; 2. G. L. Gilbreath (*Fort Payne Tribune*, 27 Nov. 1929).

De Kalb County Annual Fiddlers' Convention (described more fully in Chapter 4):

1924: 1. Jess Young; 2. Frank Davis; 3. H. Johnson; 4. Marion Blevins; 5. John Williams; 6. J. P. Moore; 7. Will Culver; 8. Frank Moore. Lady fiddler: Mrs. Ella Johnson. Oldest fiddler: W. W. Lyons. Youngest fiddler: Gipsie Samples. Ugliest fiddler: John Griffith. String bands: 1. Young's Band; 2. Samples Band (*De Kalb Republican*, 21 August 1924).

1925: Fiddlers: 1. Frank Moore, Henagar; 2. W. C. Gorman, Chavies; 3. J. P. Moore, Henagar; 4. H. Johnson, Albertville; 5. Wallace Upton, Collinsville; 6. J. M. Hunter, Round Mt. Bands: 1. Moore Band, Henagar; 2. Samples Band, Chavies. Oldest fiddler: W. W. Lyons, Valley Head, aged 87. Youngest fiddler: Jeffie Durham, Chavies (*De Kalb Republican*, 13 August 1925).

1926: 1. Frank Davis; 2. G. B. Moore; 3. W. J. Smith; 4. R. F. Moore. String bands: 1. Moore String Band; 2. Miles Family Orchestra. Oldest fiddler: W. W. Lyons. Youngest fiddler: Olin Moore (*Fort Payne Journal*, 18 August 1926).

1927: "Eleven string bands entered, some of which were from Georgia and Tennessee. However it was the good fortune of Alabama to win first prize in band, the Miles band from Boaz." Second-best band: Young Band, Jasper, Tennessee. Fiddlers: 1. Jess Young, Jasper, Tennessee; 2. Frank Davis, Rainsville; 3. Johnson, Albertville (*Fort Payne Journal*, 10 August 1927).

1928: "Carl McCool of B'ham, formerly of Fort Payne, entertained with two classical numbers. A little less than 100 musicians were present, among whom were fiddlers, banjo and guitar pickers. Nine string bands participated in the contest and it would be amiss not to compliment here the music as rendered by the Miles Band of Boaz, consisting wholly of one family—father, daughter, and 2 sons. The playing and singing of these children was exceptionally good and liberally encored by the big audience." Fiddlers: 1. Jesse Young; 2. H. Johnson; 3. T. M. McCloud; 4. Frank Davis. Best string bands: 1. Tenbroeck Band; 2. Section Band; 3. Miles Band, Boaz (*Fort Payne Journal*, 14 August 1928).

1929: Best fiddler: 1. Frank Davis; 2. John Williamson; 3. William Orr; 4. Bud Daniel. Best string bands: 1. Chavies Band; 2. Myers Band; 3. Tenbroeck Band. Oldest fiddler: J. M. Blalock (*Fort Payne Journal*, 14 August 1929).

1930: Best fiddler: 1. Emmett Cole; 2. Frank Moore; 3. Frank Davis; 4. H. Johnson. String bands: 1. Chavies Band; 2. Black Band; 3. Cherokee Band. Oldest fiddler: J. N. Hunter. Youngest fiddler: Virgil Russell (*Fort Payne Journal*, 20 August 1930).

1931: String bands: 1. Sand Mountain Night Hawks; 2. Lybrand and Coker; 3. Sample Band. Fiddlers: 1. Frank Moore; 2. C. B. Daniel; 3. J. T. Williamson. Oldest fiddler: W. M. Johnson (73). Youngest fiddler: Edwin Walker (*Fort Payne Journal*, 19 August 1931).

1932: Celebrated as 25th Annual Convention. Fiddlers: 1. Bill Hyde; 2. W. M. Jackson; 3. Jess Moore. String bands: 1. Uncle Bud and his Boll Weevils, Birmingham; 2. Chavies Band; 3. Lankford Band. Oldest fiddler: H. Johnson (*Fort Payne Journal*, 17 August 1932).

1933: Admission was reduced to 25¢ and 15¢. More than fifty fiddlers attended with "more than two score of banjo and guitar artists." Fiddlers: 1. W. H. Johnson; 2. Jesse Moore; 3. Bud Daniel. String bands: 1. Albertville String Band; 2. Johnson String Band. Oldest fiddler: W. M. Johnson, 78. Youngest fiddler: Edward Walker, 18 (*Fort Payne Journal*, 16 August 1933).

1934: No follow-up press account.

1935: Fiddlers: 1. Roy Cross of Clark Bros. Band, Chattanooga; 2. J. B. Durham. Oldest fiddler: Mat Cunningham, 79. Youngest fiddler: J. B. Durham, 14. String bands: (newspaper almost illegible at this point) Ramsey? Band of Dawson, composed of four brothers and a first cousin; 2. S—— Band of Huntsville, four brothers; 3. Happy Jack's String Band (*Fort Payne Journal*, 14 August 1935).

1936: Fiddlers: 1. Jess Moore; 2. Marion Blevins; 3. B. C. Kemsley. String Bands: 1. Kemsley Band; 2. Jones Band. Oldest fiddler: Zander Traffensted. Youngest fiddler: Virgil Pruett (*Fort Payne Journal*, 19 August 1936).

1937: Fiddlers: 1. Mark Daniel (could be "Monk" Daniels), Nixon's Chapel; 2. Jess Moore; 3. W. S. Hankford (?), Portersville. String bands: Kimsey Band; Ringgold? Georgia Band; James Band, Peeks's Corner. Oldest fiddler: Tom Oyler?, Sulphur Springs, Georgia. Youngest fiddler: J. R. Justin, 10, Chavies (*Fort Payne Journal*, 18 August 1937).

1938: Fiddlers: 1. Noah Lacy; 2. J. M. Street; 3. John Stuart. String bands: 1. Dixie Dewdrop; 2. Dixie Rhythm Makers; 3. Dixie Fiddlers. Oldest fiddler: J. T. Williamson. Youngest fiddler: Roy Justice (*Fort Payne Journal*, 22 August 1938).

1939: Fiddlers: 1. Noah Lacy; 2. Jesse Martin; 3. D. C. Kimsey. Bands: 1. Dixie Rhythm Makers; 2. Black Jacks; 3. Blevins Band (*Fort Payne Journal*, 23 August 1939).

1940: 77 contestants; winners not listed (*Fort Payne Journal*, 21 August 1940).

1941: 100 or more contestants; winners not listed (*Fort Payne Journal*, 20 August 1941).

1942: Fiddlers: 1. Paul Frazier; 2. Robert Smith; 3. Jasper Jaco? Bands: 1. Round Up Gang; 2. Prairie Riders (*Fort Payne Journal*, 28 28 August 1942).

Elmore County

Wetumpka: 3 December 1926. Fiddlers' and Harpers' Convention, also hog callers, sponsored by P.T.A. at S.S.A.S. Auditorium. Manager: Mrs. J. J. Williams (*Weekly Herald*, 18 November 1926. Winners: 1. J. R. Powell, Wetumpka; 2. H. H. Smith; 3. D. Stokes (*Weekly Herald*, 9 December 1926).

Fayette County

Fayette: March 1921. *Fayette Banner* announced winners of the fiddlers' convention: 1. W. F. Kolbey ($10); 2. A. Jones ($6); 3. Dr. Hollis ($4). (*Fayette Banner*, 10 March 1921, reprinted in *150 Yesteryears*, Fayette County Historical Society, 1971).
—— 11 March 1929. Lucy Monroe, chairman. About 1,000 people paid to attend and all standing room was taken. Winners: "The music was so entertaining that instead of giving prizes as intended, four who were decided by the judges to be outstanding were awarded $10 each: Charles Stripling, Jimmie Porter, Charles Brown, and Ed Brown" (*Fayette Banner*, 14 March 1929).
—— 10 September 1929. Courthouse was packed and every available place for standing was taken. Mayor M. L. Coons, an old-time fiddler, acted as announcer. Winners: four prizes of $10 each went to Charles Stripling, Kennedy; Jimmie Porter, Columbus; and E. E. and Charles Brown of northern Fayette County (*Fayette Banner*, 12 September 1929). In the "Kennedy News" section of the *Lamar Democrat*, Charlie Stripling was reported as the first-place winner. Also: "Some of the best fiddling talent of the state participated including Wise E. Hammonds [Y. Z. Hamilton] of Bessemer and Charlie and Epp Brown of Tuscaloosa" (*Lamar Democrat*, 18 September 1929).
—— March 1930. Winners: First place: Charlie Stripling, Kennedy; Jimmie Porter, Kennedy; Charlie Brown, Tuscaloosa; 2. Mrs. Morgan, Caledonia, Mississippi; 3. J. B. Dickey, Tuscaloosa; 4. Marvin Smith, Kennedy (*Lamar Democrat*, 19 March 1930).
—— 8 September 1930. Winners: 1. Jimmie Porter, Steens, Mississippi ($10); 2. Charlie Stripling, Kennedy; 3. Henry Ledlow, Berry; 4. Leo Freeman, Millport. Other entrants: C. W. Morris, Felix Barnes, M. L. Beasley, J. A. Fowler, Gene Morris, and H. C. Enis, of Fayette; Lloyd Miller, T. E. Miller, E. D. Freeman,

D. Stephens, and L. M. Stewart, Millport; Cooper Norris and
Everette Sanford, Bankston; J. L. Dickey and V. A. Hannah, Tus-
caloosa; Marvin Smith, and Clifton Stripling, Kennedy (*North-
west Alabamian*, 11 September 1930).
——— 13 March 1933. Winners: 1. Charlie Brown, Tuscaloosa; 2.
Charlie Stripling, Kennedy; 3. Ralph Bobo, Bluff; 4. Mr. Maddox,
Bankston; 5. J. C. Brock, Fayette (*Northwest Alabamian*, 16
March 1933). Another newspaper reported: "Charlie Stripling
won 1st prize with a number of others receiving awards also"
(*Fayette Banner*, 16 March 1933).

Greene County

Knoxville, W.O.W. Hall: 29 April 1927. Raised money for the baseball team; contest was followed by a dance. Winners: I. O. Pate
of Ralph, and Victor Phillips, from Knoxville vicinity (*Tuscaloosa News*, 1 May 1927).

Jefferson County

Birmingham Municipal Auditorium: 25 February 1925. Auspices of
the Nathan Bedford Forrest Klan. First prize, $100 in gold; sec-
ond, $75 in gold; third, $50 in gold; prizes 4–8, $25; prizes 9–
18, $10. Only those with a reputation to be accepted (*Birming-
ham Age-Herald*, 25 January and 22 February 1925). The audience numbered 3,500. Winners: 1. Y. Z. Hamilton, Bessemer;
2. A. A. Gray, Waco, Georgia; 3. Earl Johnson, Atlanta. Winners
of $25: W. A. Meek, Birmingham; Cliff Click, Birmingham;
D. S. McKee, Notasulga; C. M. Stibrbling [sic], Kentucky [sic];
and E. D. Brown, Tennessee [sic] (*Birmingham Age-Herald*, 26
February 1925).

Limestone County

Elkmont County High School: 13 March 1931 (*Limestone Democrat*, 5 March 1931). Winners: 1. L. W. Weir, of Coxey; 2. D. A.
Cole, Athens; 3. J. C. Haney, Elkmont (*Limestone Democrat*,
19 March 1931).

Old Fiddlers' Contests at Athens Agricultural School (described more fully in Chapter 4):

1924: 1. John Chambers of western Limestone County; 2. Harris Rogers, Athens; 3. Spot Starkey; 4. Mrs. Delia Mullins, Madison County; 5. Fletcher Barksdale; 6. Mrs. Roberts, Slough Beat; 7. Crudup Group; 8. Thomas Group (five brothers with fiddle, cello, and guitars). Other entrants: Mr. George Broadway, aged 76; Booker Morrell, Richard Thomas, Robert Reynolds (brother of Mrs. Mullins), Fletcher Barksdale (*Alabama Courier*, 6 March 1924).

1925: Solo: John Watkins, Levi Weir, Harris Rogers, Fletcher Barksdale. Groups: Fairmont Group, Mrs. Roberts' Group, Thomas Group (*Alabama Courier*, 5 March 1925).

1926: Winner: Mrs. Delia Mullins (*Alabama Courier*, 4 March 1926).

1927: Single fiddle: 1. J. B. Carver; 2. R. L. Reynolds; 3. D. A. Cole. Group players: 1. Coxey Group; 2. Smith Group; 3. Terry Group (*Limestone Democrat*, 3 March 1927).

1928: 1. Emma Crabtree; 2. W. C. Burns; 3. J. R. Matthews. String bands: 1. Sparkman Group; 2. Smith Group; 3. Jackson Group (*Limestone Democrat*, 8 March 1928).

1929: 1. John D. Chambers; 2. Mrs. Delia Mullins; 3. Emma Crabtree. String bands: 1. McCrag Band; 2. Louise and Beatrice Thomas; 3. W. D. Stedham (*Limestone Democrat*, 28 February 1929).

1930: Held 28 February 1930. No subsequent press coverage.

1931: Held 27 February 1931. No subsequent press coverage.

1932: D. A. Cole; 2. Tom Sutton; 3. J. F. Chambers; 4. L. W. Weir. Groups: 1. Delmore Brothers; 2. Thomas Sisters; 3. Sutton Group; 4. Decatur Happy Four. Participants (fiddlers): Osborn Echols, Emma Crabtree, D. A. Cole, L. W. Weir, J. W. Wadkins, J. W. Galton, S. F. Chambers, Fletcher Barksdale, Oscar Gosset, Lum Sutton; (group players): McLemore Hawaiian, Decatur Happy Four, Oakland Group, Four Serenaders, Delmore Brothers, Emma Crabtree Band, Thomas Group, Smith Band, Roberts and Eaves, Union Hill Group, McGrew Group, Union Group, Flannigan, Cole, Coxey, Gulley Morrell, Emerson Brothers, Barksdale, Wiley and Sutton Group (*Limestone Democrat*, 3 March 1932).

1933: 1. Osborn Echols; 2. Giles Hollingsworth; 3. Rube McGlocklin; 4. Fletcher Barksdale (*Alabama Courier*, 2 March 1933).

Lamar County

Vernon High School: 19 February 1927. Winners: 1. Mrs. Pearl Duncan Morgan; 2. Charlie Stripling; 3. Mr. Mason (*Lamar Democrat*, 23 February 1927).

Sulligent: 10 October 1928. Sponsored by the Sulligent United Daughters of the Confederacy. Manager: Professor John Clements. Winners: 1. Charlie Stripling; 2. T. A. Morris; 3. Mrs. Morgan; 4. L. A. Duncan (*Sulligent News*, 11 October 1928).

Kennedy High School: 23 November 1929. Fiddle contest and hog calling. "An array of the best fiddling in this section participated, making the judges' task an unusually hard one." Winners: 1. Charlie Stripling, Kennedy; 2. Jimmie Porter, Kennedy; 3. Leo Freeman, Millport (*Lamar Democrat*, 4 December 1929).

Vernon Courthouse: 14 April 1930. Winners: 1. Charlie Stripling, with his two young sons as accompanists; 2. Mrs. Pearl Morgan; 3. R. L. Pennington (*Lamar Democrat*, 16 April 1930).

Liberty School: 24 October 1930. "The Stripling String Band, composed of Messrs. Ira Stripling, Eura Stripling, Charlie Stripling, and two young sons competed in the old-time Fiddlers' Contest held at Liberty Friday night." The band won first prize in the band contest (*Lamar Democrat* "Kennedy News," 29 October 1930).

Liberty School: 8 October 1931. The concluding event of the Liberty District Fair. Prizes for the two top fiddlers and for band; also for best husband caller and hog caller (*Millport Messenger*, 1 October 1931). Winners: 1. Charlie Stripling; 2. Jimmie Porter (*Millport Messenger*, 15 October 1931).

Lee County

Auburn, Lee County High School Auditorium: 3 April 1926. Called East Alabama Fiddlers' Convention—fiddlers' contest and "harp" players (*Opelika Daily News*, 1 April 1926). Results: An overflow crowd attended. Winners: 1. C. S. McGee, of Notasulga; 2. W. O. McGill, Camp Hill; 3. J. E. Boone, Wedowee; 4. Prof. F. E. Guyton, Auburn (*Opelika Daily News*, 5 April 1926).

Madison County

Huntsville, County Courthouse: 15–17 March 1928. Manager: Bud Silvey. Winners: 1. Mrs. Emma Crabtree of Merrimack; 2. Probably Delia Mullins, Madison County. (This contest has been described in *The Devil's Box*, Newsletter XXVI, 1 September 1974, pp. 54–59.)

Marengo County

Linden Courthouse: 14 October 1927. Bill Glass, president; Judge Hasty, master of ceremonies. Nearly 400 persons attended, many from neighboring counties and from Mississippi. Winners: 1. Price Glass, of Meridian, $10; 2. Eddie Megginson, Thomasville, $7; 3. E. K. Headley, Myrtlewood, $5. Other entrants: A. C. Headley of Livingston; Bob McManus, Arlington; R. M Johnson, Linden; F. M. and J. L. Pogue, Meridian; L. S. Harrison, Chilton; D. M. McIntyre, Grove Hill; Bernie Crawford, Myrtlewood (*Clarke County Democrat*, 20 October 1927).

Montgomery County

Montgomery City Auditorium: 18–20 December 1926. Manager: "Tanks" Grantham, for the American Legion. Featured Fiddlin' John Carson, Riley Puckett, Clayton McMichen (*Montgomery Advertiser*, 20 December 1926). Winners: 1. Clayton McMichen; 2. J. P. Powell, Tallassee; 3. John Loche, Columbus (*Montgomery Advertiser*, 21 December 1926).

Montgomery City Auditorium: 25–27 April 1927. Manager: "Tanks" Grantham, for the American Legion. Competition between Alabama and Georgia fiddlers plus dancing, monologues, novelty numbers, and beauty contest (*Montgomery Advertiser*, 24 April 1927). Winners: 1. J. R. Bowell, of Tallassee [the fiddler who won second place in the previous contest; his name was probably J. R. Powell instead of J. P. Powell or J. R. Bowell, as given in the newspaper accounts]; 2. D. S. McKee, Notasulga; 3. A. E. James, Newville (*Montgomery Advertiser*, 28 April 1927).

Pickens County

Palmetto: 5 March 1927. Raised $77.90 to benefit the high school. Winners: 1. Charlie Stripling; 2. Ross Daffron; 3. Jimmie Porter (*Lamar Democrat*, 16 March 1927).

Palmetto High School: 5 October 1929. Prizes of $7 each were awarded to the three fiddlers judged best: Charles Stripling, of Kennedy; Jimmie Porter, Kennedy; Leo Freeman, Millport (*Lamar Democrat* "Kennedy News," 9 October 1929).

Pike County

Pike County Fairgrounds: 5 July 1926. Winners: 1. J. W. Youngblood; 2. Mrs. J. M. Rushing; 3. W. A. Brown and M. C. Carter. "Judges had a difficult time and had Mrs. Rushing and Mr. Youngblood to play the second time and even then it was hard to make a decision" (*Troy Herald*, 6 July 1926).

Banks: 14 November 1930. Sponsored by the Ladies Missionary Society (*Troy Herald*, 6 November 1930). Winner: Huey Hickman, of Brundidge; others present were Jean Rodgers, John Turner, W. H. Spivey, W. A. Brown, Mr. Sims, and Henry and Bill Hickman (*Troy Herald*, 27 November 1930).

Tuscaloosa County

Tuscaloosa "Casino": 3 March 1927. Eight well-known contestants played for an audience of 1,000; winners were decided by secret ballot. Winners: 1. Charlie Stripling ($25), of Kennedy; 2. Henry Ledlow ($15), Tuscaloosa; 3. E. D. "Monkey" Brown, Tuscaloosa (*Tuscaloosa News*, 4 March 1927).

Walker County

Carbon Hill: 3 July 1926. Part of the Fourth of July celebration. Manager: Zack P. Shepherd. Contests for best fiddler, banjo picker, French harp player, Jew's harp player, and male quartet (*Mountain Eagle*, 30 June 1926). Winners: 1. Allen Wilson, of

Galloway; 2. Cooper Norris. P.T.A. cleared $300 from drinks and admissions (*Mountain Eagle*, 7 July 1926).

Jasper, Colonial Theater: 30 April 1929. Principal part of the program to consist of a contest between ten of the best fiddlers in the fourteenth Judicial Circuit, two fiddlers to be selected from each of the five counties by the probate judge of that county. The counties: Fayette, Lamar, Marion, Winston, and Walker. Prizes of $25, $15, and $10 to be awarded. Manager: J. M. Pennington (*Fayette Banner*, 25 April 1929). Three judges presided, one from Jasper, one from Fayette, and one from Winston. Winners: 1. J. M. Tingle (Walker County); 2. C. W. Morris (Fayette); 3. J. O. Wissenhunt (Winston) (*Fayette Banner*, 2 May 1929).

Jasper: March 1936. Sponsored by the *Union News*, twenty-six groups participated. Winners: 1. Elvie Swann ($12), of Bremen; 2. Clarence Pound's band; 3. Mrs. Mae Martin, Nauvoo (*Union News*, 26 March 1936).

Preface

1. *Alabama Courier*, 6 March 1924.
2. Quoted by Archie Green, "Hillbilly Music: Source and Symbol," *Journal of American Folklore* 78 (July–September 1965): 204.
3. *Fort Payne Journal*, 10 August 1932.

Chapter 1.
The Fiddle in Alabama History

1. Marcus Bailey, "Early Alabama Fiddling," *The Devil's Box* 17 (Summer 1983): 21.
2. Albert James Pickett, *History of Alabama and Incidentally of Georgia and Mississippi, from the Earliest Period* (1851; reprint, Birmingham Book and Magazine Co., 1972), 622.
3. Allen Feldman, *The Northern Fiddler* (New York: Oak, 1979), 48, 203.
4. Dena J. Epstein, *Sinful Tunes and Spirituals* (Urbana: University of Illinois Press, 1977), 148.
5. Eileen Southern, *The Music of Black Americans: A History* (New York: W. W. Norton, 1971), 63–64.
6. W. E. Ward quoted by John W. Blassingame, *The Slave Community: Plantation Life in the Antebellum South*, 3rd ed. (New York: Oxford University Press, 1979), 22–23.
7. Thomas Perkins Abernethy, *The Formative Period in Alabama, 1814–1828* (University: University of Alabama Press, 1965), 37–43.
8. François Diard quoted by Robert Allen Kennedy, "A History and Survey of Community Music in Mobile, Alabama" (Ph.D. diss., Florida State University, 1960), 30–31.
9. Anne Kendrick Walker, *Backtracking in Barbour County, A Narrative of the Last Alabama Frontier* (Richmond: Dietz Press, 1941), 109–110.
10. Mrs. Rose Gibbons Lovett, letter to author, Summer, 1984.
11. Jane M. and Marion Turnbull quoted by Epstein, 154.
12. Frederick Law Olmsted, *The Cotton Kingdom, A Traveller's Observations on Cotton and Slavery in the American Slave States* (New York: Mason Bros., 1861), 287.

13. Federal Writers' Project, *Slave Narratives: Alabama and Indiana Narratives* 5 (St. Clair Shores: Scholarly Press, republished 1976), 243.

14. Ibid., 280.

15. Harold Courlander, *Negro Folk Music, U.S.A.* (New York: Columbia University Press, 1963), 214.

16. Charlie Johnson as told to Ruby Pickens Tartt in Virginia Pounds Brown and Laurella Owens, *Toting the Lead Row: Ruby Pickens Tartt, Alabama Folklorist* (University: University of Alabama Press, 1981), 130–131.

17. W. C. Handy, *Father of the Blues, An Autobiography*, Arna Bontemps, ed. (New York: Macmillan, 1941), 5–6.

18. Newman I. White, "The White Man in the Woodpile," *American Speech* 4 (February 1929): 207.

19. *Slave Narratives*, 239.

20. Ibid., 280.

21. Brown and Owens, *Toting the Lead Row*, 131.

22. White, 207, 211.

23. *Alabama Planter*, 27 December 1846.

24. Weymouth Jordan, *Hugh Davis and his Alabama Plantation* (University: University of Alabama Press, 1948), 84.

25. Handy, 5.

26. *Slave Narratives*, 168.

27. Mark Keller, "Alabama Plantation Life in 1860: Governor Benjamin Fitzpatrick's 'Oak Grove,'" *The Alabama Historical Quarterly* (Spring 1976): 224.

28. Alfred H. Benners, *Slavery and Its Results* (Macon, Georgia: J. W. Burke, 1923), 25–26.

29. *Slave Narratives*, 174.

30. Byron Arnold, *Folksongs of Alabama* (University: University of Alabama Press, 1950), 38.

31. *Slave Narratives*, 155.

32. Ibid., 76.

33. William Phineas Browne, letter to daughter, 26 May 1859 (Montgomery: Alabama Department of Archives and History).

34. D. Dix Hollis, personal letter, 10 July 1926.

35. Henry Lee Hudson, interview with author, Bassett Hill Community (Clarke County), 2 August 1986.

36. *Thomasville Argus*, 25 November 1897.

37. Carolyn Blackwell Scott, *Country Roads: A Journey through Rustic Alabama* (Tuscaloosa: Portals Press, 1979), 143.

38. Mattie Lou Teague Crow, *History of St. Clair County* (Hunts-

ville: Strode, 1973), 108. In 1900 a census taker indicated that the fiddler's name was "Guss Cochran" and that he was born in 1886.

39. Gilbert Chase, *America's Music: From the Pilgrims to the Present* (New York: McGraw-Hill, 1955), 435.

40. Ibid., 270.

41. Ibid., 264.

42. Southern, 114.

43. Carl Wittke, *Tambo and Bones: A History of the American Minstrel Stage* (Durham: Duke University Press, 1930), 147.

44. Hans Nathan, *Dan Emmett and the Rise of Early Negro Minstrelsy* (Norman: University of Oklahoma Press, 1977), 159–188.

45. Chase, 273.

46. Al G. Field, *Watch Yourself Go By* (Columbus, Ohio, 1912), 485, and *Birmingham Age-Herald*, 26 September 1919.

47. Henry Hotze, "The Tune of Dixie" in *The Confederate Reader*, Malcolm C. McMillan, ed. (University: University of Alabama Press, 1963), 116.

48. *Alabama Planter*, 10 December 1846.

49. *Cullman Democrat*, 15 September 1938.

50. Robert C. Toll, *Blacking Up: The Minstrel Show in Nineteenth-Century America* (New York: Oxford University Press, 1974), 32.

51. M. B. Leavett, *Fifty Years in Theatrical Management* (New York: Broadway Publishing Co., 1912), 76.

52. *Montgomery Advertiser*, 20 January 1855, quoted by Minnie Clare Boyd, *Alabama in the Fifties: A Social Study* (New York: Columbia University Press, 1931), 225–226.

53. Robert Toll has pointed out that many local companies exploited the names of famous troupes. Because Gilbert Chase noted that Christy's Minstrels toured the South around 1840–54, the troupe appearing in Montgomery in 1856 may not have been the real Christy's Minstrels (Chase, 267, and Toll, 32).

54. *Montgomery Advertiser and State Gazette*, 12 November 1856.

55. Paul H. Satterfield, "Recreation of Soldiers, 1861–65," *Alabama Historical Quarterly* 20 (1958): 604.

56. Glenn Sisk, *Alabama Black Belt; A Social History, 1875–1917* (Ph.D. diss., Duke University, 1951), 402.

57. Etowah County Centennial Committee, *A History of Etowah County, Alabama* (Birmingham: Roberts and Son, 1968), 180.

58. *Huntsville Times*, Sesquicentennial Issue, 11–17 September 1955.

59. Handy, 17, 18.

60. Ibid., 34.

61. *Northwest Alabamian*, 3 August 1927.

62. *Washington County News*, 2 July 1924.

63. *Union Banner*, 23 June 1921.

64. *Mountain Eagle News*, 27 April 1927.

65. Harry Dichter and Elliott Shapiro, *Handbook of Early American Sheet Music, 1768–1889* (New York: R. R. Bowker, 1941), 137, 149, 54.

66. Chase, 278.

67. Dichter, 141–155.

68. Isaac Goldberg, *Tin Pan Alley, A Chronicle of American Popular Music* (New York: Ungar Publishing Co., 1961), 174.

69. J. P. Cannon, *Inside Rebeldom: The Daily Life of a Private in the Confederate Army* (Washington, D.C.: National Tribune, 1900), xix.

70. Edward McMorries, *History of the First Regiment, Alabama Volunteer Infantry, CSA* (Montgomery: Brown Printing Co., 1904), 52.

71. Robert Emory Park, *Sketch of the Twelfth Alabama Infantry* (Richmond: William Ellis Jones, 1906), 101.

72. Cannon, (April 3, 1863), 90.

73. Bell I. Wiley, *The Life of Johnny Reb, The Common Soldier of the Confederacy* (Indianapolis: Bobbs-Merrill, 1943), 158.

74. Cannon, 161.

75. Norman V. Cooper, "How They Went to War: An Alabama Brigade in 1861–62," *Alabama Review* 24 (January 1971): 18–23.

76. *Elmore Standard*, September 5, 1866.

77. Unlabeled newspaper clipping in H. H. Robison collection, State of Alabama Department of Archives and History.

78. Chase, 468–471.

79. *Birmingham Age-Herald*, 23 April 1924.

80. *De Kalb Republican*, 22 January 1925.

81. Ibid., 6 August 1925.

82. *Washington County News*, 2 November 1922.

83. Oliver Read and Walter L. Welch, *From Tin Foil to Stereo: Evolution of the Phonograph* (Indianapolis and New York: Howard W. Sams & Co. and Bobbs-Merrill, 1959), 18.

84. *Sears, Roebuck and Co., Reproduction of 1900 Catalog*, Joseph J. Schroeder, Jr., ed. (Northfield, Illinois, 1970), 217.

85. William Everis Campbell, interview with author, Henderson, Alabama, 24 November 1984.

86. Roland Gelatt, *The Fabulous Phonograph, 1877–1977*, 2nd ed. (New York: MacMillan, 1977), 178.

87. *Sears, Roebuck and Co., Reproduction of 1909 Catalog* (New York: Ventura Books, 1979), 364–67.

88. Gelatt, 48.

89. David Cohn, *The Good Old Days: A History of American Morals and Manners as Seen throughout the Sears, Roebuck Catalogs, 1905 to the Present* (New York: Simon and Schuster, 1940), 31.

90. Archie Green, "Hillbilly Music: Source and Symbol," *Journal of American Folklore* 78 (July–September 1965): 209–211.

91. Arlin Moon, interview with author, Holly Pond, 7 September 1985.

92. Country Music Foundation, discographical entry sheet, "Short Creek Trio."

93. Ibid.

94. Olen Mayes, interview with author, Birmingham, 12 September 1985.

95. Information supplied in a letter by Guthrie T. Meade, 13 May 1984.

96. *Union Banner* (Clanton), 21 October 1926.

97. *Sand Mountain Banner*, 2 August 1928.

98. Ed Rickard, interview with author, Russellville, 15 September 1985. The liner notes to County Record 548, "Riding in an Old Model T," incorrectly identify Ed Rickard as the fiddler for the Dixie Ramblers, who recorded for the American Record Company in 1937. The fiddler was Oscar Stockton of Russellville, Alabama.

99. *Tuscaloosa News*, 28 March 1971.

100. *A Most Memorable 60 Years—WAPI Radio*, special commemorative (Birmingham: WAPI, 1982), 2.

101. *Opelika Daily News*, 20 March 1926.

102. *Sand Mountain Banner*, 25 March 1926.

103. *Lamar Democrat*, 21 April 1926.

104. *Opelika Daily News*, 17 April 1926.

105. Report by the U.S. Department of Agriculture, published in the *Opelika Daily News*, 8 March 1926.

106. *Mountain Eagle*, 3 March 1926.

107. *Opelika Daily News*, 9 April 1926.

108. *Union Banner* (Clanton), 21 October 1926.

109. *Birmingham News*, 3 May 1925.

110. Letter from C. Kirkpatrick, published in *The Plainsman* (Auburn), 11 February 1928.

111. *Union Banner* (Clanton), 14 October 1926.

112. *Opelika Daily News*, 7 May 1926.

113. Ibid., 26 November 1926.

114. *Auburn Plainsman*, 19 March 1927.

115. Ibid., 19 February 1927.

116. WAPI commemorative, 3.

117. Vearl Cicero, interview with author, Ensley, 9 April 1984.

118. Ibid.

119. Sullivan soon went on to national fame with the Alabama fiddler Wiley Walker (Andalusia) as the "Wiley and Gene" team which wrote and recorded such hits as "When My Blue Moon Turns to Gold Again" and "Live and Let Live."

120. Sam Busby, interview with author, Ensley, 26 August 1983.

121. Bill Harrison, "Fiddling in Limestone County: 1925 Through 1940," Newsletter XVI of the Tennessee Valley Old-Time Fiddlers' Association (15 February 1972): 8.

122. Moon interview.

123. See Joyce Cauthen, "Uncle Dave Macon in Birmingham," *The Devil's Box* 17 (Fall, 1983): 26–31.

124. Mayes interview.

125. *Northwest Alabamian*, 29 August 1929.

126. *Fort Payne Journal*, 13 August 1930.

127. Ibid., 18 August 1935.

128. Keith Sward, *The Legend of Henry Ford* (New York: Rinehart, 1948), 259–60.

129. *Gadsden Evening Star*, 12 February 1926.

130. Don Roberson, " 'Uncle Bunt' Stephens—Champion Fiddler," *The Devil's Box* 5 (Newsletter XII, 25 May 1970): 2–5.

131. *Lamar Democrat*, 21 April 1926.

132. *Fort Payne Journal*, 17 August 1932.

133. Words of one of Folsom's opponents quoted by George E. Sims, *The Little Man's Big Friend: James E. Folsom in Alabama Politics, 1946–1958* (University: University of Alabama Press, 1985), 35.

134. Carl Grafton, "James E. Folsom's 1946 Campaign," *Alabama Review* (35: 3): 176–77; see also Carl Grafton and Anne Permaloff, *Big Mules and Branchheads: James E. Folsom and Political Power in Alabama* (Athens: University of Georgia Press, 1985).

135. Quoted by Grafton, "James E. Folsom's 1946 Campaign," 189.

136. Sims, 35

137. Crow, 108.

138. Sims, 4.

139. Al Lester, interview with author, Muscle Shoals, 2 October 1985.

140. Gene Dunlap, interview with author, Birmingham, 15 July 1986.

141. Alvin Horn, interview with author, Ashland, 6 August 1984.

142. Rhoda Coleman Ellison, *Bibb County, Alabama: The First Hundred Years* (University: University of Alabama Press, 1984), 114.

143. Bob Kyle, "Old Time Music Will Never Die," *Tuscaloosa News*, 17 March 1957. Reprinted in *The Devil's Box* XII (May 1970): 6. Used by permission of the *Tuscaloosa News*.

Chapter 2.
Modest Masters of Fiddle and Bow

1. R. T. Hamner, according to newspaper advertisements, was a "Dealer in Fine Wines, Liquors, and Cigars, with 'Jug Trade a Specialty.' " *"150 Yesteryears, Fayette County, Alabama,"* Fayette County Historical Society, II (*Fayette County Broadcaster*, 1971), 68.

2. *Fayette Banner*, 2 January 1908.

3. 13th census of U.S., 1910.

4. Information supplied by Marguerite Tarwater Callahan in letter to author, 26 August 1985.

5. Alvin Horn, interview with author, Ashland, 6 August 1984.

6. Osey Kersey, interview with author, Oakey Ridge, 22 November 1984.

7. James R. Aswell, *God Bless the Devil*, reproduced by Charles K. Wolfe in "Legends About Tennessee Fiddlers," *The Devil's Box* (Fall 1984): 24.

8. *West Alabama Breeze*, 3 July 1919.

9. *Fayette Banner*, 9 January 1941.

10. Barney Dickerson, interview with author, Dothan, 23 November 1986.

11. Arlin Moon, interview with author, Holly Pond, 7 September 1985.

12. Thomas E. Hill, interview with author, Pinson, 4 June 1983.

13. Curtis Robertson, conversation with author, Northport, 31 August 1984.

14. Howard Colburn, interview with author, McCalla, 9 May 1985.

15. Horn interview.

16. Vearl Cicero, interview with author, Ensley, 9 April 1984.

17. Gaines Arnold, interview with author, Quinton, 7 May 1984.

18. Thomas E. Hill interview.

19. J. C. Brock, interview with author, Crossville, Lamar County, 30 August 1984.

20. Monk Daniels, interview with Herb Trotman, Albertville, June 1978. Used by permission.

21. Kersey interview.

22. J. V. Porter, interview with author, Steens, Mississippi, 13 December 1984.

23. Horn interview.

24. Kersey interview and letter, 26 May 1986.

25. James Cole and Estelle Carwile, interview with author, Athens, 13 September 1984.

26. Jerry McGlocklin, interview with author, Athens, 13 September 1984.

27. Cicero interview.

28. *Alabama Courier*, 4 March 1926; *Cullman Banner*, 19 May 1939; Marcus Bailey, "Early Alabama Fiddling," *The Devil's Box* (Summer 1983): 21.

29. Moon interview.

30. Kersey interview.

31. Chester Allen, interview with author, Scottsboro, 5 June 1984.

32. Brock interview.

33. Horn interview.

34. Edward Heron-Allen in Herbert K. Goodkind, *Violin Iconography of Antonio Stradivari, 1644–1737* (Larchmont: published by author, 1972), 17.

35. Joseph Wechsberg, *The Glory of the Violin* (New York: Viking Press, 1972), 129.

36. *Sears, Roebuck and Co., Reproduction of 1900 Catalog*, Schroeder, Joseph J., ed. (Northfield, Illinois, 1970), 252; and *Sears, Roebuck and Co., Reproduction of 1909 Catalog* (New York: Ventura Books, 1979), 162.

37. Goodkind, 17.

38. William Everis Campbell, interview with author, Henderson, 24 November 1984.

39. Carl Stewart, interview with author, Ketona, 13 June 1984.

40. Robert Stripling, interview with author, west Alabama, 30 August 1984.

41. Brock interview.

42. Harmon Hicks, interview with author, Pleasant Grove, 23 April 1983.

43. Kersey interview.

44. Brock interview.

45. Hicks interview.

46. A. D. Hamner, interview with author, Northport, 24 April 1984.

47. Cicero interview.

48. *Northwest Alabamian*, 25 August 1926.

49. Charlie Stripling, interview with Bob Pinson, Kennedy, 2 September 1963. Used by permission.

50. Dickerson interview.

51. The word "banjo" was pronounced by most of the fiddlers interviewed for this book just as it was in the late 1700s when Jonathan Boucher, writing a supplement of archaic and provincial words for English-language dictionaries, discussed an instrument made of a large hollow gourd with a long handle attached to it, strung with catgut, and played with the fingers. He called it a *bandore*, but said the slaves called it a *banjer*. See Dena J. Epstein, *Sinful Tunes and Spirituals* (Urbana: University of Illinois Press, 1977), 34.

52. Rhoda Coleman Ellison, *Bibb County, Alabama: The First Hundred Years, 1818–1918* (University: University of Alabama Press, 1984), 74.

53. *Alabama Planter* (Mobile), 20 December 1846, and *Daily Alabama Journal* (Montgomery), 14 April 1849.

54. Marie Bankhead Owen, *The Story of Alabama, A History of the State*, Vol. III (New York: Lewis Historical Publishing, 1949), 647.

55. Thomas E. Hill interview.

56. John Thomas Tanner, *A History of Athens*, W. Stanley Hoole and Addie S. Hoole, eds. (University: Confederate Publishing Co., 1978), 8; Betsy Hamilton (Idora McClellan Moore), *Southern Character Sketches* (Richmond: Dietz Press, 1937), 17; Joe Acee, *Lamar County History*, revised edition (Vernon: *Lamar Democrat*, 1972), 4.

57. Hamilton, 17.

58. Aubrey Phillips, interview with author, Robertsdale, 24 December 1984.

59. Hamner interview.

60. Bailey, 22.

61. Mack Blalock, interview with author, Mentone, 3 June 1985.

62. Ed Rickard, interview with author, Russellville, 15 September 1985.

63. Carl Stewart, interview with author, Ketona, 13 June 1984.

64. Charles Wolfe, "Would You Believe; Lafollette, Bud Silvey, and Huntsville, 1928," *The Devil's Box* (Newsletter XXVI, 1 September 1974): 59.

65. Blalock interview.

66. Pearl Duncan Morgan Andrews, interview with author, Caledonia, Mississippi, 27 June 1985.

67. Carter Rushing, interview with author, Henderson, 23 November 1984.

68. William Everis Campbell, interview with author, Troy, 23 December 1984.

69. Ellis Spivey, interview with author, Robertsdale, 24 December 1984.

70. Rushing interview.

71. Tom Sutton, interview with author, Athens, 13 September 1984.

72. Ibid.

73. *Alabama Courier*, 6 March 1924.

74. Ibid., 4 March 1926.

75. Cole interview.

76. Wilma Kmetko, interview with author, Huntsville, 11 January 1986.

77. E. F. DuBose, telephone conversation with author, Huntsville, 11 January 1986.

78. Dickerson interview.

79. Cicero interview.

80. Hicks interview.

81. Bob Kyle, "Old Time Music Will Never Die," *Tuscaloosa News* (17 March 1957), reprinted in *The Devil's Box*, XII (May 1970): 6. Used with permission of the *Tuscaloosa News*.

82. Berthel Adams, *Trailing Smokes, A Pictorial History of Ider School District* (Ider: Berthel Adams, 1973), 115–116. Dr. Carroll is listed as a participant in a 1907 contest in De Kalb County; see Appendix 2.

83. Quoted by John Simpson Graham in *History of Clarke County* (Birmingham Printing Co., 1923), 270. Barnes is listed as a participant in a fiddlers' convention in Jackson in 1903; see Appendix 2.

84. Mary E. Brantley, *From Cabins to Mansions* (Huntsville: Strode, 1981), 245.

85. Etowah County Centennial Commission, *A History of Etowah County, Alabama* (Birmingham: Roberts and Sons, 1968), 344.

86. Myrtle Aldridge in *150 Yesteryears, Fayette County, Alabama*, Fayette County Historical Society, II (*Fayette County Broadcaster*, 1971), 228.

87. Mitchell B. Garrett, *Horse and Buggy Days on Hatchet Creek* (University: University of Alabama Press, 1957), 214.

88. Sutton interview.

89. A. K. Callahan, interview with author, Tuscaloosa, 22 January 1984.

90. Howard Colburn, interview with author, McCalla, 9 May 1985.

91. W. A. Bryan, "Memories of Fiddling Monk Daniels," *The Devil's Box* (1 March 1975): 36–37.

92. Campbell interview.

Chapter 3.
Alabama's Brag Fiddlers

1. Tom Sutton, interview with author, Athens, 13 September 1984.

2. "Fiddlers," *Outlook* 146 (25 May 1927): 106.

3. Commercial and home recordings by all the "brag" fiddlers discussed in Chapter 3 (with the exception of "Monkey" Brown) have been reproduced on *Possum Up a Gum Stump: Home, Field, and Commercial Recordings of Alabama Fiddlers.* This album was produced in 1988 by Joyce Cauthen under the sponsorship of the Brierfield Ironworks Park Foundation with additional funding by the Alabama State Council for the Arts and the National Endowment for the Arts. While copies are available, they may be ordered from the Brierfield Ironworks Park Foundation (Route 1, Box 147, Brierfield, Alabama 35035) or from commercial distributors of country and folk music. Copies will also be available at city, regional, and university libraries within Alabama.

4. Joe G. Acee, *Lamar County History* (Vernon, Alabama: *Lamar Democrat*, 1972), 6.

5. D. Dix Hollis, letter to Mrs. Edward McGhee, 10 July 1926. Used with permission.

6. Ibid.

7. Ibid.

8. *Opelika Daily News*, 17 April 1926.

9. Acee, 6.

10. Chloe Hollis Weaver, interview with author, Sulligent, January 1984.

11. In the brochure to JEMF LP 103 *Paramount Old Time Tunes*, Norm Cohen writes that because no Paramount ledgers or files survive, discographic data are still being "painfully pieced together." Hollis's statement that he recorded twelve numbers will be interesting to those doing the piecework. The master numbers of his known recordings—"Turkey in De Straw" (Master #1790–1), "Walking in the Parlor" (#1791–1), "Dixie" and "Yankee Doodle" (#1797–1), and "The Girl Slipped Down" (#1798–1)—indicate that he recorded at least nine. As we have no reason to doubt his word that he recorded twelve, Hollis would account for twelve of the thirteen gaps in the master numbers between 1786/ 87 (Eddie Green and Billy Wilson) and 1801/ 02 (Faye Barnes).

12. *Opelika Daily News*, 17 April 1926, and the *Lamar Democrat*, 21 April 1926.

13. Ibid.

14. Mrs. Inez Gibbs, Sulligent, personal note, 7 February 1984. Mrs. Gibbs explained in a later telephone conversation that in the "fiddler's dance," the fiddler danced and played at the same time. She recalled that Hollis excelled at this and wore special dancing slippers at such performances.

15. Bob Kyle, interview with author, 22 January 1984.

16. A. D. Hamner, interview with author, Northport, 24 April 1984.

17. A. K. Callahan, interview with author, 22 January 1984.

18. Sam Busby, interview with author, Ensley, 26 August 1983.

19. *Birmingham Age-Herald*, 24 November 1932.

20. *Lamar Democrat*, 18 September 1929.

21. *Gadsden Evening Journal*, 10 March 1908; Etowah County Centennial Committee, *A History of Etowah County* (Birmingham: Roberts and Son, 1968), 181–182.

22. Record of marriage licenses, Jefferson County.

23. *Birmingham Age-Herald*, 26 February 1925.

24. *Birmingham Age-Herald*, 19 February 1926.

25. Charles Wolfe, liner notes, "The Georgia Yellow Hammers," Rounder Records 1032.

26. Discographical data sheet, "Wyzee Hamilton," Country Music Foundation, Nashville. This group was also listed as "Hamilton Harmonicans" in Gennett logs.

27. Letter to Isabelle Enderson, 7 May 1948, in Patrick collection, Birmingham Public Library Archives.

28. Discographical data sheet, "Wyzee Hamilton."

29. Kyle interview.

30. Oscar Riley, interview with author, Northport, 31 August 1984.

31. Ibid.

32. Mrs. Louis Marston, telephone conversation, 1 June 1982.

33. Busby interview.

34. Earle Drake, interview with author, 3 August 1983.

35. *Birmingham Age-Herald*, 30 June 1936.

36. *Columbus* (Mississippi) *Commercial Dispatch*, 10 September 1929.

37. "Fiddler's Jubilee," pages 41–43, mentions a tune named "Lexington on a Bum."

38. Charlie and Ira Stripling, interview by Bob Pinson, 2 September 1963. Used with permission of Bob Pinson, Country Music Foundation, Nashville. Unless otherwise noted, all further quotations of the words of Charlie and Ira Stripling are taken from this interview.

39. *Columbus* (Mississippi) *Commercial Dispatch*, 10 September 1929.

40. *Birmingham Age-Herald*, 26 February 1925.

41. *Lamar Democrat* (Vernon), 19 May 1926.

42. Wayne Daniel, "The Memphis Fiddlers' Conventions of 1925 and 1926," *The Devil's Box* (Summer 1985): 16.

43. Ibid., 18.

44. Ibid., 18.

45. Ibid., 18–19.

46. *Tuscaloosa News*, 25 February 1927.

47. Ibid., 4 March 1927.

48. Eugene Earle and Graham Wickham, "Stripling Brothers Discography," *JEMF Quarterly*, No. 4: 21.

49. Charles K. Wolfe, "The Mystery of 'The Black Mountain Rag,' " *The Devil's Box* (1 December 1982): 3–12.

50. Earle and Wickham, Discography.

51. Robert Stripling, interview with author, West Alabama, 30 August 1984.

52. Earle and Wickham, 22.

53. Fifteenth census of the U.S., 1930.

54. Joe Acee, *Lamar County History*, revised edition (Vernon: *Lamar Democrat*, 1972), 45.

55. Earle and Wickham, 22.

56. Robert Stripling interview.

57. Ibid.

58. Elsie Stripling Mordecai, interview with author, Kennedy, 30 August 1984.

59. Robert Stripling interview.

60. Mrs. Dannie Strickland, interview with author, Moore's Bridge, 30 August 1984.

61. Undated newspaper clipping in files of Elsie Stripling Mordecai.

62. A. K. Callahan, interview with author, Tuscaloosa, 22 January 1984.

63. Charlie and Ira Stripling interview.

64. Robert Stripling interview.

65. Charles Wolfe, "Five Years with the Best; Bill Shores and North Georgia Fiddling," *Old Time Music* (Spring 1977): 5.

66. Joe LaRose, "An Interview with Lowe Stokes," *Old Time Music* 39 (Spring 1984): 7.

67. Ibid., 7. A discography accompanying this article, prepared by Tony Russell and Guthrie T. Meade, notes that Stokes recorded "Katy Hill" under the title "Sally Johnson" and that this recording has been reissued on County 544, *Georgia Fiddle Bands*.

68. Wolfe, "Five Years with the Best," 5.

69. Roger Aycock, interview with author, Rome, Georgia, 20 September 1986.

70. Paul Ray, interview with author, Rome, Georgia, 20 September 1986.

71. Aycock interview.

72. Mrs. Maude Lee, telephone conversation with author, Rome, Georgia, 20 September 1986.

73. *Sand Mountain Banner*, 5 May 1927, and *Fort Payne Journal*, 23 March 1927.

74. LaRose, 7.

75. Roger Aycock, "Rome and Community: Fifty Years Ago This Week" (*Rome News-Tribune*, 17 October and 7 November 1975).

76. Wolfe, "Five Years with the Best," 5.

77. Paul Ray's recordings of Joe Lee were located through the efforts of James Bryan, a well-known Alabama fiddler. This section would not have been possible without the aid of Bryan, who encouraged the author to write about Lee and arranged the interviews used in this chapter.

78. Aycock interview.

79. Ray interview.

80. Charles Lee, interview with author, Rome, Georgia, 20 September 1986.

81. Maude Lee interview.

82. Ray interview.

83. Charles Lee interview.

84. Aycock interview.

85. Ray interview.

86. *Mountain Eagle,* 21 February 1952; *Cullman Tribune,* 21 February 1952; *Birmingham News,* 17 February 1952, section D, 7.

87. *Birmingham Age-Herald,* 19 August 1938.

88. Undocumented newspaper clipping in Freeman family scrapbook, possibly from the *Cullman Banner,* ca. 1940.

89. Interviews with Arlin Moon, Holly Pond, 5 September 1985; Bob Kyle, Tuscaloosa, 22 January 1984; Carl Stewart, Ketona, 13 June 1984; and Bob Kyle, "Fiddle Music Will Never Die," reprinted in *The Devil's Box* XII (May 1970): 8. Used by permission of the *Tuscaloosa News.*

90. Former Congressman Carl Elliott, interview with author, Jasper, 3 October 1985.

91. Margaret Jean Jones, *Combing Cullman County* (Cullman: Modernistic Printers, 1972), 19.

92. Tom Freeman, "The Bug Tussle Murders" (unpublished manuscript), 1941. The original manuscript, which is in the possession of Freeman's granddaughter, consists of approximately 200 pages containing about 85 words per page, a high percentage of which are misspelled. There is almost no punctuation. For the reader's convenience, the author has corrected the spelling and inserted punctuation, while leaving the wording unchanged. Any words inserted for clarity that are not Freeman's are indicated by brackets. All further quotations of Tom Freeman come from this manuscript unless otherwise noted.

93. Carrie Freeman, interview with author, Bremen, 19 September 1985.

94. Wesley S. Thompson, *"The Free State of Winston;" A History of Winston* (Winfield: Pareil Press, 1968), 176.

95. Circuit Court, Cullman County, "The State of Alabama, Cullman County, vs Tom Freeman," October Term, 1925, 168.

96. Margaret Jean Jones, *Cullman County Across the Years* (Cullman: Modernistic Printers, 1975), 17.

97. *Birmingham News,* 31 March 1938.

98. *Mountain Eagle* (Jasper), 21 July 1938; *Birmingham Age-Herald,* 19 August 1938; and *Birmingham News,* 19 August 1938.

99. *Cullman Banner*, 7 September 1939.

100. Gene Wiggins, "Roosevelt's Fiddler: Bun Wright," *The Devil's Box* (1 December 1982): 50–56.

101. Undocumented newspaper clipping in Freeman family scrapbook.

102. Ed Rickard, interview with author, Russellville, 15 September 1985.

103. *Birmingham Age-Herald*, 19 August 1938.

104. Elliott interview.

105. Ibid.

106. Ibid.

107. Unlabeled newspaper clippings in Freeman family scrapbook.

108. *Cullman Banner*, 7 September 1939.

109. *Birmingham News*, 17 December 1950.

110. *Cullman Banner*, 19 May 1939.

111. *Cullman Tribune*, 21 February 1952.

112. Ibid.

113. J. C. Freeman, interview with author, Bremen, 19 September 1985.

114. *Cullman Tribune*, 21 February 1952.

115. J. C. Freeman interview.

116. Elliott interview.

117. *Cullman Tribune*, 21 February 1952.

118. Freeman manuscript.

119. *Cullman Banner*, 28 April 1940.

120. *Cullman Banner*, 5 May 1939.

121. Carl Carmer, *Stars Fell on Alabama* (1934). Reprint (University: University of Alabama Press, 1985), 44.

122. J. Wayne Flynt, introduction to *Stars Fell on Alabama*, xii.

123. Many details in Part II of the book seem to have been suggested by a Master's thesis, supervised by Carmer: S. M. Taylor, "A Preliminary Survey of Folk-Lore in Alabama," University of Alabama, 1925.

124. Carmer, "Author's Note."

125. Charlie Brown, telephone conversation, Tuscaloosa, 20 August 1986.

126. Carmer, 43.

127. Bob Kyle, *Tuscaloosa News*, 28 March 1971.

128. Nancy Callahan, "Monkey Brown: A Remembrance," *Bluegrass Unlimited* (August 1984), 27. The author appreciates permission granted by Callahan and *Bluegrass Unlimited* to quote from this article extensively.

129. Ibid., 28.

130. Ibid., 27.

131. Ibid., 24.

132. *Tuscaloosa News*, 28 March 1971.

133. A. K. Callahan, interview with author, 22 January 1984.

134. Nancy Callahan, 28.

135. Ibid., 28–29.

136. Ibid., 26.

137. Ibid., 26–27.

138. *Tuscaloosa News*, 28 March 1971.

139. Nancy Callahan, 30.

140. *Tuscaloosa News*, 29 March 1971.

141. Carmer, 48.

142. *Johnson Family History*, an unpublished manuscript. Used by permission.

143. Guy, Byron, and Ruth Johnson, interview with author, Albertville, 23 June 1983. Unless otherwise noted, all information comes from this interview and subsequent discussions with Guy and Juanita Johnson in Birmingham.

144. *De Kalb Republican*, 6 August 1925.

145. W. A. Bryan, interview with author, Boaz, 18 August 1983.

146. *Sand Mountain Banner*, 11 February 1924.

147. *Gadsden Evening Star*, 18 June 1926.

148. *Sand Mountain Banner*, 24 March 1926.

149. Ibid., 16 August 1927.

150. *Johnson Family History*.

151. Archie Green, "Hillbilly Music: Source and Symbol, *Journal of American Folklore* 78 (July–September 1965), 204–228.

152. Discographical entry sheet, "Johnson Brothers," Country Music Foundation, Nashville.

153. Richard Rachelson, "Lil McClintock's 'Don't You Think I'm Santa Claus,' " *JEMF Quarterly* 6 (Autumn 1970): 134.

154. This record, along with recordings of Johnson Family radio shows, is on file at the Country Music Foundation, Nashville.

155. *Marshall-De Kalb Monitor News Leader*, 9 January 1975.

156. E. C. Littlejohn, interview with author, Nashville, 13 August 1984.

157. Earle Drake, interview with author, Birmingham, 3 August 1983.

158. Undated newspaper clipping in Johnson family papers.

159. Mitch Mendelson, *Birmingham Post-Herald*, 4 June 1984.

Chapter 4.
Fiddling the Buttons Off Their Sleeves

1. Lucille Griffith, *Alabama, A Documentary History to 1900*, revised edition (University: University of Alabama Press, 1972), 301.

2. See Chapter III, *Plain Folk of the Old South* by Frank Lawrence Owsley (Baton Rouge: Louisiana State University Press, 1949), for a detailed description of such events.

3. Fred S. Watson, *The Back Forty* (Dothan: Moonlighters, 1968), 10.

4. Ed Rickard, interview with author, Russellville, 15 September 1985.

5. *Fort Payne Journal*, 20 March and 3 April 1907.

6. *Clarke County Democrat*, 2 July and 9 July 1925.

7. Joe Acee, *Lamar County History* (Vernon: *Lamar Democrat*, 1972), 4.

8. Francis Bartow Lloyd, *Sketches of Country Life; Humor, Wisdom and Pathos from the "Sage of Rocky Creek"* (Birmingham: Roberts and Sons, 1898), 159.

9. Harmon Hicks, interview with author, Pleasant Grove, 23 April 1983.

10. Bill Harrison, "Fiddling in Limestone County, 1925–1940," *The Devil's Box* (15 February 1972): 8.

11. James Cole, interview with author, Athens, 13 September 1984.

12. Elsie Stripling Mordecai, interview with author, Kennedy, 30 August 1984.

13. J. V. Porter, interview with author, Steens, Mississippi, 13 December 1984.

14. Thomas E. Hill, interview with author, Pinson, 4 June 1983.

15. Gaines Arnold, interview with author, Quinton, 7 May 1984.

16. Cole interview.

17. Porter interview.

18. Captain W. L. Fagan, "History of Marion, 1818–'35" in the *Marion Standard*, 30 April 1909. *Breakdown* and *hoedown* are terms which describe vigorous dancing with showy footwork. They also apply to the tunes that inspire such dancing.

19. *Centerville Press*, 7 July 1898.

20. Mrs. Dannie Strickland, interview with author, Moore's Bridge, 30 August 1984.

21. Hicks interview.

22. Matthew D. Hill, interview with author, Chalkville, 30 May 1982.

23. Cecil J. Sharp and Maud Karpeles, *The Country Dance Book, Part V* (New York: H. W. Gray, 1918), 7–12.

24. Lloyd Shaw, *Cowboy Dances*, revised edition (Caldwell, Idaho: Caxton Printers, 1952), 30.

25. Porter, Hill, and Rickard interviews.

26. Marguerite Tarwater Callahan, letter to author, 26 August 1985.

27. Claude Cassidy, interview with author, Fort Payne, 4 June 1985.

28. David Campbell and David Coombs, "Skyline Farms: A Case Study of Community Development and Rural Rehabilitation," *Appalachian Journal* 10 (Spring 1983): 244–254.

29. Janelle Warren-Findley, "Musicians and Mountaineers: The Resettlement Administration's Music Program in Appalachia, 1935–37," *Appalachian Journal* (Autumn–Winter 1979–1980): 106.

30. Chester Allen, interview with author, Scottsboro, 5 June 1984; and *Birmingham Age-Herald*, 13 May 1938.

31. Earle Drake, interview with author, Birmingham, 3 August 1983.

32. Sandy Gable, interview with author, Eastern Valley (Jefferson County), 23 August 1984.

33. Tom Sutton, interview with author, Athens, 13 September 1984.

34. Shaw, 36.

35. Gene Dunlap, interview with author, Birmingham, 15 July 1986.

36. Dunlap interview.

37. Thomas E. Hill interview.

38. *Alabama Courier*, 6 March 1924.

39. Richard Hulan, "The 1st Annual Country Fiddlers' Contest," *Devil's Box* (15 March 1969): 15–18.

40. *South Alabamian*, 25 July 1903, reprinted in *Historical Sketches of Clarke County, Alabama; A Story of the Communities of Clarke County, Alabama*, Clarke County Historical Society (Huntsville: Strode Publishers, 1977), 277.

41. *Clarke County Democrat*, 20 August 1903.

42. John Simpson Graham, *History of Clarke County* (Birmingham: Birmingham Printing Co., 1923), 246–47.

43. *Chilton County News*, 1 June 1922.

44. *Sand Mountain Banner*, 8 March 1923.

45. *Alabama Courier*, 23 February 1933.

46. Ibid., 10 March 1932.

47. *Limestone Democrat*, 15 March 1934.

48. *Clarke County Democrat*, 8 December 1938.

49. *A History of Chatom in Words and Pictures* (Chatom: *Call-News Dispatch*, 1979), 71.

50. *Sand Mountain Banner*, 8 December 1921.

51. *Birmingham News*, 13 April 1927.

52. Arlin Moon, interview with author, Holly Pond, 29 January 1986.

53. Julia L. Willard, "Reflections of an Alabama Teacher, 1875–1950," *The Alabama Historical Quarterly* (Winter, 1976): 303.

54. E. F. DuBose, telephone conversation with author, Huntsville, 11 January 1986.

55. Willard, 303.

56. *Cullman Democrat*, 29 December 1938.

57. Willard, 299.

58. Elizabeth Counselman and Vera Coate Stringer, "Coffeeville," *Historical Sketches of Clarke County, Alabama*: Clarke County Historical Society (Huntsville: Strode Publishers, 1977), 107–121.

59. *Clarke County Democrat*, 19 December 1935.

60. *Chilton County News*, 19 February 1925.

61. *Mountain Eagle*, 12 February 1930.

62. *Union Banner*, 25 October 1925.

63. Willard, 302.

64. *Mountain Eagle*, 12 February 1930.

65. *Cullman Democrat*, 20 October 1938.

66. *Union Banner*, 17 February 1927.

67. Ibid., 11 March 1926.

68. Ibid., 27 October 1921.

69. Robert Stripling, interview with author, Warrior, 21 May 1984.

70. *Sulligent News*, 9 April 1928.

71. *Clarke County Democrat*, 25 October 1934.

72. Porter interview.

73. *Clarke County Democrat*, 9 May 1929.

74. James W. Jackson, interview with author, Huntsville, 18 September 1984.

75. *Union Banner*, 29 September 1921.

76. *Clarke County Democrat*, 9 May 1929.

77. S. M. Taylor, "A Preliminary Survey of Folk-Lore in Alabama," Master's thesis (University of Alabama, 1925), 32.

78. *Clarke County Democrat*, 16 May 1929.

79. Bob Kyle, interview with author, Tuscaloosa, 22 January 1984.

80. Arnold interview.

81. Kyle interview.

82. Everis Campbell, interview with author, Troy, 24 November 1984.

83. Charlie Stripling, interview with Bob Pinson, Kennedy, 2 September 1963.

84. *Union Banner*, 29 September 1921.

85. *Clarke County Democrat*, 16 May 1929.

86. *Limestone Democrat*, 28 February 1929.

87. *Clarke County Democrat*, 25 February 1937.

88. Ibid., 9 December 1937.

89. Ibid.

90. Ibid., 25 October 1934.

91. Bob Kyle and A. K. Callahan, interview with author, Tuscaloosa, 22 January 1984.

92. *Collinsville New Era*, 20 October 1932.

93. Alton Delmore, *Truth Is Stranger Than Publicity* (Nashville: Country Music Foundation Press, 1977), 25.

94. Harrison: 5–7.

95. Delmore, 28–29.

96. *Alabama Courier*, 6 March 1924.

97. Ibid.

98. Ibid., 5 March 1925.

99. Ibid., 4 March 1926.

100. *Limestone Democrat*, 3 March 1927.

101. By "old fiddlers," Johnson may have meant "old-time fiddlers," as the winner of the competition, Mrs. Emma Crabtree, was 30 years old at the time.

102. *Limestone Democrat*, 23 February 1928.

103. Ibid., 28 February 1929.

104. *Alabama Courier*, 20 February 1930.

105. Ibid., 3 March 1932.

106. Delmore, 28–29.

107. *Limestone Democrat*, 3 March 1932, and *Alabama Courier*, 3 March 1932.

108. *Alabama Courier*, 2 March 1933.

109. Harrison: 8.

110. Bill Harrison, notes on program of Tennessee Valley Old-Time Fiddlers' Convention, 4 October 1969.

111. Wellington Vandiveer, in *Sketches of Talledega County, Alabama; A Collection* (Birmingham: Works Progress Administration, 1938), 126.

112. Owsley, 116.

113. Mattie McAdory Huey, *History of the Alabama Division, United Daughters of the Confederacy* (Opelika: Post Publishing Co., 1937), 268–269.

114. Henry Wadsworth Longfellow, "The Day Is Done," reprinted in the *Northwest Alabamian*, 25 August 1926.

115. *Northwest Alabamian*, 4 September 1930.

116. *Fayette Banner*, 17 January 1929.

117. Marguerite T. Callahan, discussion with author, Tuscaloosa, 26 June 1985.

118. Stripling interview by Pinson.

119. *Northwest Alabamian*, 11 September 1930.

120. Stripling interview by Pinson.

121. *Fayette Banner*, 14 March 1929.

122. Porter interview.

123. Huey, 269.

124. *Birmingham News-Age Herald*, 10 May 1936.

125. *Fort Payne Journal*, 16 August 1933.

126. W. Stanley Hoole and Addie S. Hoole, *Early History of Northeast Alabama and Incidentally of Northwest Georgia* (University: Confederate Publishing Co., 1979), 8.

127. *De Kalb Republican*, 14 August 1924.

128. *Fort Payne Journal*, 7 August 1929.

129. Ibid.

130. Ibid., 10 August 1932.

131. Ibid., 5 August 1931.

132. Ibid., 19 August 1936.

133. Ibid., 20 August 1930.

134. Ibid., 14 August 1929. J. M. Blalock, who was called Joe, not Jim, composed a number of tunes that have been preserved by Blalock family musicians and recorded by James Bryan on Rounder Record 0175.

135. Ibid., 10 August 1932.

136. Ibid., 13 August 1941.

137. Ibid., 11 August 1928.

138. Ibid., 14 August 1935.

139. Buddy Durham, "The Buddy Durham Story," *The Devil's Box* (Spring 1985): 28–33.

140. *De Kalb Republican*, 21 August 1924.

141. *Fort Payne Journal*, 10 August 1927.

142. Ibid., 8 August 1928.

143. Ibid., 17 August 1932.

144. Ibid.

145. Ibid., 14 August 1929.

146. Ibid., 13 August 1942.

147. Ibid., 4 August 1943.

148. Ibid., 19 August 1936.

149. Ibid., 17 August 1938 and 16 August 1939.

150. *De Kalb Republican*, 14 August 1924.

151. *Mountain Eagle*, 24 April 1929.

152. *Fayette Banner*, 2 May 1929, and *Mountain Eagle*, 1 May 1929.

153. *Sand Mountain Banner*, 5 May 1927.

154. Charles Wolfe, "Would You Believe; Lafollette, Bud Silvey, and Huntsville, 1928," *The Devil's Box* (Newsletter XXVI, 1 September 1974): 59.

155. *Birmingham News*, 15 May 1927.

156. Ibid., 19, 22, 23 May 1925, and *Birmingham Age-Herald*, 19 May 1925.

157. *Birmingham Age-Herald*, 25 January 1925, and 22 February 1925.

158. Ibid., 26 February 1925.

159. *Tuscaloosa News*, 17 April 1927. E. E. Akins, better known as "Silas" Akins, was a well-known Birmingham fiddler who played on the radio and recorded "There Ain't No Flies on Auntie" and "I Walked and Walked" (Columbia 15348). Jack Jackson, at the time, was the fiddler with the Gibbs Brothers Band of Huntsville.

160. Porter interview and W. A. Bryan, interview with author, Boaz, 18 August 1983.

161. *Montgomery Advertiser*, 18 December 1926.

162. Ibid., 24 April 1927.

163. *Columbus Enquirer-Sun*, 12 December 1926.

164. *Montgomery Advertiser*, 24 and 28 April 1927.

165. Dick Vance, "More on Natchee the Indian," *The Devil's Box* (1 September 1980): 13.

166. "Happy" Hal Burns, interview with author, Birmingham, 15 April 1986.

167. Vance: 12–13.

168. Ivan M. Tribe, "Curly Fox: Old Time and Novelty Fiddler Extraordinary," *The Devil's Box* (1 December 1974): 10.

169. Vance: 11.

170. Burns interview.

171. Tribe: 11.

172. Untitled clipping from scrapbook of Earline Guined, Birmingham.

173. Burns interview.

174. *Birmingham Age-Herald*, 31 March 1938.

175. Burns interview.

176. Nancy Callahan, "Keeping Old-Time Music Alive," *Bluegrass Unlimited* (June 1980): 56–60. Tapes of Callahan's conventions and those he attended in other states are archived in the Southern Folklore Collection of the University of North Carolina at Chapel Hill.

177. *De Kalb Republican*, 21 August 1924.

Chapter 5.
Fiddling and Associated Sins

1. John Gorman Barr, *Rowdy Tales from Early Alabama; The Humor of John Gorman Barr*, G. Ward Hubbs, ed. (University: University of Alabama Press, 1981), 163. The latter set of quotation marks indicates Barr's quotation of George Powell, Esq., who had submitted a sketch of Blount County to the Alabama Historical Society.

2. Barr, 163–64.

3. *Historical Records of Randolph County, Alabama, 1832–1900*, compiled by Marilyn Davis Barefield (Easley, South Carolina: Southern Historical Press, 1985), 8.

4. Mattie Lou Teague Crow, *History of St. Clair County (Alabama)* (Huntsville: Strode Publishers, 1973), 147.

5. "Fiddling to Henry Ford," *Literary Digest* 88 (2 January 1926): 34.

6. Herbert Halpert, "The Devil and the Fiddle," *Hoosier Folklore Bulletin* 2 (1943): 39–43.

7. Francis Bartow Lloyd, *Sketches of Country Life; Humor, Wisdom and Pathos from the "Sage of Rocky Creek"* (Birmingham: Roberts and Son, 1898), 289–90.

8. Lloyd, 21.
*Fiddler's Green: According to the folklore of fishermen, a land of perpetual dancing, drinking, music, and singing.

9. Lloyd, 23.

10. Howell Raines, *Whiskey Man* (New York: Viking Press, 1977).

11. Dickson D. Bruce, Jr., *And They All Sang Hallelujah; Plain-folk Camp-Meeting Religion, 1800–1845* (Knoxville: University of Tennessee Press, 1974), 126.

12. George Pullen Jackson, *White Spirituals in the Southern Uplands* (Chapel Hill: University of North Carolina Press, 1933), 146.

13. Glenn N. Sisk, *Alabama Black Belt, A Social History, 1875–1917*, PhD dissertation (Duke University, 1951), 241.

14. *Alabama Baptist*, 18 August 1887.

15. Captain W. L. Fagan, "History of Marion, 1818–'35," in *Marion Standard*, 9 April 1909.

16. Tom Sutton, interview with author, Athens, 13 September 1984.

17. Monk Daniels, interview with Herb Trotman, June 1978. Used by permission.

18. Vearl Cicero, interview with author, Quinton, 7 May 1984.

19. *Cullman Democrat*, 24 September 1925; *Sand Mountain Banner*, 9 April 1936.

20. Gaines Arnold, interview with author, Quinton, 7 May 1984.

21. Betsy Hamilton (Idora M. Moore), *Southern Character Sketches* (Richmond: Dietz Press, 1937), 27–28; copyright renewed 1965 by Otis D. Smith. Used by permission.

22. Hamilton, 27.

23. H. C. Nixon, *Lower Piedmont Country* (New York: Duell, Sloan and Pearce, 1946), 85.

24. *Fruitdale Herald*, 3 October 1900.

25. *Hayneville Citizen-Examiner*, 24 July 1913, as quoted by Sisk, 396.

26. *Alabama Baptist*, 7 April 1887.

27. Ibid.

28. Mitchell B. Garrett, *Horse and Buggy Days on Hatchet Creek* (University: University of Alabama Press, 1957), 214.

29. Eddie B. Rozelle, *Recollections—My Folks and Fields* (privately published by E. B. Rozelle, Talledega, 1960), 84. Used by permission.

30. Byron Johnson, interview with author, Albertville, 23 June 1983.

31. Lloyd, 160.

32. Ibid.

33. Garrett, 171.

34. Rhoda Coleman Ellison, *Bibb County, Alabama: The First Hundred Years, 1818–1918* (University: University of Alabama Press, 1984), 70.

35. Sisk, 245.

36. Geneva Gaines, interview with Alice Crocker, Leeds, 20 October and 1 November 1975, for Oral History Research Office, University of Alabama in Birmingham.

37. *Union Banner*, 6 October 1921.

38. Rozelle, 84.

39. W. P. Wilkes, *An Alabama Boy, 1880 to 1902* (3rd edition of an undated collection of memoirs first published in the *Troy Daily Messenger and Weekly Herald*), 48.

40. *Marengo News-Journal*, 9 June 1883, cited in Sisk, 246.

41. *Clarke County Democrat*, 15 November 1934 and 2 December 1937; *Tuscaloosa News*, 23 May 1927; *Chilton County News*, 8 April 1926.

42. Ed Rickard, interview with author, Russellville, 15 September 1985.

43. Marion Bailey Brunson, *Pea River Reflections; Intimate Glimpses of Area Life During Two Centuries*, 3rd ed. (Tuscaloosa: Portals Press, 1984), 39–44. Used by permission.

44. Brunson, 169–70.

45. *"A Night with the Hants" and Other Alabama Folk Experiences*, Ray B. Browne, ed. (Bowling Green, Ohio: Popular Press, 1979), 133–34.

46. Ibid., 167.

47. D. Dix Hollis, letter to Mrs. Edward McGhee, 10 July 1926. Hollis's reference is to passages in I Samuel 16.

Books

Abernethy, Thomas Perkins. *The Formative Period in Alabama, 1814–1828*. University: University of Alabama Press, 1965.

Acee, Joe. *Lamar County History*. Revised Edition. Vernon: *Lamar Democrat*, 1972.

Adams, Berthel. *Trailing Smokes, A Pictorial History of Ider School District*. Ider: Berthel Adams, 1973.

Arnold, Byron. *Folksongs of Alabama*. University: University of Alabama Press, 1950.

Barr, John Gorman. *Rowdy Tales from Early Alabama: The Humor of John Gorman Barr*, G. Ward Hubbs, ed. University: University of Alabama Press, 1981.

Benners, Alfred H. *Slavery and Its Results*. Macon, Georgia: J. W. Burke, 1923.

Blassingame, John W. *The Slave Community: Plantation Life in the Antebellum South*. 3rd ed. New York: Oxford University Press, 1979.

Boyd, Minnie Clare. *Alabama in the Fifties: A Social Study*. New York: Columbia University Press, 1931.

Brantley, Mary E. *From Cabins to Mansions*. Huntsville: Strode, 1981.

Brown, Virginia Pounds, and Laurella Owens. *Toting the Lead Row: Ruby Pickens Tartt, Alabama Folklorist*. University: University of Alabama Press, 1981.

Browne, Ray B., ed. *"A Night with the Hants" and Other Alabama Folk Experiences*. Bowling Green, Ohio: Popular Press, 1979.

Bruce, Dickson D., Jr. *And They All Sang Hallelujah: Plain-folk Camp-Meeting Religion, 1800–1845*. Knoxville: University of Tennessee Press, 1974.

Brunson, Marion Bailey. *Pea River Reflections: Intimate Glimpses of Area Life During Two Centuries*. 3rd ed. Tuscaloosa: Portals Press, 1984.

Cannon, J. P. *Inside Rebeldom: The Daily Life of a Private in the Confederate Army*. Washington, D.C.: National Tribune, 1900.

Carmer, Carl. *Stars Fell on Alabama*. New York: Farrar and Rinehart, 1934. Reprint, University: University of Alabama Press, 1985.

Chase, Gilbert. *America's Music: From the Pilgrims to the Present.* New York: McGraw-Hill, 1955.

Clarke County Historical Society. *Historical Sketches of Clarke County, Alabama: A Story of the Communities of Clarke County, Alabama.* Huntsville: Strode, 1977.

Cohn, David. *The Good Old Days: A History of American Morals and Manners as Seen throughout the Sears, Roebuck Catalogs, 1905 to the Present.* New York: Simon and Schuster, 1940.

Courlander, Harold. *Negro Folk Music, U.S.A.* New York: Columbia University Press, 1963.

Crow, Mattie Lou Teague. *History of St. Clair County.* Huntsville: Strode, 1973.

Delmore, Alton. *Truth Is Stranger Than Publicity.* Nashville: Country Music Foundation Press, 1977.

Dichter, Harry, and Elliott Shapiro. *Handbook of Early American Sheet Music, 1768–1889.* New York: R. R. Bowker, 1941.

Ellison, Rhoda Coleman. *Bibb County, Alabama: The First Hundred Years, 1818–1918.* University: University of Alabama Press, 1984.

Epstein, Dena J. *Sinful Tunes and Spirituals.* Urbana: University of Illinois Press, 1977.

Etowah County Centennial Commission. *A History of Etowah County, Alabama.* Birmingham: Roberts and Sons, 1968.

Fayette County Historical Society. *150 Yesteryears, Fayette County, Alabama.* Fayette: *Fayette County Broadcaster*, 1971.

Federal Writers' Project. *Slave Narratives: Alabama and Indiana Narratives.* Vol. 5. St. Clair Shores: Scholarly Press. Republished 1976.

Feldman, Allen. *The Northern Fiddler.* New York: Oak, 1979.

Field, Al G. *Watch Yourself Go By.* Columbus, Ohio, 1912.

Garrett, Mitchell B. *Horse and Buggy Days on Hatchet Creek.* 2nd ed. University: University of Alabama Press, 1957.

Gelatt, Roland. *The Fabulous Phonograph, 1877–1977.* 2nd ed. New York: MacMillan, 1977.

Goldberg, Isaac. *Tin Pan Alley, A Chronicle of American Popular Music.* New York: Ungar, 1961.

Goodkind, Herbert K. *Violin Iconography of Antonio Stradivari, 1644–1737.* Larchmont: published by author, 1972.

Grafton, Carl, and Anne Permaloff. *Big Mules and Branchheads: James E. Folsom and Political Power in Alabama.* Athens: University of Georgia Press, 1985.

Graham, John Simpson. *History of Clarke County*. Birmingham Printing Co., 1923.

Griffith, Lucille. *Alabama, A Documentary History to 1900*. Revised ed. University: University of Alabama Press, 1972.

Hamilton, Betsy (Idora McClellan Moore). *Southern Character Sketches*. Richmond: Dietz Press, 1937.

Handy, W. C. *Father of the Blues, An Autobiography*. Edited by Arna Bontemps. New York: Macmillan, 1941.

Historical Records of Randolph County, Alabama, 1832–1900. Compiled by Marilyn Davis Barefield. Easley, South Carolina: Southern Historical Press, 1985.

A History of Chatom in Words and Pictures. Chatom: *Call-News Dispatch*, 1979.

Hoole, W. Stanley, and Addie S. Hoole. *Early History of Northeast Alabama and Incidentally of Northwest Georgia*. University: Confederate Publishing Co., 1979.

Huey, Mattie McAdory. *History of the Alabama Division, United Daughters of the Confederacy*. Opelika: Post Publishing Co., 1937.

Jackson, George Pullen. *White Spirituals in the Southern Uplands*. Chapel Hill: University of North Carolina Press, 1933.

Jones, Margaret Jean. *Combing Cullman County*. Cullman: Modernistic Printers, 1972.

———. *Cullman County Across the Years*. Cullman: Modernistic Printers, 1975.

Jordon, Weymouth. *Hugh Davis and his Alabama Plantation*. University: University of Alabama Press, 1984.

Leavett, M. B. *Fifty Years in Theatrical Management*. New York: Broadway Publishing Co., 1912.

Lloyd, Francis Bartow. *Sketches of Country Life: Humor, Wisdom and Pathos from the "Sage of Rocky Creek."* Birmingham: Roberts and Sons, 1898.

McMillan, Malcolm C., ed. *The Confederate Reader*. University: University of Alabama Press, 1963.

McMorries, Edward. *History of the First Regiment, Alabama Volunteer Infantry, CSA*. Montgomery: Brown Printing Co., 1904.

Moore, A. B. *History of Alabama*. Tuscaloosa: Alabama Book Store, 1934.

A Most Memorable 60 Years—WAPI Radio. Special Commemorative. Birmingham: WAPI, 1982.

Nathan, Hans. *Dan Emmett and the Rise of Early Negro Minstrelsy*. Norman: University of Oklahoma Press, 1977.

Nixon, H. C. *Lower Piedmont Country*. New York: Duell, Sloan and Pearce, 1946, Reprint. University: University of Alabama Press, 1984.

Olmsted, Frederick Law. *The Cotton Kingdom, A Traveller's Observations on Cotton and Slavery in the American Slave States*. New York: Mason Bros., 1861.

Owen, Marie Bankhead. *The Story of Alabama, A History of the State*. Vol. III. New York: Lewis Historical Publishing, 1949.

Owsley, Frank Lawrence. *Plain Folk of the Old South*. Baton Rouge: Louisiana State University Press, 1949.

Park, Robert Emory. *Sketch of the Twelfth Alabama Infantry*. Richmond: William Ellis Jones, 1906.

Pickett, Albert James. *History of Alabama and Incidentally of Georgia and Mississippi, from the Earliest Period*. 1851. Reprint. Birmingham Book and Magazine Co., 1972.

Raines, Howell. *Whiskey Man*. New York: Viking Press, 1977.

Read, Oliver, and Walter L. Welch. *From Tin Foil to Stereo: Evolution of the Phonograph*. Indianapolis and New York: Howard W. Sams & Co. and Bobbs-Merrill, 1959.

Scott, Carolyn Blackwell. *Country Roads: A Journey through Rustic Alabama*. Tuscaloosa: Portals Press, 1979.

Sears, Roebuck and Co. Reproduction of 1900 Catalog. Joseph J. Schroeder, Jr., ed. Northfield, Illinois, 1970.

Sears, Roebuck and Co. Reproduction of 1909 Catalog. New York: Ventura Books, 1979.

Sharp, Cecil J., and Maud Karpeles. *The Country Dance Book, Part V*. New York: H. W. Gray, 1918.

Shaw, Lloyd. *Cowboy Dances*. Revised ed. Caldwell, Idaho: Caxton Printers, 1952.

Sims, George E. *The Little Man's Big Friend: James E. Folsom in Alabama Politics, 1946–1958*. University: University of Alabama Press, 1985.

Southern, Eileen. *The Music of Black Americans: A History*. New York: W. W. Norton, 1971.

Stanfield, Mattie Cole. *Sourwood Tonic & Sassafras Tea*. New York: Exposition Press, 1963.

Sward, Keith. *The Legend of Henry Ford*. New York: Rinehart, 1948.

Tanner, John Thomas. *A History of Athens*. W. Stanley Hoole and Addie S. Hoole, eds. University: Confederate Publishing Co., 1978.

Thompson Wesley S. *"The Free State of Winston": A History of Winston*. Winfield: Pareil Press, 1968.

Toll, Robert C. *Blacking Up: The Minstrel Show in Nineteenth-Century America*. New York: Oxford University Press, 1974.

Walker, Anne Kendrick. *Backtracking in Barbour County, A Narrative of the Last Alabama Frontier*. Richmond: Dietz Press, 1941.

Watson, Fred S. *The Back Forty*. Dothan: Moonlighters, 1968.

Wechsberg, Joseph. *The Glory of the Violin*. New York: Viking Press, 1972.

Wiley, Bell I. *The Life of Johnny Reb, The Common Soldier of the Confederacy*. Indianapolis: Bobbs-Merrill, 1943.

Wilkes, W. P. *An Alabama Boy, 1880 to 1902*. Published by *Troy Daily Messenger and Weekly Herald*.

Wittke, Carl. *Tambo and Bones: A History of the American Minstrel Stage*. Durham: Duke University Press, 1930.

Works Progress Administration. *Sketches of Talledega County, Alabama: A Collection*. Birmingham, 1938.

Articles

Bailie, Marcus. "Early Alabama Fiddling." *The Devil's Box* 17 (Summer 1983): 21–23.

Bryan, W. A. "Memories of Fiddling Monk Daniels." *The Devil's Box* (1 March 1975): 36–38.

Callahan, Nancy. "Monkey Brown: A Remembrance." *Bluegrass Unlimited* (August 1984): 24–31.

———. "Keeping Old-Time Music Alive." *Bluegrass Unlimited* (June 1980): 56–60.

Campbell, David, and David Coombs. "Skyline Farms: A Case Study of Community Development and Rural Rehabilitation." *Appalachian Journal* 10 (Spring 1983): 244–54.

Cauthen, Joyce. "Uncle Dave Macon in Birmingham." *The Devil's Box* 17 (Fall 1983): 26–31.

Cooper, Norman V. "How They Went to War: An Alabama Brigade in 1861–62." *Alabama Review* 24 (January 1971): 17–50.

Daniel, Wayne W. "The Memphis Fiddlers' Conventions of 1925 and 1926." *The Devil's Box* (Summer 1985): 15–21.

Durham, Buddy. "The Buddy Durham Story." *The Devil's Box* (Spring 1985): 28–33.

Earle, Eugene, and Graham Wickham. "Stripling Brothers Discography." *JEMF Quarterly*. Vol. 4: 21–23.

"Fiddlers." *Outlook* 146 (25 May 1927): 105–106.

"Fiddling to Henry Ford." *Literary Digest*, 88 (2 January 1926): 34.

Grafton, Carl. "James E. Folsom's 1946 Campaign." *Alabama Review* (35: 3): 172–199.

Green, Archie. "Hillbilly Music: Source and Symbol." *Journal of American Folklore* 78 (July–September 1965): 204–228.

Halpert, Herbert. "The Devil and the Fiddle." *Hoosier Folklore Bulletin* 2 (1943): 39–43.

Harrison, Bill. "Fiddling in Limestone County: 1925 Through 1940." *The Devil's Box* (Newsletter XVI, 15 February 1972): 4–9.

Hulan, Richard. "The 1st Annual Country Fiddlers' Contest." *Devil's Box* (15 March 1969): 15–18.

Keller, Mark. "Alabama Plantation Life in 1860: Governor Benjamin Fitzpatrick's 'Oak Grove.' " *Alabama Historical Quarterly* (Spring 1976): 218–227.

Kyle, Bob. "Old Time Music Will Never Die." *Tuscaloosa News* (17 March 1957). Reprinted in *The Devil's Box* XII (May 1970): 6–7.

LaRose, Joe. "An Interview with Lowe Stokes." *Old Time Music* 39 (Spring 1984): 6–11.

Rachelson, Richard. "Lil McClintock's 'Don't You Think I'm Santa Claus.' " *JEMF Quarterly* 6 (Autumn 1970): 132–35.

Roberson, Don. " 'Uncle Bunt' Stephens—Champion Fiddler." *The Devil's Box* (Newsletter XII, 25 May 1970): 2–5.

Satterfield, Paul H. "Recreation of Soldiers, 1861–65." *Alabama Historical Quarterly* 20 (1958): 601–610.

Tribe, Ivan. "Curly Fox: Old Time and Novelty Fiddler Extraordinary." *The Devil's Box* (1 December 1974), 8–21.

Vance, Dick. "More on Natchee the Indian." *The Devil's Box* (1 September 1980): 11–15.

Warren-Findley, Janelle. "Musicians and Mountaineers: The Resettlement Administration's Music Program in Appalachia, 1935–37." *Appalachian Journal* (Autumn–Winter 1979–1980): 105–123.

White, Newman I. "The White Man in the Woodpile." *American Speech* 4 (February 1929): 207–214.

Wiggins, Gene. "Roosevelt's Fiddler: Bun Wright." *The Devil's Box* (1 December 1982): 50–56.

Willard, Julia L. "Reflections of an Alabama Teacher, 1875–1950." *Alabama Historical Quarterly* (Winter 1976): 291–304.

Wolfe, Charles K. "Five Years with the Best: Bill Shores and North Georgia Fiddling." *Old Time Music* (Spring 1977): 4–8.

———"Legends About Tennessee Fiddlers." *The Devil's Box* (Fall 1984): 19–26.

————"The Mystery of 'The Black Mountain Rag.' " *The Devil's Box*
(1 December 1982): 3–12.
————"Would You Believe; Lafollette, Bud Silvey, and Huntsville,
1928." *The Devil's Box* (Newsletter XXVI, 1 September 1974):
54–59.

Newspapers

Alabama Baptist, 1887.
Alabama Courier, 1924–33.
Alabama Planter, 1846.
Auburn Plainsman, 1927.
Birmingham Age-Herald, 1919, 1924–38.
Birmingham News, 1925–52.
Birmingham Post-Herald, 1984.
Centerville Press, 1898.
Chilton County News, 1922–26.
Clarke County Democrat, 1903–38.
Collinsville New Era, 1932.
Columbus (Georgia) Enquirer, 1926.
Commercial Dispatch (Columbus, Mississippi), 1929.
Cullman Banner, 1938–40.
Cullman Democrat, 1925, 1938.
Cullman Tribune, 1952.
Daily Alabama Journal (Montgomery), 1849.
De Kalb Republican, 1924–25.
Fayette Banner, 1908–41.
Fort Payne Journal, 1907–43.
Fruitdale Herald, 1900.
Gadsden Evening Journal, 1908.
Gadsden Evening Star, 1926.
Huntsville Times, 1955.
Lamar Democrat, 1926–29.
Limestone Democrat, 1929–34.
Marion Standard, 1909.
Marshall-De Kalb Monitor News Leader, 1975.
Montgomery Advertiser, 1855–1927.
Mountain Eagle News, 1926–52.
Northwest Alabamian, 1926–30.
Opelika Daily News, 1926.

Rome (Georgia) *News-Tribune*, 1975.
Sand Mountain Banner, 1921–36.
Sulligent News, 1928.
Thomasville Argus, 1897.
Tuscaloosa News, 1927, 1957, 1971.
Union Banner (Clanton), 1921–27.
Washington County News, 1922–24.
West Alabama Breeze, 1919.

Theses, Letters, and
Other Unpublished Works

Browne, William Phineas. Papers. Alabama Department of Archives and History, Montgomery.

Callahan, Marguerite Tarwater. Letter to author. 26 August 1985.

Country Music Foundation. Discographical entry sheets, "Short Creek Trio," "Wyzee Hamilton," and "D. Dix Hollis." Nashville. Undated photocopies.

Freeman, Tom. "The Bug Tussle Murders." Bremen, 1941. Handwritten manuscript.

Gibbs, Mrs. Inez. Letter to author. Sulligent, 7 February 1984.

Hollis, D. Dix. Letter to Mrs. Edward McGhee. Sulligent, 10 July 1926.

Johnson Family History. Prepared by the Johnson family of Albertville. Undated photocopy.

Kennedy, Robert Allen. "A History and Survey of Community Music in Mobile, Alabama." Ph.D. diss. Florida State University, 1960.

Lovett, Mrs. Rose Gibbons. Letter to author. Summer 1984.

Meade, Guthrie T. Discographical information supplied to author. 13 May 1984.

Patrick, Luther. Papers. Birmingham Public Library Archives.

Rozelle, Eddie B., *Recollections—My Folks and Fields*. Talladega, 1960. Photocopy.

Russell, Tony. Notes from a forthcoming discography of early country music supplied to author, 21 August 1986.

Sisk, Glenn N. *Alabama Black Belt: A Social History, 1875–1917*. Ph.D. diss. Duke University, 1951.

Taylor, S. M. "A Preliminary Survey of Folk-Lore in Alabama." Master's thesis. University of Alabama, 1925.

Recordings

ALBUMS

Georgia Yellow Hammers. Rounder Records 1032. Liner notes by
    Charles K. Wolfe.
Lookout Blues. James Bryan. Rounder Records 0175.
Old-Time Fiddle Classics. County 507.
Paramount Old Time Tunes. John Edwards Memorial Foundation
    LP 103. Liner notes by Norm Cohen.
*Possum up a Gum Stump: Home, Field and Commercial Recordings
    of Alabama Fiddlers.* Alabama Traditions 103.
Riding in an Old Model T. County 548.
The Stripling Brothers. County 401.

78 RPM RECORDINGS

Akins Birmingham Boys. Private collection.
Chester Allen and Skyline Farms String Band. Library of Congress,
    Archive of Folksong, Washington, D.C.
D. Dix Hollis. Archives, Country Music Foundation, Nashville.
Hugh Gibbs String Band. Archives, Country Music Foundation,
    Nashville.
Joe Lee and Paul Ray. Home recording. Private collection.
Johnson Brothers String Band. Archives, Country Music Foundation,
    Nashville.
Short Creek Trio. Archives, Country Music Foundation, Nashville.
"Wyzee" Hamilton. Archives, Country Music Foundation, Nash-
    ville.
[Note: The recordings above are those discussed within the text of
    the book. A listing of commercially recorded fiddlers will be
    available in a forthcoming discography of early country music
    compiled by Tony Russell, editor of *Old-Time Music* (London,
    England).]

Interviews

Allen, Chester. Scottsboro, 5 June 1984.
Andrews, Pearl Duncan Morgan. Caledonia, Mississippi, 27 June
    1985.
Arnold, Gaines. Quinton, 7 May 1984.

Aycock, Roger. Rome, Georgia, 20 September 1986.

Blalock, Mack. Mentone, 3 June 1985.

Brock, J. C. Crossville (Lamar County), 30 August 1984.

Brown, Charlie. Telephone conversation with A. K. Callahan, Tuscaloosa, 20 August 1986.

Bryan, W. A. Boaz, 8 August 1983.

Burns, "Happy" Hal. Birmingham, 15 April 1986.

Busby, Sam. Ensley, 26 August 1983.

Callahan, A. K. Tuscaloosa, 22 January 1984.

Callahan, Marguerite T. Tuscaloosa, 26 June 1985.

Campbell, William Everis. Henderson, 24 November 1984, and Troy, 23 December 1984.

Carwile, Estelle. Athens, 13 September 1984.

Cicero, Vearl. Ensley, 9 April 1984.

Colburn, Howard. McCalla, 9 May 1985.

Cole, James. Athens, 13 September 1984.

Daniels, Monk. Interviewed by Herb Trotman, Albertville, June 1978.

Dickerson, Barney. Dothan, 23 November 1986.

Drake, Earle. Birmingham, 3 August 1983.

DuBose, E. F. Telephone conversation, Huntsville, 11 January 1986.

Dunlap, Gene. Birmingham, 15 July 1986.

Elliott, Carl. Jasper, 3 October 1985.

Freeman, Carrie and John. Bremen, 19 September 1985.

Gable, Sandy. Eastern Valley, 23 August 1984.

Gaines, Geneva. Interview by Alice Crocker for Oral History Research Office, University of Alabama in Birmingham. Leeds, 20 October and 1 November 1975.

Gibbs, Inez. Sulligent, 7 February 1984.

Hamner, A. D. Northport, 24 April 1984.

Hicks, Harmon. Pleasant Grove, 23 April 1983.

Hill, Matthew D. Chalkville, 30 May 1982.

Hill, Thomas E. Pinson, 4 June 1983.

Horn, Alvin. Ashland, 6 August 1984.

Jackson, James W. Huntsville, 18 September 1984.

Johnson, Byron, Guy, and Ruth. Albertville, 23 June 1983.

Kersey, Osey. Oakey Ridge, 22 November 1984.

Kmetko, Wilma. Huntsville, 11 January 1986.

Kyle, Bob. Tuscaloosa, 22 January 1984.

Lee, Charles. Rome, Georgia, 20 September 1986.

Lee, Mrs. Maud. Telephone conversation, Rome, Georgia, 20 September 1986.

Lester, Al. Muscle Shoals, 2 October 1985.

Littlejohn, E. C. Nashville, 13 August 1984.

Marston, Mrs. Louis. Telephone conversation, Birmingham, 1 June 1982.

Mayes, Olen. Birmingham, 12 September 1985.

McGlocklin, Jerry. Athens, 13 September 1984.

Moon, Arlin. Holly Pond, 7 September 1985.

Mordecai, Elsie Stripling. Kennedy, 30 August 1984.

Phillips, Aubrey. Robertsdale, 24 December 1984.

Porter, J. V. Steens, Mississippi, 13 December 1984.

Ray, Paul. Rome, Georgia, 20 September 1986.

Rickard, Ed. Russellville, 15 September 1985.

Riley, Oscar. Northport, 31 August 1984.

Robertson, Curtis. Northport, 31 August 1984.

Rushing, Carter. Henderson, 23 November 1984.

Spivey, Ellis. Robertsdale, 24 December 1984.

Stewart, Carl. Ketona, 13 June 1984.

Strickland, Mrs. Dannie. Moore's Bridge, 30 August 1984.

Stripling, Charles and Ira. Interviewed by Bob Pinson, Kennedy, 2 September 1963.

Stripling, Robert. Conversations on car trip to west Alabama, 30 August 1984.

Sutton, Tom. Athens, 13 September 1984.

Weaver, Chloe Hollis. Sulligent, 15 January 1984.

About the Author

Joyce H. Cauthen has worked with the Alabama Folklife Association, the Alabama State Council on the Arts, the Birmingham Country Dance Society, and other organizations in a variety of activities celebrating and preserving the old-time musical traditions of the state. She received her B.A. from Texas Christian University and her M.A. from Purdue University and has taught English on the secondary and college levels.